Inclusive Tourism Development

This comprehensive volume seeks out ways in which those who are typically marginalized by, or excluded from, tourism can be brought into the industry in ways that directly benefit them. It addresses the central questions asked by an inclusive tourism approach: Who is included? On what terms? With what significance?

Tourism is often understood and experienced as an exclusive activity, accessible only to the relatively wealthy. This volume seeks to counter that tendency by exploring how marginalized groups can gain more control over tourism. The book starts by defining the concept of inclusive tourism and discussing seven different elements which might indicate inclusivity in tourism. Research from a wide range of geographical contexts – from Cambodia to Australia, Sweden, Turkey and Spain – have been drawn upon to illustrate the need for more inclusive tourism. The examples encompass the actions of a multinational tour operator, hotel owners, and social enterprises, while also examining how to ensure tourism is accessible for those with disabilities. Inclusive tourism is offered here as both an analytical concept and an aspirational ideal.

The authors hope that this book inspires a restless quest to find ways to include new actors and new places in tourism on terms that are equitable and sustainable. The chapters were originally published as a special issue of the journal *Tourism Georgraphies*.

Regina Scheyvens is Professor of Development Studies at Massey University, Palmerston North, New Zealand. Her research probes ways in which tourism in small island states can be more sustainable, inclusive and empowering for local populations.

Robin Biddulph is Associate Professor of Human Geography at the University of Gothenburg, Sweden. His recent research projects include analyses of tourism livelihoods in the rural areas around Siem Reap, Cambodia, land reform in Mozambique and Tanzania, and social enterprises in Scandinavia and Southeast Asia.

Inclusive Tourism Development

Edited by
Regina Scheyvens and Robin Biddulph

LONDON AND NEW YORK

First published 2021
by Routledge
2 Park Square, Milton Park, Abingdon, Oxon, OX14 4RN

and by Routledge
52 Vanderbilt Avenue, New York, NY 10017

Routledge is an imprint of the Taylor & Francis Group, an informa business

© 2021 Taylor & Francis

Chapter 1 © 2018 Robin Biddulph and Regina Scheyvens. Originally published as Open Access.

Chapter 3 © 2018 María José Zapata Campos, C. Michael Hall and Sandra Backlund. Originally published as Open Access.

With the exception of Chapters 1 and 3, no part of this book may be reprinted or reproduced or utilised in any form or by any electronic, mechanical, or other means, now known or hereafter invented, including photocopying and recording, or in any information storage or retrieval system, without permission in writing from the publishers. For details on the rights for Chapters 1 and 3, please see the chapters' Open Access footnotes.

Trademark notice: Product or corporate names may be trademarks or registered trademarks, and are used only for identification and explanation without intent to infringe.

British Library Cataloguing-in-Publication Data
A catalogue record for this book is available from the British Library

ISBN13: 978-0-367-62177-3

Typeset in Myriad Pro
by codeMantra

Publisher's Note
The publisher accepts responsibility for any inconsistencies that may have arisen during the conversion of this book from journal articles to book chapters, namely the inclusion of journal terminology.

Disclaimer
Every effort has been made to contact copyright holders for their permission to reprint material in this book. The publishers would be grateful to hear from any copyright holder who is not here acknowledged and will undertake to rectify any errors or omissions in future editions of this book.

Contents

	Citation Information	vi
	Notes on Contributors	viii
1	Introducing inclusive tourism *Robin Biddulph and Regina Scheyvens*	1
2	Understanding inclusive tourism development *Regina Scheyvens and Robin Biddulph*	7
3	Tour operators and corporate social responsibility: Can they promote more inclusive tourism? *María José Zapata Campos, C. Michael Hall and Sandra Backlund*	28
4	Social enterprise and inclusive tourism. Five cases in Siem Reap, Cambodia *Robin Biddulph*	51
5	Too precarious to be inclusive? Hotel maid employment in Spain *Ernest Cañada*	71
6	Challenges to inclusive tourism experiences for wheelchair users at historic sites *Ayşe Nilay Evcil*	93
7	Stakeholder collaboration in the development of accessible tourism: A framework for Inclusion *Julie Nyanjom, Kathy Boxall and Janine Slaven*	111
	Index	135

Citation Information

The chapters in this book were originally published in the *Tourism Geographies*, volume 20, issue 4 (October 2018). When citing this material, please use the original page numbering for each article, as follows:

Chapter 1
Introducing inclusive tourism
Robin Biddulph and Regina Scheyvens
Tourism Geographies, volume 20, issue 4 (October 2018) pp. 583–588

Chapter 2
Understanding Inclusive tourism development
Regina Scheyvens and Robin Biddulph
Tourism Geographies, volume 20, issue 4 (October 2018) pp. 589–609

Chapter 3
Tour operators and corporate social responsibility: Can they promote more inclusive tourism?
María José Zapata Campos, C. Michael Hall and Sandra Backlund
Tourism Geographies, volume 20, issue 4 (October 2018) pp. 630–652

Chapter 4
Social enterprise and inclusive tourism. Five cases in Siem Reap, Cambodia
Robin Biddulph
Tourism Geographies, volume 20, issue 4 (October 2018) pp. 610–629

Chapter 5
Too precarious to be inclusive? Hotel maid employment in Spain
Ernest Cañada
Tourism Geographies, volume 20, issue 4 (October 2018) pp. 653–674

Chapter 6
Barriers and preferences to leisure activities for wheelchair users in historic places
Ayşe Nilay Evcil
Tourism Geographies, volume 20, issue 4 (October 2018) pp. 698–715

Chapter 7
Towards inclusive tourism? Stakeholder collaboration in the development of accessible tourism
Julie Nyanjom, Kathy Boxall and Janine Slaven
Tourism Geographies, volume 20, issue 4 (October 2018) pp. 675–697

For any permission-related enquiries please visit:
http://www.tandfonline.com/page/help/permissions

Contributors

Sandra Backlund Department of Political Sciences, University of Gothenburg, Sweden.

Robin Biddulph Human Geography Unit, Department of Economy & Society, University of Gothenburg, Sweden.

Kathy Boxall School of Arts and Humanities, Edith Cowan University (South West Campus), Bunbury, Australia.

María José Zapata Campos Department of Business Administration, School of Business, Economics and Law, University of Gothenburg, Sweden.

Ernest Cañada Alba Sud – Research and Communication for Development, Barcelona, Spain. School of Tourism, Hospitality & Gastronomy, Barcelona University, Spain.

Ayşe Nilay Evcil Faculty of Engineering and Architecture, Beykent University, Istanbul, Turkey.

C. Michael Hall Department of Marketing, University of Canterbury, New Zealand.

Julie Nyanjom School of Business and Law, Edith Cowan University, Bunbury, Australia.

Regina Scheyvens Institute of Development Studies, Massey University, Palmerston North, New Zealand.

Janine Slaven Edith Cowan University (South West Campus), Bunbury, Australia.

∂ OPEN ACCESS

Introducing inclusive tourism

Robin Biddulph ⓘ and Regina Scheyvens ⓘ

ABSTACT
Tourism is often understood and experienced as an exclusive activity. In supporting the concept of inclusive tourism, this volume seeks to counter that tendency by seeking out ways in which those who are typically marginalized by, or excluded from tourism can be brought into the industry in ways that directly benefit them, or that they can gain more control over tourism. This introduction to the special issue first presents a conceptual article that defines the concept of inclusive tourism and discusses seven different elements, which may constitute lines of inquiry in investigations of tourism's inclusiveness. It then presents five empirical articles that illustrate some of the ways in which an inclusive tourism approach might inform discussion of the potentials and limitations for tourism to generate wider social and economic benefits. The examples provided are from a wide range of geographical contexts, from Cambodia to Australia, Sweden, Turkey and Spain. Inclusive tourism is offered here as both an analytical concept and an aspirational ideal. We do not ever envisage minimum standards for inclusive tourism. We rather hope that there will be a restless quest to find ways to include new actors and new places in tourism on terms that are equitable and sustainable.

For as long as there has been tourism, there have been scholars interested in its wider social benefits and seek to understand how those benefits may be maximised. This special

---

This is an Open Access article distributed under the terms of the Creative Commons Attribution-NonCommercial-NoDerivatives License (http://creativecommons.org/licenses/by-nc-nd/4.0/), which permits non-commercial re-use, distribution, and reproduction in any medium, provided the original work is properly cited, and is not altered, transformed, or built upon in any way.

issue asserts that the concept of inclusive tourism may be a valuable addition to the family of terms (e.g. responsible tourism, social tourism, peace through tourism, pro-poor tourism, accessible tourism) which constitute this field of scholarship. As presented in this special issue, inclusive tourism is defined as 'Transformative tourism in which marginalized groups are engaged in ethical production or consumption of tourism and the sharing of its benefits' (Scheyvens & Biddulph, this volume). Our impulse is normative: tourism should be inclusive, and scholars should be seeking to identify ways in which it can be more inclusive. Our impulse is also, of course, critical, highlighting the need to ask how inclusive any particular initiative really is, and to investigate structural limits to inclusion both within the industry and in the wider political economy.

In recent decades almost every country around the globe has had campaigns seeking to develop and grow their tourism sector. There is an assumption that such growth is good because it leads to jobs, government revenue and other national benefits, such as preservation of natural and cultural heritage. With the development of communications and transport technology and reduced costs for travel in many cases, along with growing numbers in the middle classes around the world, tourism has duly grown and money has flowed. But the shine of tourism is rubbing off for many. As an industry it has been criticised for causing environmental problems, cultural desecration, negative social impacts and economic inequality. Things came to a head in the summer of 2017 when residents of European hotspots such as Venice, Barcelona and Dubrovnik protested, violently in some cases, against 'over tourism' which had led to crowding of their streets and parks, increased prices for housing and a lower quality of life for locals: these places are now bracing themselves for the summer ahead (Papathanassis, 2017; Seraphin, Sheeran, & Pilato, 2018; Sharpley, 2018b). It is time to find a new way forward. Can 'inclusive tourism' offer any guidance on this?

The central questions asked by an inclusive tourism approach 'Who is included? On what terms? With what significance?' (Scheyvens & Biddulph, this volume) are not geographically restrictive. Tourism can be more or less inclusive in any region of the world. The cases that first prompted us to reflect on inclusiveness were local initiatives that our colleagues at the Centre for Tourism in Gothenburg were collaborating with, for example, Gothenburgo (http://www.gbgo.se/om-oss.html), a small NGO which made tourist maps for wards in the city which are not usually considered tourist attractions, or Tikitut (http://tikitut.se/home/), a social enterprise in a marginalized area of the city which offers homestays, cooking experiences and guided walking tours, all of which alert visitors to the social and natural richness and diversity in an area of the city which many city residents would not otherwise consider visiting. These local initiatives, which included new people and new places in tourism in ways that promised social, spatial and economic integration, in various ways reminded us of other initiatives in areas of the Global South which also had similar effects (e.g. Scheyvens, 2006).

Tourism is often understood – and also marketed – as an exclusive activity. The more exotic the destination, the more lavish the experience, the higher the price that can be demanded. As we go to press, there is renewed talk of opportunities for space tourism: with costs of US\$100 million per person for a space walk (with untold environmental implications), this may be the ultimate example of exclusive tourism. In supporting the concept of inclusive tourism this volume seeks to turn that notion on its head, seeking out ways in which those who are typically marginalized by or excluded from tourism can be brought into the industry in ways that directly benefit them, or that they can gain more control over tourism. This could be as producers of tourism products (see Biddulph on social enterprises in Cambodia, this volume), as consumers of tourism (see Evcil's article on wheelchair users as tourists, this volume), as those influencing policy and practice (see Nyanjom et al., this volume), as beneficiaries of enlightened corporate policies (see Zapata Campos et al., this volume), or as employees whose rights and wellbeing are assured (see Cañada, this volume, who shows why this is desperately needed).

The conceptual article by Scheyvens and Biddulph (this volume) which begins this special issue situates inclusive tourism as a response to tendencies towards social, economic and spatial exclusion in tourism. These authors provide a definition and a conceptual framework featuring seven different elements which may constitute lines of inquiry in investigations of tourism's inclusiveness. The article distinguishes inclusive tourism from other similar-sounding terms such as all-inclusive tourism and inclusive business approaches, and also sets it in the comparative context of existing concepts which are also concerned with the wider social benefits of tourism. Finally, the article uses the elements of the conceptual framework to review illustrative cases of inclusive tourism within existing literature concluding with a discussion of factors that constrain tourism inclusiveness.

Robin Biddulph's article (this volume) on five social enterprises in Siem Reap, Cambodia, provides insights into how inclusive forms of tourism are being implemented in practice. The Soria Moria initiative, for example, demonstrates how tourism can transform power relations. It describes how the Norwegian owners of a hotel in Siem Reap handed over ownership and control of their award-winning boutique establishment to the staff, many of whom had grown up living hand-to-mouth lives in poor rural villages. This ambition was not fully realized, but, as Biddulph suggests, it provides lessons and may act as a source of inspiration for other similar worker cooperatives to allow them to find a more substantial foothold in the tourism market. In another example, Phare circus shows how young Cambodians have authored variations on traditional Cambodian performance for tourist audiences, which in turn raise funds for cultural schools for budding performers in another province, far away from the tourist eye. Biddulph suggests that this is illustrative of a growing range of social enterprises which seek not only to generate a tourism product, but also to create spaces for self-expression and cultural development which are grounded in host preferences and tastes, rather than primarily being attuned to tourists' whims. Founded as all social enterprises are, on a social mission, such enterprises thus show considerable potential for delivering on inclusive tourism; however it is important to reflect that they are only a niche of the tourism sector currently and are unlikely to be able to significantly transform tourism overall.

Truly transformational tourism could occur if the multinational companies which dominate the hotel and tour operator segments would change their policies and practices, making the mass tourism sector more inclusive. Two-thirds of the European market is dominated by a few tour operators, a consolidation of power which characterizes the contemporary industry. As the employers of people from many marginalized groups, at least indirectly, and being able to influence supplier procurement policies, large tour operators can actually wield significant influence in terms of encouraging sustainable and inclusive practices. To date, Corporate Social Responsibility (CSR) efforts by tourism companies have been somewhat tokenistic (de Grosbois, 2012; Hughes & Scheyvens, 2016; Kalisch,

2002). However, Maria José Zapata Campos, Michael Hall and Sandra Backlund (this volume) alert us to possibilities for corporates to adopt more inclusive approaches. Specifically, they analyse the CSR policy and practices of Swedish tour operator, Apollo. While Apollo has made positive strides in terms of implementing its parent company, Kuoni's, Travelife system and supplier code of conduct, Zapata Campos et al. show that codes of conduct risk becoming a type of 'symbolic compliance' because they are not monitored. Thus, based on an analysis of the processes by which inclusive tourism issues might become part of a CSR agenda, these authors caution against superficial adoption of inclusive tourism principles by multinational tourism businesses; they concurrently assert the need for a focus on the social dimensions of their practice and on equity. Encouragingly, this article demonstrates how Apollo was able to exert influence over its parent organization, Kuoni, by bringing concerns of inclusivity into its transnational CSR policy.

One component of inclusive tourism spelled out by Scheyvens and Biddulph is the transformation of oppressive power relations. The importance of this is exemplified in Ernest Cañada's research (this volume) which focuses on the erosion of labour rights in the tourism sector in the face of economic restructuring. Unfortunately, labour rights and employee wellbeing are relatively neglected areas of tourism research (Baum, 2007; Baum et al., 2016). Cañada specifically examines how, following the global financial crisis, there were changes in Spanish law involving deregulation and outsourcing, which have left hotel maids effectively in a race to the bottom, competing for jobs which are ever more precarious and poorly paid. There are over 400,000 hotel workers in this 'socially invisible' group who clean, dust, wash, vacuum, mop and pick up our rubbish so that we – the privileged – can enjoy a holiday in the sun. For too long the assumption has been that job creation equals good development. Inclusive tourism demands that we look well beyond this and instead focus on the International Labour Organization's concept of 'decent work' when considering whether tourism is actually contributing to inclusive development. To read Canada's study of maids in Spain is to be reminded of the forces in the wider political economy which work against attempts to provide decent work and instead create a society which is more exclusive. Cañada's findings about the decrease in pay of maids, job insecurity, work overload and declining health of maids, do not lead him to dismiss the concept of inclusive tourism. Rather, he uses it to argue that it is vital that there is the opportunity for a wide range of actors to make decisions about tourism, noting that in this case, freedom for trade unions and women's organisations is important so they can assert worker's demands for better labour relations, working conditions and to be treated with dignity. Cañada's work also stresses that inclusive tourism must consider class and gender divisions in order to develop a more equitable model for labour in the tourism industry.

It is notable that in this special issue we have two articles that go to the roots of inclusivity in tourism, in that the term inclusive has, to date, mostly been used in discussions of accessible tourism for those whose mobility is impaired (e.g. Darcy & Dickson, 2009). Both articles point to the importance of hearing the voice of people with disabilities when planning for tourism development. Their lived experience of disability offers unique insights into ways in which tourism destinations could better plan to cater for those whose mobility is impaired. Julie Nyanjom, Kathy Boxall and Janine Slaven's article approaches this from the perspective of how stakeholders need to cooperate effectively to develop accessible tourism. Their research with 19 participants in the town of Margaret River in Australia, found that there was minimal evidence of collaboration among government agencies, tourism providers, agencies for people with disabilities, and disabled people themselves. In particular, they argue that people with disabilities need to be the main stakeholder group at the collaborative table, and they need to not only be dialogue partners, but also to have significant influence in governance and decision-making.

Following this, Ayşe Nilay Evcil provides an interesting case study of issues faced by wheelchair users in one of the pre-eminent tourism attractions of Turkey, Sultanahmet Square in Istanbul. 125 respondents noted that they had particular problems with sidewalks, ramps, stairs and parking. Reflecting on the value of the concept of 'universal design', which is based on the principal of equity, Evcil thus notes that conservation and restoration goals in a heritage location such as this can clash with accessibility goals for those with disabilities. Essentially, a lack of accessibility creates social inequality.

As laid out in this volume then, inclusive tourism is offered as an analytical concept and as an aspirational ideal. It can be used to evaluate current tourism practices to help to detect where changes are needed, as well as to guide new tourism development. We neither hope nor expect that inclusive tourism will be adopted as a form of certification or an industry-brand where businesses can be defined as 'inclusive' or not. Other concepts clearly perform this valuable function, but in doing so their analytical usefulness can be compromised (Burrai & Hannam, 2018; Sharpley, 2018a; Wheeller, 1990). One danger is that this certification function can lead to a focus on avoiding negative consequences, rather than maximizing benefits. Another is that it can reduce analysis to rather simple, closed, check-list binaries. We therefore hope that the pursuit of inclusive tourism, both as research project and ethical tourism practice, will be seen as an on-going process.

Overall, this special issue gives the reader insights into the potential of inclusive tourism as a concept, while also cautioning that a lot needs to be done for this to come into place effectively in practice. Thus whilst small-medium scale initiatives – such as the social enterprises discussed by Biddulph - may meet with success, creating industry-wide change is a challenge of quite a different order, requiring much broader mobilization. To encourage fundamental changes to the practices of multinational hotels and tour operators, governments that are willing will have to effectively regulate development, something that many have been shy to do for fear of losing market share in the extremely competitive neoliberal environment in which they operate. There would also be a need for systematic monitoring and evaluation of tourism endeavours to ensure they were complying with their commitments to more inclusive forms of development. As some of the examples in this volume show, however, aiming for inclusion is worth the effort if we want tourism endeavours to contribute to a more sustainable, equitable world.

Acknowledgements

We would like to thank all participants in the Centre for Tourism Symposium on Inclusive Tourism in Gothenburg in April 2016, particularly co-organiser Dr Kristina Lindström and keynote speakers Professors Dianne Dredge and Wineaster Anderson.

Disclosure statement

No potential conflict of interest was reported by the authors.

Funding

Professor Scheyvens' contributions to this special issue were supported by the International Visiting Professor Programme at the School of Business Economics and Law at the University of Gothenburg, while Dr Biddulph's contributions were supported by the Swedish Research Board for Sustainable Development, FORMAS grant number 259-2011-1315 .

ORCID

Robin Biddulph http://orcid.org/0000-0003-2485-9867
Regina Scheyvens http://orcid.org/0000-0002-4227-4910

References

Baum, T. (2007). Human resources in tourism: Still waiting for change. *Tourism Management, 28*(6), 1383–1399.
Baum, T., Cheung, C., Kong, H., Kralj, A., Mooney, S., Nguyễn Thị Thanh, H., ... Siow, M. (2016). Sustainability and the tourism and hospitality workforce: A thematic analysis. *Sustainability, 8*(8), 809.
Burrai, E., & Hannam, K. (2018). Challenging the responsibility of 'responsible volunteer tourism'. *Journal of Policy Research in Tourism, Leisure and Events, 10*(1), 90–95.
Darcy, S., & Dickson, T. J. (2009). A whole-of-life approach to tourism: The case for accessible tourism experiences. *Journal of Hospitality and Tourism Management, 16*(1), 32–44.
de Grosbois, D. (2012). Corporate social responsibility reporting by the global hotel industry: Commitment, initiatives and performance. *International Journal of Hospitality Management, 31*(3), 896–905.
Hughes, E., & Scheyvens, R. (2016). Corporate social responsibility in tourism post-2015: A development first approach. *Tourism Geographies, 18*(5), 469–482.
Kalisch, A. (2002). *Corporate futures: Social responsibility in the tourism industry; consultation on good practice*, London, Tourism Concern.
Papathanassis, A. (2017). Over-tourism and anti-tourist sentiment: An exploratory analysis and discussion. *Ovidius University Annals, Economics Sciences Series, 17*(2), 288–293.
Scheyvens, R. (2006). Sun, sand, and beach fale: Benefiting from backpackers–the Samoan Way. *Tourism Recreation Research, 31*(3), 75–86.
Seraphin, H., Sheeran, P., & Pilato, M. (2018). Over-tourism and the fall of Venice as a destination. *Journal of Destination Marketing & Management.* doi:https://doi.org/10.1016/j.jdmm.2018.01.011
Sharpley, R. (2018a). Responsible volunteer tourism: Tautology or oxymoron? A comment on Burrai and Hannam. *Journal of Policy Research in Tourism, Leisure and Events, 10*(1), 96–100.
Sharpley, R. (2018b). *Tourism, tourists and society*, Abingdon, Routledge.
Wheeller, B. (1990). Responsible tourism. *Tourism Management, 11*(3), 262–263.

Understanding inclusive tourism development

Regina Scheyvens ⓘ and Robin Biddulph

ABSTRACT
In the light of growing inequality globally, it is important to consider how to make tourism, one of the world's largest industries, more inclusive. This concern is set in the context of, first, the growing use of tourism as a tool for social integration in Europe, not least in relation to making refugees welcome, and second, new expectations in the sustainable development goals (SDGs) that development should be inclusive and that the Global North and the private sector will take more responsibility for this. We provide a definition and suggest elements of an analytical framework for inclusive tourism, and note where inclusive tourism sits in relation to other terms that engage with the social and economic development potentials of tourism. Elements of inclusive tourism are illustrated with reference to a range of examples from around the world. This illustrates how marginalized people might be ethically and beneficially included in the production and consumption of tourism. However, it also demonstrates how formidable the challenges are to achieve substantial social change through inclusive tourism given constraints both within the sector and in the wider political economy.

1. Introduction

One of the most enduring critiques of tourism in social science discourse relates to its exclusive nature. Tourism is accused of providing opportunities for the privileged middle and upper classes to travel and enjoy leisure activities in 'other' places, creating profits particularly for large companies and creating exclusive enclaves for rich, while development opportunities associated with tourism are not open to those who are poor and marginalized (Gibson, 2009, p. 1280; Harrison, 1992; Jamal & Camargo, 2014). In this article, we recognize the validity of these criticisms but start with a different proposition: that the concept of inclusive tourism development can help us to think constructively and critically about ways of approaching tourism that so that it can provide a holistic range of benefits and lead to more equitable and sustainable outcomes.

A concern with inclusiveness enables analytical links to be made between the stated ambitions of global policy-making and a range of grass-roots initiatives. These involve a plethora of different actors in diverse settings seeking to widen the range of people involved in producing tourism, consuming tourism, and benefiting from tourism. In many cases, these initiatives involve challenging existing geographies of tourism. In other words, inclusive tourism development attempts not only to widen access to consumption, production and benefit-sharing in existing tourism sites, but also to re-draw the tourism map in order to create new sites of experience and interaction.

At the global level, inclusion is one of the central principles behind the United Nations' sustainable development goals (SDGs) which were ratified in September 2015. As noted by UNDP, 'Many people are excluded from development because of their gender, ethnicity, age, sexual orientation, disability or poverty... Development can be inclusive – and reduce poverty – only if all groups of people contribute to creating opportunities, share the benefits of development and participate in decision-making' (United Nations Development Program, 2016). Seen in this light, a focus on tourism development as inclusive would include attention to including previously silenced voices in decision-making about tourism, as well as ensuring that a broader spread of the benefits of tourism.

In this article, we will define 'inclusive tourism', and show how it sits in relation to other conceptualizations of socially and economically beneficial tourism development like pro-poor and responsible tourism. We argue that this term can add value to tourism knowledge and understandings by seeking to explicitly overcome the exclusionary tendencies of tourism and to ensure that a wider range of people participate in and benefit from tourism endeavours.

2. Conceptualizing inclusive tourism

Before defining what we mean by inclusive tourism, it is important to distinguish it from some of the ways that the concept of inclusion has previously been linked to tourism and to development more broadly, in both the scholarly literature and in development industry material.

First, when talking about inclusive tourism we are not referring to 'all-inclusives' whereby tourists pay a travel agent in advance for a package including the costs of flights, transfers, accommodation, meals and tours at a foreign destination. In fact, all-inclusive tourism often offers the opposite of what we see as inclusive tourism. For the last two to three decades social scientists have critiqued all-inclusive resorts because they tend to result in enclaves which are out of bounds to the local population, they limit opportunities for local entrepreneurs to benefit by selling goods or services to tourists, and they result in high levels of leakage of tourist spending, with much going to foreign hotel chains and travel agents (Britton, 1982; Gibson, 2009; Scheyvens, 2011). As Saarinen (2017, p. 425) concludes, 'enclave tourism spaces with all-inclusive products can turn out to be all-exclusive for local communities in development'.

Second, tourism is sometimes viewed through an 'inclusive business' lens. Within international development discourse and among businesses wishing to exhibit their social responsibility, a specific body of work has formed around the notion of inclusive business. Here the focus is on how for-profit businesses can contribute to poverty reduction by including people from low-income communities in the value chain (www.businessfordevelopment.org). In tourism, proponents emphasise how low-income populations can benefit from tourism growth (www.inclusivebusinesshub.org; see also www.inclusive-business.org). For example, the ITC training guide examines ways in which handicraft producers can be linked to tourism markets (International Trade Centre, 2012). Growth in tourism, it is proclaimed,

> offers a unique opportunity for unlocking opportunities through inclusive business (IB) models. Tourism can create employment and income-generating opportunities along an expansive value chain... For this growth to create meaningful and sustainable impact for local populations however, innovative inclusive business models need to be put into place that allow low-income people to have better employment and entrepreneurship opportunities and catalyse more systemic poverty reduction effects. (Deutsche Gesellschaft für Internationale Zusammenarbeit, 2016)

The inclusive business approach has much in common with the inclusive growth agenda which is currently a dominant thread in discussions by aid donors and development banks. According to Bakker and Messerli (2017), inclusive growth is based on a long-term agenda to expand employment opportunities and the size of the economy: it is not specifically about redistribution of resources to the poor. These authors believe that the concept of inclusive growth offers more promise to the tourism sector than a pro-poor tourism (PPT) approach. While few tourism scholars have tested the notion of tourism-led inclusive growth, it is significant that Hampton, Jeyacheya, and Long (2017) work in Ha Long Bay, Vietnam, concluded that despite the rapid growth of tourism in this area, the research raised significant doubts about whether tourism could contribute to inclusive growth. In fact, the local supply chain was weakening, and business and employment opportunities were less equitable than in the past.

Notably, the inclusive business approach supports a neoliberal model of economic growth, which assumes that including the poor in the market economy is a direct route out of poverty. It limits itself to economic dimensions and is not linked to a political agenda such as efforts to overcome structural inequalities which are barriers to development for the poor. We support the views of a number of scholars who see flaws in this approach (Blowfield & Dolan, 2014; Kumi, Arhin, & Yeboah, 2014; José Carlos Marques & Peter Utting, 2010). For example, a number of big business actors are primarily interested in the business case for responsible practice: in one study of 40 large corporations the motivation to pursue sustainable and inclusive business practices ranged from 'maintaining competitive position' as the leading motivator, followed by 'avoiding reputational damage,' 'avoiding future supply disruptions,' and 'capturing revenues and building loyalty'' (Chakravorti, Macmillan, & Siesfeld, 2014, pp. 2–3). Our understanding of 'inclusive tourism' should thus not be conflated with an inclusive business or inclusive growth approach.

Third, a broader, more holistic perspective on 'inclusive development' has emerged as seen in the following UNDP definition:

> People are excluded from development because of their gender, ethnicity, age, sexual orientation, disability or poverty... Development can be inclusive – and reduce poverty – only if all groups of people contribute to creating opportunities, share the benefits of development and participate in decision-making. (www.undp.org)

Lawson (2010) takes this argument forward, arguing that inclusive development requires an understanding of economic development as being intrinsically embedded in place, politics and society. She completes her critique of the 2009 Human Development Report with the statement that 'Inclusive development begins from an embedded conceptualization of economic development which is informed by an ethical concern for people and care, not just economic growth' (Lawson, 2010, p. 359). International actors, including donors, have become well versed in the language of inclusive development partly through the post-2015 focus on the SDGs. While the notion that economic growth is essential to inclusive development comes through in the SDGs, overall there is a broader perspective of inclusive development than that found in business-centric approaches. There are associated social development objectives embedded in the SDGs including enhancing human dignity and overcoming inequalities.

Inclusive development is, therefore, a more holistic concept than inclusive growth, implying an interest in a broader sense of welfare than one simply measured by per capita GDP. It also goes beyond societal averages (as found in headline Human Development Index figures) or impacts on particular groups (as in pro-poor figures), but takes an interest in whether marginalized groups improve their overall share of welfare, such as narrowing the gap between the poor and the rest of society (Rauniyar & Kanbur, 2010). Drawing on these understandings of the meaning of inclusive development allows us to broaden the scope of inclusive tourism development beyond economic criteria, and to deliberately steer it away from notions of 'inclusive business' and 'all-inclusive' tourism.

3. A definition

The authors have noted that a small group of researchers is starting to link 'tourism' and 'inclusive development', so the following discussion represents our efforts to provide clearer parameters around this term. Inclusive tourism can be understood as

> Transformative tourism in which marginalized groups are engaged in ethical production or consumption of tourism and the sharing of its benefits.

This means something can only be considered inclusive tourism if marginalized groups are involved in ethical production of it, or they are involved in ethical consumption of it, and in either case, marginalized groups share the benefits. Who is marginalized will vary from place to place but this could include the very poor, ethnic minorities, women and girls, differently abled people and other groups who lack power and/or voice. Ethical production and consumption is a key component of the definition of inclusive tourism. This includes responsibility for other people, and for the environment. In terms of 'transformative', this could mean addressing inequality, overcoming the separation of different groups living in different places, challenging stereotypes or generalized histories, and opening people up to understanding the situation of minorities.

A strength of this definition is its applicability to the Global North and South, blurring conventional boundaries. It encourages us to ask the same questions of tourism as an inclusive development activity no matter whether it is occurring in a village in England or a megacity in China, the mountains of Kenya or the coast of Australia.

In social terms, inclusion invites two sets of crucial questions: (1) who is included (and excluded) and (2) on what terms are they included? As such, a discussion of inclusion can never be adequate if it only attends to one case or group. Similarly, if a narrow group of stakeholders are included in a tokenistic way in order to create the impression of progress, or if some marginalized people are included but in a superficial manner – as represented in the literature by terms such as green-wash, pink-wash – then tourism is not being inclusive in any meaningful way. It is, to borrow the terms used by Marques and Utting (2010), ameliorative rather than transformative.

Using 'inclusion' alerts us to who is not there as well. Since the 1970s, tourism has been widely critiqued by academics for being *exclusive*, that is, dominated by multinational interests, mainly accessible to those who are members of national and global elites, exploitative of local people and resources, and leading to dependency. The saga of Ochheuteal Beach in Cambodia, where local stallholders are negotiating under threat of eviction with provincial and national authorities who are seeking to beautify and develop the seafront (Sotheary, 2016), is but one of many examples of struggles around the terms on which local people are included in or excluded from the spaces, activities and benefits of tourism. An interesting prospect is Cukier's notion of the value of 'explosions of niches' in tourism in Cuba, as a contrast to exclusive enclaves (Cukier, 2011). The discussion of inclusive tourism is a direct attempt to acknowledge that many people have been excluded by tourism in the past, and to find ways to overcome this so that more people can benefit from tourism. However, it also acknowledges that some people may choose not to be included because of concerns they have about tourism (Craven, 2016).

Implicit in the concept of inclusive tourism are the following components, which are further depicted in the seven elements of Figure 1:

(1) Overcoming barriers to disadvantaged groups to access tourism as producers or consumers.
(2) Facilitating self-representations by those who are marginalized or oppressed, so their stories can be told and their culture represented in ways that are meaningful to them.
(3) Challenging dominant power relations.
(4) Widening the range of people who contribute to decision-making about development of tourism.
(5) Providing opportunities for new places to be on the tourism map.
(6) Encouraging learning, exchange and mutually beneficial relationships which promote understanding and respect between 'hosts' and 'guests'.

Analytically, then, these elements provide a conceptual framework: the degree to which tourism development is inclusive may be assessed in terms of its ambitions and achievements in relation to these seven elements. There are examples of inclusive approaches to tourism which incorporate these elements in Section 5. Before this,

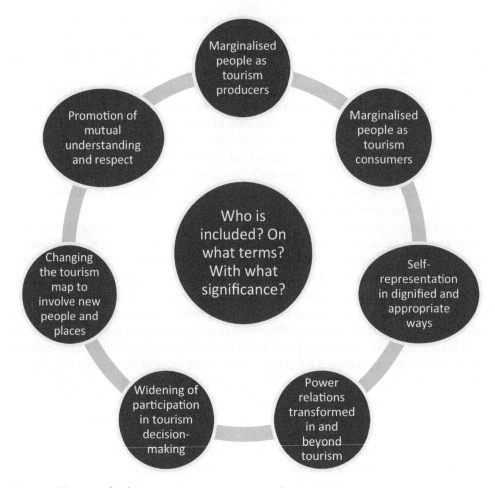

Figure 1. Elements of inclusive tourism.

however, we elaborate on how the concept of inclusive tourism development builds upon and is distinctive from related terms in tourism scholarship and practice.

4. How does 'inclusive tourism' compare with other related terms regarding tourism and development?

The dual notions that tourism itself can be improved, and also that tourism can act as an agent of improvement for wider society, have spawned a broad family of overlapping concepts deployed to varying extents by scholars and practitioners. Some of these, such as responsible tourism and eco-tourism, are part of mainstream practice and will be familiar to many consumers and producers of tourism. Others are probably more recognizable to scholars and policy-makers, such as PPT and social tourism. Others cater for smaller niches, such as tourism for peace and community-based tourism. Such terms are outlined in Table 1, noting their key elements and what makes inclusive tourism distinct from them.

The concept of inclusive tourism adds one more distinctive term to this family of overlapping concepts. As such it does not seek to usurp or supersede any of them. We

Table 1. Distinctions between inclusive tourism and other related forms of tourism.

	Commonalities with inclusive tourism	Inclusive tourism focus is different because:
Accessible tourism	Focuses on access to tourism by differently abled people as consumers of tourism	Inclusive tourism is interested more broadly in access to consumption *and* productive of tourism, by *all* forms of marginalized people
Pro-poor tourism	Focuses on increasing poor people's economic share of benefits from tourism in the Global South	Inclusive tourism focuses on economic and *social* inclusion of poor and other marginalized groups, and applies to both the Global North and South
Social tourism	Focuses on widening access of marginalized groups as consumers of tourism	Inclusive tourism also focuses on widening of access of marginalized people, but as both as *producers* and consumers of tourism, and as *decision-makers*
Peace through tourism	Focuses on tourists as ambassadors for peace	Inclusive tourism is *broader* in focus, but shares this interest in building mutual understanding between hosts and guests
Community-based tourism	Focuses on empowerment and development of community members as producers of tourism	Inclusive Tourism is interested in these things, but not only at the community level; it focuses on *all forms and scales of tourism*
Responsible tourism	Focuses on ethical tourism, with a general interest in improving the terms under which tourism takes place	Inclusive Tourism does not share the focus on environment found in responsible tourism, and is more focused on *quality of relationships and empowerment of hosts*

envisage inclusive tourism to be an analytical term rather than one that will be taken up and used in marketing or certification or campaigning. The distinctive contributions of the term to the analytical mix relate to

(1) focusing attention on an innovation frontier where new people and new places are incorporated into tourism consumption and production, and
(2) using tourism to counter socio-economic exclusions and divisions.

As such the interest is both quantitative (to what extent are new people and places being included) and qualitative (what are the terms and meanings of that inclusion).

4.1. Accessible tourism

When the inclusiveness of tourism is discussed it is often in terms of its accessibility for tourists who are differently abled. The concept has been variously defined in order to pay more or less attention to issues of physical ability, cognitive ability and issues relating to age (Darcy, 2006; Darcy & Dickson, 2009). While accessibility is generally the key term in this literature, inclusive approaches and inclusive attitudes are identified as key to providing accessibility (Darcy & Pegg, 2011; Yau, McKercher, & Packer, 2004).

Accessible tourism is based on advocating for the rights of differently abled people to enjoys holidays and tourism, which necessitates removing barriers which might prevent this from occurring (Pagán, 2012). Others have described inclusive tourism along these lines as well, for example: 'Inclusive Tourism is an environment where people of all abilities are felt welcome and wanted as customers and guests' (TravAbility.com). For us inclusive tourism relates to both production and consumption of tourism, so in terms of differently abled people an inclusive tourism perspective would also focus on their roles as owners, entrepreneurs, employees and regulators. Accessible tourism has value in that it seeks to ensure that tourism is produced with people of all abilities in mind, and can be consumed by people of all abilities. As such, accessible tourism is just one aspect of inclusive tourism as the latter is interested in all forms of social and economic exclusion and division.

4.2. PPT

PPT emerged as an analytical concept around the turn of the century and is associated with some of the same academic-practitioners as responsible tourism (Ashley, Boyd, & Goodwin, 2000; Ashley & Roe, 2002; Goodwin & Font, 2007). It follows a long-term interest arising from the expansion of mass tourism in relatively poor settings in the Global South (Britton, 1982; de Kadt, 1979; Harrison, 1992) and seeks ways of ensuring that a greater proportion of the tourist spend finds its way directly or indirectly into the hands of poor people (Mitchell & Ashley, 2010). An inclusive tourism approach shares this concern with economic inclusion, but also extends it to the Global North, and is interested not only in tourism's economics but also in its potential to promote social inclusion and integration.

4.3. Social tourism

Social tourism is concerned with guests rather than hosts, and has focused more on the Global North rather than the Global South: social tourism is thus almost a mirror image of the concerns of PPT. Historically, social tourism has been concerned with enabling economically disadvantaged people to participate in tourism (Haulot, 1981). Academic interest has focused on eligibility for social tourism, on the particular interests and needs of different age groups, and on the social and economic costs and benefits of social tourism (Caffyn & Lutz, 1999; McCabe & Diekmann, 2015; Minnaert, Maitland, & Miller, 2011; Morgan, Pritchard, & Sedgley, 2015). The interest in overcoming exclusion is a shared perspective with inclusive tourism. Again, though, inclusive tourism's scope is broader, encompassing guests and hosts, the Global North and the Global South, and also being interested in opening new geographical frontiers for tourism.

4.4. Peace through tourism

Peace through tourism has investigated the proposition that tourism can be mobilized as a means of avoiding war or securing peace (Cho, 2007), and is associated with a practitioner-academic movement which seeks to rebrand tourism as the first global peace industry (D'Amore, 2009). Tourism's potentials as a promoter of peace are examined in two ways: firstly, on a structural level where the financial incentives provided and organizational cooperation required by tourism are seen as having potential to steer countries towards peace (Kim, Prideaux, & Prideaux, 2007), and secondly, at a personal level where bringing people together in situations where they better understand and empathize with each other might undermine popular support for conflict (Gelbman, 2008; Sonmez & Apostolopoulos, 2000). To the extent that pro-peace tourism in involves people and places that would not normally be included in tourism (for example in the growth of food tourism and homestays in Palestine), then peace through tourism shares some concerns with inclusive tourism. However, while the peace through tourism literature chiefly engages with theories from international relations (Kim et al., 2007), inclusive tourism's interests are more broadly aligned with sociological and geographical literatures on exclusion and integration (Higgins-Desbiolles, 2003; Lawson, 2010).

4.5. Community-based tourism

Community-based tourism may be motivated by a variety of economic, social, cultural or environmental concerns, and usually involves an element of control over the tourism enterprise by local communities (Okazaki, 2008; Salazar, 2012; Zapata, Hall, Lindo, & Vanderschaeghe, 2011). Community-based tourism is usually small-scale and as such it may be a site for piloting ways of doing things which can be scaled up, but it may also function as a cul-de-sac, as approaches which work in small, resource-intensive, often personalized niches prove difficult to scale up to larger scales and mass markets (Goodwin, 2009). From an inclusive tourism perspective, just as with responsible tourism and PPT, community-based tourism can be a promising site of innovation. However, key questions revolve around the extent to which inclusiveness extends either within the local community (Blackstock, 2005; Manyara & Jones, 2007), or beyond it into areas that are of interest to inclusive tourism such as wider societal structures and industry practices.

4.6. Responsible tourism

One of the broadest and most long-standing concepts associated with tourism and socio-economic improvement is responsible tourism. This was initially adopted in preference to the label 'alternative tourism' (Wheeller, 1990), which it critiqued as being impotent to deal with the fact that mass tourism was already a fact of life and that seeding alternatives would do nothing to curb the negative effects of mass tourism (Wheeller, 1991). Since this time it has become much more broad in its scope, and especially since the establishment of the International Centre for Responsible Tourism centred around Leeds Metropolitan University in the mid-1990s it has become a movement which seeks to influence the behaviour of producers and consumers in the mass market as well as in specialized niche markets (Goodwin & Font, 2007).

Responsible tourism as a concept stresses doing no harm. However, its definition, as laid out by those who propagate it, is not just concerned with the ethics of tourism actors, but with the wider operation of socio-economic processes relating to tourism. Within the Cape Town Declaration (Spenceley, 2012, p. 5), it is clear that responsible tourism includes engendering respect and building local pride, generating greater economic benefits – especially for local people – and involving them in decision-making, encouraging meaningful connections between guests and local people, and respecting cultural and natural diversity. Responsible Tourism requires that operators, hoteliers, governments, local people and tourists take responsibility, and take action to make tourism more sustainable. It has thus become a framework for evaluating any tourism sector from a broad range of research perspectives (Bramwell, Lane, McCabe, Mosedale, & Scarles, 2008). For example, a responsible tourism lens has been applied to cruise tourism (Klein, 2011), slum tourism (Booyens, 2010), and tourism for the promotion of peace (Isaac, 2010). Interpreted broadly, then, responsible tourism is the term which has the largest overlap with the notion of inclusive tourism.

5. Inclusive tourism in practice

We have framed inclusive tourism as comprising a concern with widening the participation of marginalized groups in tourism, on terms that are favourable to them and that might have broader transformative influence within and beyond the tourism industry. Using the elements from our framework above (Figure 1) as sub-headings, we now focus on how inclusive tourism is being sought in practice by drawing on examples from the wider literature, and also noting where barriers exist.

5.1. Marginalized people as tourism producers

In the Global South, the inclusion of local people as producers in and for the tourism market is a long-term and continuing struggle. For example, small farmers are one group which has typically not benefited greatly from growth of tourism, even where there is significant interest in utilizing local fresh produce in tourist restaurants (Telfer & Wall, 2000; Torres, 2002). Thus, many newly emerging inclusive tourism initiatives are concerned with engaging different groups of people as tourism producers. For example, the Fair Trade in Tourism (FTT) movement is actively trying to change the poor deal that some producers get from the tourism industry: specifically, it aims to ensure that tourism producers (of handicrafts, accommodation, produce, etc.) get a fair deal, and to raise the awareness of consumers about FTT. In South Africa, a national FTT organization certifies tourism businesses and thus provides a guarantee for consumers regarding a business's ethics (Scheyvens, 2011, p. 34).

Arguably, one of the biggest challenges for inclusive tourism is to encourage responsible production of tourism by existing tourism businesses. Mainstream operators can take an inclusive approach to tourism production by transforming their core activities, such as providing decision-making roles and ownership opportunities for staff; mentoring local people in relation to starting their own small businesses associated with tourism; introducing inclusive procurement strategies; and offering dignified work, good training, and fair remuneration (Ashley, Haysom, & Spenceley, 2008; Walmsley, 2012; Hughes & Scheyvens, 2016). Interestingly, when inclusive tourism was promoted by local authorities in the rural town of Dullstroom in South Africa, the emphasis was on upskilling of employees for quality jobs, not just on job creation (Butler & Rogerson, 2016).

Tren Ecuador provides an example of a business offering a luxury tourist experience – a train journey across Ecuador, from the Andes to the Pacific – but doing so in a sustainable and responsible way. One of the state-owned business's key goals is to contribute to improving the quality of life of local communities along the length of its journeys (Monge, Yagüe, & Perales, 2016). As such, rather than creating an exclusive comfort zone on board that separates travellers from local populations, Tren Ecuador encourages tourists to eat at restaurants along the way, buy crafts at one of 14 artisan squares, and purchase snacks from over 20 locally run station cafes. It is estimated that Tren Ecuador now supports the livelihoods of over 5,000 people living along its routes, which is why it was awarded 'Best in poverty reduction and inclusion' in the 2016 Responsible Tourism Awards (http://www.responsibletravel.com/awards/categories/economic.htm).

5.2. Marginalized people as tourism consumers

Another way to ensure that tourism is inclusive is through widening access to non-mainstream consumers – building on traditions such as social tourism (for lower socio-economic groups) and accessible tourism (for those with disabilities), as discussed in Section 4. For example, in the United Kingdom it has been found that economically disadvantaged older people gain numerous well-being benefits from the ability to participate in specially designed trips which allow them to escape their everyday lives, reminisce and connect with others (Morgan et al., 2015).

Tourism can also become less exclusive through ensuring that destinations are frequented by both tourists and locals, which can be encouraged through domestic marketing campaigns, encouraging schools to take students on extended field trips, and support for social tourism initiatives. There are both economic and sociocultural benefits of such domestic tourism, including breaking down barriers between different ethnic groups and increasing appreciation of cultural, linguistic and religious differences; helping to build a sense of national pride and identity; revitalizing social ties between extended family and community groups; encourage local servicing of tourist demands; and spreading economic benefits to areas not frequented by international tourists (Mawdsley, 2009; Scheyvens, 2007). Socially and politically, nationals of any country should feel able to enjoy the attractions of their own country but due to neo-colonial attitudes there can be barriers which prevent access. In Fiji, Uprising Resort provides a contrast to the enclave-type development of many other tourist resorts which leave indigenous people feeling unwelcome and excluded, by encouraging Fijians to enjoy the resort's facilities and participate in activities such as sports events (Scheyvens, 2011).

5.3. Changing the tourism map to involve new people and places

We also argue that there is a territorial dimension to inclusive tourism in that it opens up more places and spaces as sites of tourism. As Kitchin and Dodge have argued, '...mapping is a process of constant reterritorialization' (Kitchin & Dodge, 2007, 331). Thus, places not conventionally frequented by tourists – such as under-resourced or lower socio-economic neighbourhoods – can be reimagined as tourist spaces, and included on the tourist map. In doing so, individuals have the opportunity to encounter new locations and landscapes in multiple, nuanced ways (Edensor, 2015).

This process of remapping tourism and involving new people and places is evident in Sweden's second largest city, Gothenburg. Anna Cederberg Gerdrup wrote a book based on riding the No.11 tram line in Gothenburg from one end to the other, passing through a range of socio-economic areas and getting off at each stop to meet people, to eat and to collect recipes which are reproduced in a cookbook. Her book is encouraging residents to explore their own city more actively and make contact with people of different ethnicities and walks of life (personal communication, April 2016).

We do not wish to suggest, however, that the provision of a few 'novel' or 'out of the way' places and spaces for tourism necessarily constitutes 'inclusive tourism'. Favela, slum or shantytown tours are a good case to consider here. Twenty years ago, such tours were virtually unheard of and only the most intrepid tourists would venture into these somewhat marginalized zones of the city, whereas now they are another box to tick on the itinerary of many conventional tourists visiting the likes of Rio de Janeiro, Mumbai or Johannesburg. Whether or not these tours are inclusive, however, depends on how they are established, with whose input, and how they are carried out. Criticisms abound relating to concerns about voyeurism, representation of the poor, exploitation and commercialization of poverty, and lack of direct benefits to the people of these marginalized areas (Frenzel, 2014; Selinger, 2009). In practice, however, some of these tours have enabled poorer residents to be directly involved in the production of tourism by constructing and running tours, or developing small enterprises that engage tourists; meanwhile tourists consuming these tours have the opportunity to deepen their understanding of the history and politics of the people and places visited, in the case of those tours providing good information (Basu, 2012; Mekawy, 2012).

In the Global North, 'changing the tourism map' is sometimes an implicit component of agendas to promote social integration, such as with the Tikitut initiative in Gothenburg, Sweden. Tikitut attracts domestic and international tourists to an outlying district which has previously suffered from a reputation as a deprived and dangerous area. A network of local hosts who are migrants to Sweden and have no background in tourism or hospitality industries offer home stays and cooking experiences (http://tikitut.se/home). This fundamental shift in who produces the tourism product (see Section 5.1) has led to a number of related inclusive tourism benefits such as integration of marginalized groups, and promoting mutual understanding and respect between hosts and guests (see Section 5.5).

5.4. Widening of participation in tourism decision-making

Who controls and makes decisions about tourism development has a big influence on whether tourism will contribute to inclusive development. Tourism industry players are centrally concerned with profit maximization thus if they are left to self-regulate and adopt unmonitored policies on corporate social responsibility (see Section 5.1), it is unlikely that the industry will always act responsibly and reflect the interests of wider society. This is why Pingeot (2014), referring to the influence of big business over the development of the SDGs, cautions against giving corporations 'undue influence on policymaking and ignoring their responsibility in creating and exacerbating many of the problems that the Post-2015 agenda is supposed to tackle' (Pingeot, 2014, p. 6). When we look closely at what is proposed by business actors in relation to the SDGs, self-interest is a clear driver: this is why there is a focus on voluntary change rather than regulation, and soft measures to reduce environmental impacts rather than fundamental changes in production and consumption (Pingeot, 2014, p. 29). This is of even greater concern when we consider that recent years have seen consolidation of the power of the largest tourism-related organizations through mergers and growth, rather than a dismantling of their power (Scheyvens, 2011).

A counter to this, and a strategy for more inclusive tourism, is to enhance citizens' active participation in tourism decision-making. Timothy (2007, p. 203), for example, shows how decentralizing decision-making power by empowering 'people locally on the ground' can lead to more effective development outcomes. After conducting research with Tibetan youths living in a suburban area of Lhasa, Tibet, and asking them to compare the value of two tourism parks in their area, Wu and Pearce (2016) discovered that the young people preferred strong community control over tourism rather than tourism that is managed by an outside company. This might run counter to some people's views that outside companies are preferred because of advantages they bring in terms of investment potential and business know-how; however this does not reflect the views of at least one large segment of the community. It is vital that more research which actively listens to community voices is conducted to counter industry-centric perspectives and inform inclusive approaches to tourism development.

Following on from this point, Smith and Pappalepore (2015) discuss the case of Deptford, an economically marginal area of London's docklands which was controversially promoted as a tourist destination by the New York Times. Their discussions with local residents lead them to recommend that tourism development should be based on the preferences of these people. They note that this is somewhat 'idealistic' thus they pair it with a more practical recommendation of stimulating events as a means of catalysing movement in and out of such areas and thereby allowing a more organic growth of tourism rather than one that is derived from marketing or journalism which may oversell or mis-sell a place (see Section 5.6).

5.5. Promotion of mutual understanding and respect

While government officials are often preoccupied with economic benefits of tourism, the social benefits can be very important too. An inclusive approach to tourism can, for example, result in enhanced unity in rural, urban or beach locations, less crime, a better sense of security, and a more pleasant place to live. With growing inequality and associated social dysfunction in many societies in the Global North and South, there is now greater interest in the value of breaking down barriers between people (including those living in different suburbs within the same city), providing opportunities to develop mutual understanding, and overcoming negative stereotypes. For example, Higgins-Desbiolles (2016, p. 1280) points out that in Australia indigenous festivals can result in 'positive visibility' for indigenous people and even have a 'role of reconciliation' in situations of past harm from a settler society. Much depends, however, on whose interests are reflected in the resulting tourism, and in this case there were concerns that the festival was transformed in ways that grew tourist numbers while undermining the social and cultural value of the festival, especially from an indigenous perspective (Higgins-Desbiolles, 2016).

In South Africa, the government has tuned into the language of inclusive tourism, and sees this as a means of providing opportunities for people on the margins. As South Africa's Minister of Tourism, Derek Hanekom, said in 2015,

> We want to make the entire sector more inclusive and representative by bringing people who have been marginalised in to the mainstream tourism economy (cited in Butler & Rogerson, 2016, p. 265)

When this concept was applied to the town of Dullstroom, mentioned above, which has seen growth in second home tourism, fly fishing and agritourism, Butler and Rogerson (2016) found clear evidence of an inclusive tourism development approach. Surveyed residents noted social benefits as being highly significant to them. Interestingly, apart from oft-cited benefits such as capability and empowerment, these residents valued the enhanced safety of their town associated with growth of tourism, along with important strides to overcome mistrust between ethnic groups (who were now more likely to be working together in tourism enterprises): 'An additional example of social empowerment concerned the development of positive relationships between black and white community members' (Butler & Rogerson, 2016, p. 276).

In recent years, a rise in the share of the votes in elections by anti-foreigner political parties in Europe has coincided with a refugee crisis prompted by the Syrian conflict which has also flowed over into Europe. Rights to asylum have been challenged even in places where they have for decades been taken for granted. Amongst the many efforts seeking to ensure that refugees are given asylum have been those emanating from the tourism sector. Social enterprises such as the Good Hotel in Amsterdam and London and the Magdas Hotel in Vienna have been set up to provide employment for refugees and to create opportunities for social interaction as part of a movement to use tourism to ensure that refugees are welcomed and integrated in European societies (Coldwell, 2016). Similarly, the Kitchen on the Run project saw a small group of Germans build a kitchen in a container which they toured around European cities for five months during summer 2016; they used the container to host several dinner parties per week for 25–35 refugees and locals who cooked together and ate together in 'a space that encourages and supports intimate get-togethers between refugees from all over the world and locals in Europe around the kitchen table' (Kitchen on the run, 2016). They cooked with a total of over 2000 people from 65 different countries, and planned to repeat the initiative with multiple containers taking different routes in 2017 (Persson, 2016).

5.6. Self-representation in dignified and appropriate ways

One persistent critique of tourism is that it has a tendency to objectify and exoticize the 'other'. This is a process that is entrenched. As quickly as tourists move beyond the tourist track in search of 'authentic' interactions, those interactions themselves become susceptible to commercialization and commodification (MacCannell, 1992, 2008). This process of objectification is part of what critics find abhorrent about orphanage tourism and some forms of voluntourism (Guiney & Mostafanezhad, 2015).

One of the foci of inclusive tourism, then, is to find ways that host communities, including indigenous people, and vulnerable and poor people in host communities, can represent themselves in ways that they find appropriate and dignified. Thus, for example, rather than being represented by others as having a 'static', 'traditional' culture, Māori people of New Zealand are, through their tourism businesses, re-negotiating the way in which they are represented to tourists and showing how they interact with and draw from other cultures as well: '..."difference" is not so much a pre-given and static trait of 'fixed' tradition but a complex ongoing negotiation' (Amoamo & Thompson, 2010, p. 47). In another example, Seiver and Matthews (2016) provide a fascinating comparison of representations of Aboriginal people in destination images for four regions in Australia. While one region virtually overlooks Aboriginal peoples, in other destinations Aboriginal tourism incorporates Aboriginal perspectives and presents the culture as living and dynamic, which helps to disrupt stereotypes.

5.7. Power relations transformed in and beyond tourism

All of the elements of inclusive tourism which we have discussed above provide potentially incremental contributions to the larger, long-term goal of transforming power relations and ending social exclusion. Direct attempts at overturning power relations, however, whether within the tourism industry or in wider society, are inevitably battling the odds. Social structures and systems which marginalize and impoverish may have a high degree of resilience and path dependency (Baird, Chaffin, & Wrathall, 2017). Thus some new initiatives such as Private-Community Partnerships in Uganda, which are set up specifically to share ownership of a tourism venture such as a high-end ecolodge, have fallen short in achieving true 'partnership' (Ahebwa, Van der Duim, & Sandbrook, 2012). Nevertheless there are examples of transformations of social and economic life such that marginalized and poor individuals and groups are included on terms that are decent and fair, and of shared ownership which genuinely transfers power to previously exploited groups.

Positive initiatives include those that hand over ownership and control of a tourism business to (former) employees. An interesting example from North Cyprus is the Dome Hotel, which used to be state-owned, and became employee-owned after trade unions and employees sought an alternative to planned privatization of the hotel. It is now owned by 49 hotel employees and the Tourism Workers Union, and operated by Solidarity Tourism Company (Timur & Timur, 2015). Through this system, every full time employee has one vote over decisions which span marketing, wages, profit distribution, and investments. The employee ownership system is widely appreciated by the new owners and by the wider community, which benefits from the hotel's 'support your local economy' policy, and also experiences social benefits such as discounted access to the hotel facilities. Interestingly, the hotel has also gained direct benefits from this, including more stable local employment, more return customers (partly related to the relationships developed with long-term staff), and preservation of an iconic hotel (Timur & Timur, 2015). This may provide a source of inspiration for other similar employee ownership or worker cooperative schemes, to allow them to find a more substantial foothold in the tourism market thus disrupting the consolidation of power in the hands of a small number of major hotel and tour operators.

6. Constraints to achieving inclusive tourism

However, a few success stories are not enough to 'prove' that an inclusive approach to tourism is valuable. The power of larger companies in the tourism sector is becoming entrenched, making it difficult for those wanting to start their own initiatives: 15 per cent of businesses which are internationally branded chains have 52 of the business, thus claiming a 'dominant' position in the industry (Niewiadomski, 2014, p. 50). It is important for us to confront the constraints on inclusiveness in practice, with the key constraint being the prevailing ideology of neoliberalism. Essentially, whether there is a tag-on agenda of poverty-alleviation or sustainability, under neoliberal logic the premise is that economic growth is the basis of development (Mowforth & Munt, 2009, p. 34). Such an approach fails to consider how economic growth can undermine sociocultural well-being and the environment. Thus, encouraging the inclusion of new sites for people to find leisure or escape may compromise quality of life for some people in those locales by impinging on livelihood options (not always positively), overcrowing, limiting public access to social spaces, and so forth. Under neoliberal policy much faith has been placed in private sector entities working as development actors, despite the fact that, for example, global tour operators, multinational hotel chains and the like are not skilled in overcoming inequality, empowering the poor or delivering on socio-economic goals (McEwan, Mawdsley, Banks, & Scheyvens, 2017). Neoliberalism has led to a rise in the number and types of enclavic spaces in tourism, making more places inaccessible to local people (unless they enter as cleaners, gardeners and so forth) (Saarinen, 2017). Allowing markets to drive growth is thus unlikely to work as a strategy to support inclusive tourism; rather, it is more likely to reinforce the wealth of some and entrench the poverty of others.

There are significant barriers to overcome to achieve inclusive tourism in terms of opportunities for those who are poor or marginalized. In many cases, poorer local people, even when in sight of wealthier tourists and without physical or policy barriers erected against them, will lack the language, skills, networks or capital to engage with those tourists on their own initiative (e.g. Biddulph, 2015, pp. 107–9). They also tend to face various forms of discrimination. Even when they have an opportunity to, for example, operate a community-based tourism enterprise, they might simultaneously experience empowerment and forms of disempowerment, the latter because they are still subject to domination by others (Knight & Cottrell, 2016).

Furthermore, a lot of tourism products are still built on difference (between rich and poor, between different cultures) rather than breaking down differences and building mutual understanding. The industry explicitly exploits this 'difference', for example, when rich tourists visit the poor via cultural tourism, and when tourists from urban jungles are enticed to meet the 'primitive' minorities in tropical jungles (Scheyvens, 2011, p. 83). This is what Mowforth and Munt (2009, p. 81) refer to as the 'ultimate aestheticism of reality… [through] which racism and class struggle actually seem to be enjoyed'. Thus initiatives espoused under the banner of inclusive tourism might simply provide a distraction from the fundamental structural inequalities upon which tourism is base. For example, a nice tourism-related social enterprise to help former-refugees in an outer suburb to economically integrate into a new country might deflect attention from more pressing needs and challenges they face in their new communities. Tourism, inclusive or not, will not always be a suitable strategy to achieve holistic development.

7. Conclusion

This article has defined and conceptualized inclusive tourism, demonstrating why the authors feel that it provides a valuable analytical perspective to tourism in the Global North and South. Travel can broaden the mind by exposing the traveller to places and people and perspectives that s/he would not encounter at home. Tourism, by commodifying travel, always risks robbing it of what is most enriching and promising about it. Initiatives to make tourism more inclusive can be seen as attempts to improve the quality of human interaction, and to ensure that tourism delivers benefits to those who have in the past been excluded from, or marginalized by, its production and consumption. Given the fierce competition within the industry with drives to keep the mass market low cost and standardized and the luxury market exclusive and enclaved, such initiatives are likely to be battling against the odds. This is especially the case in a neoliberal climate which expects change to be led not through the consolidated, organized power of the state, but via the fragmentary, uncoordinated decisions of individual consumers.

Nevertheless, the discussion above has demonstrated ways in which an inclusive approach to tourism is playing out in practice in specific locations. Some of the examples could provide inspiration to actors wishing to support more inclusive outcomes from tourism development. We have shown how marginalized people are becoming more involved in the production and consumption of tourism, with Tren Ecuador's support for the livelihoods of thousands of people along its routes and Uprising Hotel in Fiji welcoming indigenous customers while challenging notions of the resort as an exclusive enclave. We have demonstrated why it is important for more people to have a say over decision-making around tourism, whether the economically marginalized of Deptford or the youth of Lhasa. Our examples show that indigenous people are now choosing how they represent themselves to tourists, after years of being misrepresented. We have explained how tourism can be a mechanism for the economic empowerment and social inclusion of refugees, such as through the Good Hotel in Amsterdam, and how a business can come to be owned and controlled by former employees, as with the Dome Hotel in Cyprus.

We believe that inclusive tourism provides a way forward in terms of thinking that will help to overcome some of the barriers noted in the discussion above. Our ambition is not that inclusive tourism will become a source of branding or certification initiatives, but rather that it will provide a source of critical and innovative thinking. We hope that it will prompt a certain analytical restlessness as the questions 'how inclusive is this development?' and 'how could this tourism enterprise be more inclusive?' are repeatedly posed and improvements sought. Furthermore, it is apparent that for inclusive tourism to be fully realized we cannot rely on private sector initiative or good intentions alone, rather, national and international regulatory frameworks have a critical role to play.

Disclosure statement

No potential conflict of interest was reported by the authors.

ORCID

Regina Scheyvens http://orcid.org/0000-0002-4227-4910

References

Ahebwa, W. M., Van der Duim, V. R., & Sandbrook, C. G. (2012). Private-community partnerships: Investigating a new approach to conservation and development in Uganda. *Conservation and Society, 10*(4), 305.

Amoamo, M., & Thompson, A. (2010). (re) Imaging Māori tourism: Representation and cultural hybridity in postcolonial New Zealand. *Tourist Studies, 10*(1), 35–55.

Ashley, C., & Roe, D. (2002). Making tourism work for the poor: Strategies and challenges in Southern Africa. *Development Southern Africa, 19*(1), 61–82. doi:10.1080/03768350220123855

Ashley, C., Boyd, C., & Goodwin, H. (2000). *Pro-poor tourism: Putting poverty at the heart of the tourism agenda*. London:ODI (Overseas Development Institute).

Ashley, C., Haysom, G., & Spenceley, A. (2008). The development impacts of tourism supply chains: Increasing impact on poverty and decreasing our ignorance. In A. Spenceley (Ed.) *Responsible Tourism: Critical issues for Conservation and Development*. London: Earthscan. 129–156.

Baird, T. D., Chaffin, B. C., & Wrathall, D. J. (2017). A disturbance innovation hypothesi s: Perspectives from human and physical geography. *The Geographical Journal*, 183(2), 201–208. doi:10.1111/geoj.12206

Bakker, M., & Messerli, H. R. (2017). Inclusive growth versus pro-poor growth: Implications for tourism development. *Tourism and Hospitality Research*, 17(4), 384–391 doi:10.1177/1467358416638919

Basu, K. (2012). 4 Slum tourism: For the poor, by the poor. *Slum Tourism: Poverty, Power and Ethics*, 32, 66.

Biddulph, R. (2015). Limits to mass tourism's effects in rural peripheries. *Annals of Tourism Research*, 50, 98–112.

Blackstock, K. (2005). A critical look at community based tourism. *Community Development Journal*, 40(1), 39–49. doi:10.1093/cdj/bsi005

Blowfield, M., & Dolan, C. S. (2014). Business as a development agent: Evidence of possibility and improbability. *Third World Quarterly*, 35(1), 22–42. doi:10.1080/01436597.2013.868982

Booyens, I. (2010). Rethinking township tourism: Towards responsible tourism development in South African townships. *Development Southern Africa*, 27(2), 273–287. doi:10.1080/03768351003740795

Bramwell, B., Lane, B., McCabe, S., Mosedale, J., & Scarles, C. (2008). Research perspectives on responsible tourism. *Journal of Sustainable Tourism*, 16(3), 253–257. doi:10.1080/09669580802208201

Britton, S. G. (1982). The political economy of tourism in the third world. *Annals of Tourism Research*, 9(3), 331–358. doi:10.1016/0160-7383(82)90018-4

Butler, G., & Rogerson, C. M. (2016). Inclusive local tourism development in South Africa: Evidence from dullstroom. *Local Economy*, 31(1–2), 264–281.

Caffyn, A., & Lutz, J. (1999). Developing the heritage tourism product in multi-ethnic cities. *Tourism Management*, 20(2), 213–221. doi:10.1016/S0261-5177(98)00075-2

Chakravorti, B., Macmillan, G., & Siesfeld, T. (2014). *Growth for good or good for growth? How sustainable and inclusive activities are changing business and why companies aren't changing enough.* Retrieved from http://www.citifoundation.com/citi/foundation/pdf/1221365_Citi_Foundation_Sustainable_Inclusive_Business_Study_Web.pdf

Cho, M. (2007). A re-examination of tourism and peace: The case of the Mt. Gumgang tourism development on the Korean Peninsula. *Tourism Management*, 28(2), 556–569. doi:10.1016/j.tourman.2006.04.019

Coldwell, W. (2016, 27th June). Floating hotel to open in London as part of social enterprise project. *The Guardian*. 20 June 2016. Retrieved from https://www.theguardian.com/travel/2016/jun/27/floating-hotel-to-open-london-social-enterprise-project

Craven, C. E. (2016). Refusing to be toured: Work, tourism, and the productivity of 'Life' in the Colombian Amazon. *Antipode*, 48(3), 544–562. doi:10.1111/anti.12208

Cukier, J. (2011). Development tourism: Lessons from Cuba. *Annals of Tourism Research*, 38(1), 333–335. doi:10.1016/j.annals.2010.11.004

D'Amore L. (2009). Peace through tourism: The birthing of a new socio-economic order. *Journal of Business Ethics*, 89(4), 559–568. doi:10.1007/s10551-010-0407-3

Darcy, S. (2006). Setting a research agenda for accessible tourism. In C. Coober, T. D. Lacy, & L. Jago (Eds.), *Sustainable Tourism Cooperative Research Centre technical report series*. Gold Coast, Australia.

Darcy, S., & Dickson, T. J. (2009). A whole-of-life approach to tourism: The case for accessible tourism experiences. *Journal of Hospitality and Tourism Management*, 16(1), 32–44. doi:10.1375/jhtm.16.1.32

Darcy, S., & Pegg, S. (2011). Towards strategic intent: Perceptions of disability service provision amongst hotel accommodation managers. *International Journal of Hospitality Management*, 30(2), 468–476. doi:10.1016/j.ijhm.2010.09.009

Deutsche Gesellschaft für Internationale Zusammenarbeit. (2016). *How can we unlock the power of inclusive tourism?* Paper presented at the 2nd Inclusive Business Asia Forum, Manila. http://www.

inclusivebusinesshub.org/wp-content/uploads/2016/05/IBAsiaForumTourismSessionGIZRIBHOutline.pdf

Edensor, T. (2015). The gloomy city: Rethinking the relationship between light and dark. *Urban Studies, 24,* 422–438.

Frenzel, F. (2014). Slum tourism and its controversies from a management perspective. In M. Gudic, A. Rosenbloom and C. Parkes (Eds.). *Socially Responsive Organizations and the Challenge of Poverty* (pp. 123–135). Leeds: Greenleaf.

Gelbman, A. (2008). Border tourism in Israel: Conflict, peace, fear and hope. *Tourism Geographies, 10* (2), 193–213. doi:10.1080/14616680802000022

Gibson, C. (2009). Geographies of tourism: Critical research on capitalism and local livelihoods. *Progress in Human Geography, 33*(4), 527–534.

Goodwin, H. (2009). Reflections on 10 years of pro-poor tourism. *Journal of Policy Research in Tourism, Leisure and Events, 1*(1), 90–94. doi:10.1080/19407960802703565

Goodwin, H., & Font, X. (2007). *Advances in responsible tourism.* Retrieved from Leeds:

Guiney, T., & Mostafanezhad, M. (2015). The political economy of orphanage tourism in Cambodia. *Tourist Studies, 15*(2), 132–155. doi:10.1177/1468797614563387

Hampton, M., Jeyacheya, J., & Long, P. H. (2017). Can tourism promote inclusive growth? Supply chains, ownership and employment in Ha Long Bay, Vietnam. *The Journal of Development Studies.* Online advance publication. doi:10.1080/00220388.2017.1296572

Harrison, D. (Ed.) (1992). *Tourism and the Less Developed Countries.* London: Belhaven Press.

Haulot, A. (1981). Social tourism. *International Journal of Tourism Management, 2*(3), 207–212. doi:10.1016/0143-2516(81)90007-4

Higgins-Desbiolles, F. (2003). Reconciliation tourism: Tourism healing divided societies! *Tourism Recreation Research, 28*(3), 35–44. doi:10.1080/02508281.2003.11081415

Higgins-Desbiolles, F. (2016). Sustaining spirit: A review and analysis of an urban indigenous Australian cultural festival. *Journal of Sustainable Tourism, 24*(8-9), 1280–1297. doi:10.1080/09669582.2016.1149184

Hughes, E., & Scheyvens, R. (2016). Corporate social responsibility in tourism post-2015: A development first approach. *Tourism Geographies, 18*(5), 469–482.

International Trade Centre. (2012). *Linking the handicraft sector to tourism markets.* Geneva. Retrieved from: http://www.intracen.org/uploadedFiles/intracenorg/Content/Exporters/Sectoral_Information/Service_Exports/Tourism/Linking the Handicraft Sector reprint 9 10 2012 for web.pdf

Isaac, R. K. (2010). Moving from pilgrimage to responsible tourism: The case of Palestine. *Current Issues in Tourism, 13*(6), 579–590. doi:10.1080/13683500903464218

Jamal, T., & Camargo, B. A. (2014). Sustainable tourism, justice and an ethic of care: Toward the just destination. *Journal of Sustainable Tourism, 22*(1), 11–30.

Kim, S. S., Prideaux, B., & Prideaux, J. (2007). Using tourism to promote peace on the Korean Peninsula. *Annals of Tourism Research, 34*(2), 291–309. doi:10.1016/j.annals.2006.09.002

Kitchen on the run. (2016). Kitchen on the run. Retrieved from http://www.kitchenontherun.org/about/

Kitchin, R., & Dodge, M. (2007). Rethinking maps. *Progress in Human Geography, 31*(3), 331–344.

Klein, R. A. (2011). Responsible cruise tourism: Issues of cruise tourism and sustainability. *Journal of Hospitality and Tourism Management, 18*(1), 107–116. doi:10.1375/jhtm.18.1.107

Knight, D. W., & Cottrell, S. P. (2016). Evaluating tourism-linked empowerment in Cuzco, Peru. *Annals of Tourism Research, 56,* 32–47.

Kumi, E., Arhin, A. A., & Yeboah, T. (2014). Can post-2015 sustainable development goals survive neoliberalism? A critical examination of the sustainable development–neoliberalism nexus in developing countries. *Environment, Development and Sustainability, 16*(3), 539–554.

Lawson, V. (2010). Reshaping economic geography? producing spaces of inclusive development. *Economic Geography, 86*(4), 351–360.

MacCannell, D. (1992). *Empty meeting grounds.* London: Routledge.

MacCannell, D. (2008). Why it never really was about authenticity. *Society, 45*(4), 334–337. doi:10.1007/s12115-008-9110-8

Manyara, G., & Jones, E. (2007). Community-based tourism enterprises development in Kenya: An exploration of their potential as avenues of poverty reduction. *Journal of Sustainable Tourism, 15*(6), 628–644. doi:10.2167/jost723.0

Marques, J. C., & Utting, P. (2010). *Corporate social responsibility and regulatory governance: Towards inclusive development?* Basingstoke: Palgrave Macmillan.

Marques, J. C., & Utting, P. (2010). Introduction: Understanding business power and public policy in a development context. *Business, politics and public policy* (pp. 1–29). New York: Spring er.

Mawdsley, E. (2009). Development update: Domestic tourism. *Geography Review, 22*(3), 32–33.

McCabe, S., & Diekmann, A. (2015). The rights to tourism: Reflections on social tourism and human rights. *Tourism Recreation Research, 40*(2), 194–204. doi:10.1080/02508281.2015.1049022

McEwan, C., Mawdsley, E., Banks, G., & Scheyvens, R. (2017). Enrolling the private sector in community development: Magic bullet or sleight of hand? *Development and Change, 48*(1), 28–53.

Mekawy, M. A. (2012). Responsible slum tourism: Egyptian experience. *Annals of Tourism Research, 39*(4), 2092–2113.

Minnaert, L., Maitland, R., & Miller, G. (2011). What is social tourism? *Current Issues in Tourism, 14*(5), 403–415. doi:10.1080/13683500.2011.568051

Mitchell, J., & Ashley, C. (2010). *Tourism and poverty reduction: Pathways to prosperity.* (1st ed.). London: Earthscan.

Monge, J., & Yagüe Perales, R., (2016). Sustainable tourism development: Tren Crucero del Ecuador. *Estudios y Perspectivas en Turismo, 25*(1), 57–72.

Morgan, N., Pritchard, A., & Sedgley, D. (2015). Social tourism and well-being in later life. *Annals of Tourism Research, 52*, 1–15. doi:10.1016/j.annals.2015.02.015

Mowforth, M., & Munt, I. (2009). *Tourism and sustainability: Development and new tourism in the third world*. London: Routledge.

Niewiadomski, P. (2014). Towards an economic-geographical approach to the globalisation of the hotel industry. *Tourism Geographies, 16*(1), 48–67.

Okazaki, E. (2008). A community-based tourism model: Its conception and use. *Journal of Sustainable Tourism, 16*(5), 511–529. doi:10.1080/09669580802159594

Pagán, R. (2012). Time allocation in tourism for people with disabilities. *Annals of Tourism Research, 39*(3), 1514–1537.

Persson, K. (2016, July 30). Kök på resa genom Europa skapar möten. *Göteborgsfria*. Retrieved from https://www.goteborgsfria.se/artikel/123903

Pingeot, L. (2014). *Corporate influence in the Post-2015 process* (Working Paper). Aachen, Berlin, Bonn: Misereor, Brot fur die Welt, Global Policy Forum. Retrieved from http://www19.iadb.org/intal/intalcdi/PE/2014/13575.pdf

Rauniyar, G., & Kanbur, R. (2010). Inclusive growth and inclusive development: A review and synthesis of Asian Development Bank literature. *Journal of the Asia Pacific Economy, 15*(4), 455–469.

Saarinen, J. (2017). Enclavic tourism spaces: Territorialization and bordering in tourism destination development and planning. *Tourism Geographies, 19*(3): 425–437. doi:10.1080/14616688.2016.1258433

Salazar, N. B. (2012). Community-based cultural tourism: Issues, threats and opportunities. *Journal of Sustainable Tourism, 20*(1), 9–22. doi:10.1080/09669582.2011.596279

Scheyvens, R. (2007). Poor cousins no more valuing the development potential of domestic and diaspora tourism. *Progress in Development Studies, 7*(4), 307–325.

Scheyvens, R. (2011). *Tourism and poverty*. New York, NY: Routledge.

Seiver, B., & Matthews, A. (2016). Beyond whiteness: A comparative analysis of representations of aboriginality in tourism destination images in New South Wales, Australia. *Journal of Sustainable Tourism, 24*(8–9), 1298–1314. doi:10.1080/09669582.2016.1182537

Selinger, E. (2009). Ethics and poverty tours. *Philosophy & Public Policy Quarterly, 29*(1/2), 2–7.

Smith, A., & Pappalepore, I. (2015). Exploring attitudes to edgy urban destinations: The case of Deptford, London. *Journal of Tourism and Cultural Change, 13*(2), 97–114. doi:10.1080/14766825.2014.896371

Sonmez, S. F., & Apostolopoulos, Y. (2000). Conflict resolution through tourism cooperation? The case of the partitioned island-state of Cyprus. *Journal of Travel & Tourism Marketing*, *9*(3), 35–48. doi:10.1300/J073v09n03_03

Sotheary, P. (2016, April 11). Eviction of beach businesses begins at Ochheuteal. *The Phnom Penh Post*. Retrieved from http://www.phnompenhpost.com/national/eviction-beach-businesses-begins-ochheuteal

Spenceley, A. (Ed.) (2012). *Responsible tourism: Critical issues for conservation and development*. London: Earthscan.

Telfer, D. J., & Wall, G. (2000). Strengthening backward economic linkages: Local food purchasing by three Indonesian hotels. *Tourism Geographies*, *2*(4), 421–447. doi:10.1080/146166800750035521

Timothy, D. (2007). Empowerment and stakeholder participation in tourism destination communities. In T. C. Andrew Church (Ed.), *Tourism, power and space* (pp. 203–216). London: Routledge.

Timur, S., & Timur, A. T. (2015). Employee ownership and sustainable development in tourism: A case in North Cyprus. *Sustainable Development*, *24* (2), 89–100.

Torres, R. (2002). Toward a better understanding of tourism and agriculture linkages in the Yucatan: Tourist food consumption and preferences. *Tourism Geographies*, *4*(3), 282–306. doi:10.1080/14616680210147436

United Nations Development Program. (2016). Inclusive Development. Retrieved from http://www.undp.org/content/undp/en/home/ourwork/povertyreduction/focus_areas/focus_inclusive_development.html

Walmsley, A. (2012). Decent work and tourism wages: An International comparison. *Progress in responsible tourism*, *2*(1), 90–99.

Wheeller, B. (1990). Responsible tourism. *Tourism Management*, *11*(3), 262–263. doi:10.1016/0261-5177(90)90050-J

Wheeller, B. (1991). Tourism's troubled times. *Tourism Management*, *12*(2), 91–96. doi:10.1016/0261-5177(91)90062-X

Wu, M. Y., & Pearce, P. L. (2016). A tale of two parks: Tibetan youths' preferences for tourism community futures. *Journal of Tourism and Cultural Change*, *15*(4), 359–379. doi:10.1080/14766825.2016.1156687

Yau, M. K.-s., McKercher, B., & Packer, T. L. (2004). Traveling with a disability: More than an access issue. *Annals of Tourism Research*, *31*(4), 946–960. doi:10.1016/j.annals.2004.03.007

Zapata, M. J., Hall, C. M., Lindo, P., & Vanderschaeghe, M. (2011). Can community-based tourism contribute to development and poverty alleviation? Lessons from Nicaragua. *Current Issues in Tourism*, *14*(8), 725–749. doi:10.1080/13683500.2011.559200

de Kadt, E. (1979). *Tourism: Passport to development?* New York, NY: Oxford University Press.

🔓 OPEN ACCESS

Tour operators and corporate social responsibility: Can they promote more inclusive tourism?

María José Zapata Campos, C. Michael Hall and Sandra Backlund

ABSTRACT
Outbound tour operators are key actors in international mass tourism. However, their contribution to more sustainable and inclusive forms of tourism has been critically questioned. Drawing from new institutional theories in organization studies, and informed by the case of one of the largest Scandinavian tour operators, we examine the corporate social responsibility (CSR) and sustainability work in large tour operators and the challenges faced in being more inclusive. On the basis of in-depth interviews with corporate officers, document analysis and media reports, we show how top-down coercive and normative pressures, coming from the parent company and the host society shape the ability of the daughter corporation to elaborate a more inclusive agenda. However, daughter companies do not merely comply with these institutional pressures and policy is also developed from the 'bottom-up'. We show how the tour operator's sustainability work is also the result of organizational responses including buffering, bargaining, negotiating and influencing the parent organization. By creating intra and inter-sectoral learning and collaborative industry platforms, MNCs not only exchange and diffuse more inclusive practices among the industry, but also anticipate future normative pressures such as legislation and brand risk. Daughter organizations help shape their institutional arrangements through internal collaborative platforms and by incorporating local events and societal concerns into the multinational CSR policy, especially when flexible policy frameworks operate, and the corporate CSR agenda and organizational field are under formation. However, risks do exist, in the absence of institutional pressures, of perpetuating a superficial adoption of more inclusive practices in the mass tourism industry.

This is an Open Access article distributed under the terms of the Creative Commons Attribution License (http://creativecommons.org/licenses/by/4.0/), which permits unrestricted use, distribution, and reproduction in any medium, provided the original work is properly cited.

Introduction

Outbound tour operators are major actors in the tourism industry (Alegre & Sard, 2015; Cvelbar, Dwyer, Koman, & Mihalič, 2016; Tveteraas, Asche, & Lien, 2014). Tour operators are one of the largest facilitators of information between suppliers and customers and, consequently, are significant influencers of how the travel market can evolve towards more inclusive and responsible tourism, affecting both suppliers and demand. Inclusiveness for major operators has historically been interpreted more in terms of packages for tourists rather than considering the groups and stakeholders that are excluded from the tourism system. For the purposes of this paper, inclusive tourism is regarded as the voluntary inclusion of otherwise marginalized interests in the consumption and production of tourism (also see Scheyvens & Biddulph, 2017). From this perspective inclusivity is identified as a relative and contested, rather than an absolute, concept, the interpretation of which belongs to the involved parties. The identification of inclusivity depends on the stakeholders involved and the nature of inclusion, with inclusivity defined either by one party or by both producers and marginalized interests (Figure 1). A tourism producer may seek to include marginal interests but such interests may not recognize their inclusivity despite producer efforts, leading to a staged inclusivity or non-inclusive practices. You may even have situations where producers and marginalized interests believe that the relationship is inclusive but tourists do not recognize it as such, thereby missing the opportunity to communicate more fully inclusive tourism practices and with them the chance to show alternative practices for a more inclusive tourism. Importantly, the notion of inclusion is one that varies over socio-cultural contexts and that will change over time in response to shifts in the business,

Nature of inclusion	Tourist's perception of inclusivity of marginalised interests into tourism system	
	Genuine	Inauthentic/staged
Multi-party (both producers and marginalised interests see it as inclusive)	Fully inclusive	Denied inclusivity
Only one party (producer or marginalised group see it as inclusive)	Staged inclusivity	Non-inclusive / exploitative

Figure 1. Types of inclusive tourism.

political and socio-economic environments; the composition of interests and stakeholders, and new interpretations of what constitutes inclusive and sustainable tourism.

Given their role in tourism, the practices of large tour operators can influence the wider industry in becoming more inclusive and sustainable (Bricker & Black, 2016; Erskine & Meyer, 2012). However, while there is significant academic interest in the role of tour operators with respect to sustainability, this has often been focussed more on niche tourism areas or specific environmental practices, such as emissions or waste reduction (Gössling, Hall, & Scott, 2015), rather than the equity and social dimensions of sustainability that may provide an operational and strategic focus for inclusive tourism (Hall, 2008).

Outbound tour operators are key actors in mass tourism and hold critical positions in the tourism value chain, especially for developing countries, where they can act as major gatekeepers of tourism flows and influence practices (de Sausmarez, 2013; Dieke, 2013). Therefore, any account of the extent to which international mass tourism can be made more inclusive must include assessment of the role of outbound tour operators and the way in which they develop particular practices that relate to inclusiveness. This paper draws from new institutional theories in organization studies to understand the practice of sustainability and social responsibility work in large tour operators. Specifically, it examines the challenges to transforming mass tourism into becoming more inclusive in terms of recognizing and incorporating new practices, as informed by the case of one of the largest Scandinavian operators, Apollo, and its corporate social responsibility (CSR) and sustainability work.

This paper draws from in-depth interviews with company officers, and document analysis of CSR and sustainability reports. In order to understand what the CSR agenda of a large tour operator looks like, how it is shaped and the challenges faced in being more inclusive, this paper is structured around two questions: how are the institutional pressures and the organizational characteristics of MNCs and subsidiaries shaping tour operators' sustainability practices? and what are the firm's organizational responses to these pressures?

In the next section, the literature on sustainability, inclusive tourism and the tour operators sector is presented, followed by the methods to collect and analyse the data. The case study of Apollo Sweden is then presented. Next, the theoretical framework used to analyse the case is explained. Thereafter, the empirical study is analysed and discussed. This paper closes with reflections on how large corporations can be encouraged to provide more inclusive tourism services.

Sustainability, inclusive tourism and the tour operator sector

The tour operator sector has become increasingly consolidated in recent decades. A few large tour operators dominate the sector and account for almost two-thirds of the European market (Schwartz, Tapper and Font, 2008). German and British large tour operators alone dominate more than 45% of the European market, with four companies estimated to control over 90% of the UK holiday market (Budeanu, 2009).

Large tour operators draw together thousands of employees in travel agencies, hotels, airlines and other tourism firms in hundreds of destinations around the world. However, inclusiveness in terms of the participation of marginalized actors in the consumption and production of tourism has not historically been a priority. The concentration of power in the hands of a few global operators has led to conflicts between operators, suppliers and destinations. Large tour operators have often been seen more as agents of exclusion than inclusion, with this often being combined with related environmental degradation, sociocultural ignorance or disruption, limited returns to local economies, human rights abuse and other negative impacts (Hall & Brown, 2006). In general, mass-market operators offering mainstream packages (i.e. all-inclusive – where a single price covers includes all charges for lodging, meals and soft drinks, most alcoholic drinks, gratuities, and possibly other services, such as sports and other activities), and have not traditionally considered sustainability in business processes in the same way as specialist operators selling 'more sustainable products' (Bricker & Black, 2016; Bruni, Cassia, & Magno, 2017; Gössling et al., 2015; Hall, Gössling & Scott, 2015). Yet, the critical role of tour operators in the mass tourism market value chain means that they must become a focal point of any initiative that seeks to make tourism more inclusive of otherwise marginalized groups and issues. For example, via their role as employers of marginalized groups in local destinations in which the notion of inclusiveness includes aspects of decent work and fair salaries as well as more socially and environmentally inclusive procurement policies (Saarinen, Rogerson, & Hall, 2017), such as purchasing from local food suppliers (Hall & Gössling, 2016).

Given how strategic priorities are set in tourism corporations, CSR and sustainability policies, codes of conduct and certification systems are likely to be the main practices through which corporations would approach inclusive tourism. Therefore, improvements in our understanding of these areas (e.g. decent work, procurement policies and monitoring strategies), and recognition of any initiatives that bear the hallmarks of inclusive tourism, can help shed light on the mechanisms by which greater inclusiveness can be encouraged and achieved.

The factors shaping the adoption of sustainability practices by tour operators show how sustainability strategies, practices and standards, to which we would potentially add inclusive tourism, are likely conceived primarily as a means of risk management (to buffer or prevent negative public image), as a competitive advantage (e.g. brand value and reputation), and as a regulation avoidance strategy (Schwartz et al., 2008), rather than as a means to provide improved services to customers, cost savings or business opportunities (Budeanu, 2007), or inclusion. Compared to other sectors, such as accommodation, the tour operator sector arguably lags behind in the integration of sustainability in business practices due to a combination of reasons: tour operators do not always take a long-term view of destination development, as their operations are more spatially flexible and easier to move between destinations compared to suppliers such as hotels; and they may claim a lack of control over impacts in destinations. Operators operate on small profit margins and the resultant pressure on suppliers to reduce prices can limit supplier capacity to invest in quality improvements (Alegre & Said, 2015) or other strategies that do not have a relatively immediate return. The industry also works with a multitude of suppliers operating under different national regulations and interests which can make it more difficult to develop consistent sustainability and CSR programs. On the demand side, customers' interest in responsible tourism services and products, and willingness to pay extra for inclusive practices in general, appears significantly lower compared to, for example, specific elements such as local food (Hall & Gössling, 2016). In relation to the regulatory environment, most of the tour package legislation is quality, health and safety related, and there is usually very little specific regulatory pressure for improved environmental or social performance in tour operator's operations. In addition, cost savings from adopting practices are not so clearly identified for tour operators as, for example, for hotels (Budeanu, 2007; Gössling et al., 2015; Tepelus, 2005).

Methods

Scandinavia is routinely cited as a global leader in CSR and sustainability (Strand, Freeman, & Hockerts, 2015). Apollo is one of the three largest tour operators in Sweden and one of the Nordic pioneers of proactively adopting CSR and sustainability practices in tourism (Schyst Resande, 2008). This paper adopts a 'critical case' approach (Flyvbjerg, 2001). Informed by this approach we have selected as favourable a setting as possible, one of the top leading Swedish tour operators working proactively with sustainability, for examining the integration of sustainability in large tour operators. A critical case approach provides the opportunity to draw valid insights from a single case that has strategic importance for a general problem, such as the challenges that large operators face in making mass tourism a more inclusive activity.

Data collection involved analysis of documents such as ethical guidelines, policies, standards, sustainability and assessment reports, voluntary performance schemes, and codes of conduct (Supplemental data). The websites of the parent (Kuoni) and daughter company (Apollo) as well as those of CSR-related stakeholders and collaboration partners were also reviewed. Semi-structured interviews were carried out with officials at Apollo and Kuoni. The interviews served to complement and triangulate the information coming from documents and electronic sources. All interviews were recorded and transcribed. The number of interviews conducted and the positions of those interviewed at Apollo and Kuoni is not stated here as this would potentially publicly identify participants.

The documents, websites and interviews were analysed through qualitative content analysis, structured by the two research questions and guided by the concepts stemming from the institutional theories used in the analysis (presented later after the case): coercive, normative and mimetic isomorphism as well as the organizational responses (strategies and tactics) of the firm to these pressures. The data coming from the personal interviews with employees at Apollo is triangulated with text documents, interview material from the parent company (Kuoni) and electronic sources. Combining methods helps to overcome the limitations of using a single case with limited interview opportunities. Interviews were conducted during spring 2015. The Apollo Nordic division was acquired by the German REWE-travel group in summer 2015. No significant changes have been observed in terms of sustainability work since then, although this new situation has not been the focus of this study.

Apollo Sweden, sustainability strategy and work

In this section we present the case of Apollo Sweden and its sustainability work, informed by corporate documents, websites, news, reports and interviews. After we present our analytical framework, the empirical data will be analysed and discussed.

Apollo Sweden

In Sweden three large tour operators (Ving, Apollo and Fritidsresor) account for 80% of the outbound tour operator market (SwedWatch and Fair Action, 2015). Apollo was founded by Fotios Costoulas in 1986 and ran as a family business providing travel from Sweden to Greece. In 2001 it was bought by Kuoni Holding Ltd, a Switzerland-based provider of services to the international travel industry and governments. Its activities are centred on global travel, travel services distribution, visa provision and tour operating, including hotel, accommodation, and land and transportation services, tours and activities. Apollo Sweden, together with its Finnish, Norwegian and Danish counterparts, and the airline Novair, belongs to the Apollo Travel Group. With approximately 900 employees and one million international travellers annually, Apollo Travel Group has an annual turnover of over US$ 590 million (Apollo, 2016a). In mid-2015 Apollo was sold to the German REWE-group and became part of the DER Touristik travel division as DER Touristik Nordic AB including Apollo Sweden, Denmark, Norway and Finland. Apollo offers travel to 20 countries in Europe, 10 in Asia, 5 in Africa, 5 in the Americas and 1 in Oceania. Among the most popular tourist destinations are Greece, Turkey, Spain, Cyprus, Thailand, Jordan, Tobago and Cuba.

Managing and strategizing sustainability at Apollo

CSR and sustainability management are integrated with the communication management department in Apollo. There were two employees working directly with sustainability at management level: one responsible for sustainability and communication; and another who worked part-time mostly on the Travelife system (a business-to-business sustainability certification program implemented by Apollo, explained below) with their suppliers. Plans, strategies, and practices that fall under the category of sustainability, CSR and ethics have existed at Apollo since it became part of the Kuoni group in 2001. However, CSR and sustainability 'was not the highest prioritized issue by the former manager of the firm' (Apollo employee).

Kuoni's Group CSR Strategy was the framework within which all work with sustainability matters at group level was assembled from 2001 until 2015. The Kuoni CSR agenda was reviewed every three years and was formulated by the central board of directors at Kuoni's headquarters in Zurich. The strategy consisted of six core areas: employees, human rights, sustainable products, natural environment, stakeholder management and sustainable supply chain management. The mapping and priority setting of sustainability topics was based on stakeholder dialogues carried out in wider and inner stakeholder consultation circles (Kuoni, 2014). Inner stakeholders were members and employees at all levels within the Kuoni Group, including the central board of directors and CSR officials from business units. Apollo participated in the stakeholder consultations for the development of Kuoni's Group CSR strategy as an internal stakeholder. External stakeholders include international, national and local non-governmental organizations (NGOs), investors, experts, suppliers, consultants, and international organizations. The strategy was also built on a range of international conventions, codes of conduct and sustainability charters including the *UN Global Compact*, the *Universal Declaration of Human Rights*, the *UN Guiding Principles on Business and Human Rights*, the OECD *Guidelines for Multinational*

Enterprises and ECPAT's *Code of Conduct*. Significantly, from an inclusive tourism perspective, even though such agreements are often held up as cornerstones of CSR practice, local communities had only a limited role in such dialogues.

Internally, Kuoni had a 'CSR steering group', in which Apollo participated, that met twice a year (Kuoni, 2016). This group consisted of representatives from Kuoni's business units, core corporate functions and external CSR specialists. The purpose of the committee was to plan CSR strategies and activities for the entire group, as well as review performance and ensure that the Group CSR strategy was aligned between business units. This was also a platform where Apollo exchanged experiences with other participants, provided inputs to the board of directors and contributed to central CSR objectives.

Apollo's sustainability strategy

Kuoni's Group CSR strategy served as the guiding framework for Apollo's work but they were encouraged to design their own corporate strategy for sustainability by taking a point of departure in the core areas of this agenda (Kuoni interview). How the Kuoni's Group CSR strategy was implemented by Apollo was neither strictly stipulated nor regulated. Apollo's CSR agenda did not need the approval of the central board of Kuoni (Kuoni Interview). Apollo's sustainability/CSR strategy has been divided into four areas: human rights, climate change, sustainable supply chain management and sustainable products (Apollo, 2016b). The following projects, dealing with the social dimension of sustainability and integrated in Apollo's human rights and supply chain areas (Table 1), are described below before subsequent analysis.

ECPAT – the code

ECPAT is an international NGO working against sexual exploitation of children since 1992 in Thailand and other South Asian countries. ECPAT Sweden was created after the World Congress against Commercial Sexual Exploitation of Children was hosted by the Swedish Government in 1996. The Code, which is a guideline consisting of six measures aimed at helping tourism businesses to protect children, was the result of this congress. Apollo states on its website that the protection of children is one of the most prioritized issues in Apollo's work with sustainability. An Apollo officer emphasizes the focus on children due to the empathy showed by travellers and employees when they come in contact with suffering children in destinations, as also observed via customer evaluation forms. Concerns raised in Sweden regarding the harmful impacts of tourism on children in South-East Asia destinations are also behind this prioritization. In the words of an Apollo official regarding ratification of the Code:

> It reaches a point where we understand that we neither can nor want to be held accountable for certain things, for which we feel that we must act and take on our responsibility (...) The

Table 1. Summary of the social components of Apollo's CSR agenda.

Human rights	Sustainable supply chain management
• Suppliers' Code of Conduct, 2008	• Suppliers' Code of Conduct, 2008
• Statement of Commitment on Human Rights, 2012	• Travelife Sustainability System, 2009
• ECPACT – The Code, 2001	
• Collaboration with SOS Children's Villages, 2004	

risks of not doing anything is that we acquire a bad reputation. In the end, caring for the corporate image and the reputation is a strong driving force.

In order to prevent their services being misused for exploitative purposes, Apollo joined forces with fellow signatories such as the Swedish government, ECPAT, industry partners and tour operators such as Fritidsresor and Ving. This collaborative strategy was motivated by the 'pleasant feeling of being united and not having to stand alone, and to be able to show a united front' (Apollo officer). The signatories to The Code in Sweden meet twice a year to discuss topics and strategies related to child trafficking. The Code was ratified independently by Apollo in 2001. Apollo and Nordic partners also encouraged Kuoni to ratify this policy.

SOS children's villages

Apollo's ratification of the ECPAT Code led to the collaboration in Sweden with SOS Children's Villages in 2004. SOS Children's Villages is an international organization giving family-based childcare to children without families in order to allow them to grow up in safety. Apollo donates one million SEK per year to a SOS village in Phuket. This money funds a kindergarten and three SOS families in the village. Since 2015 Apollo is partner to SOS Children's Villages at the Nordic Kuoni level, and funds an emergency help program for families in Syria. An Apollo officer states that such cooperation is a good way to show their commitment to children's right issues in a concrete way. The NGO's good reputation is also important to choosing the partner: 'Since SOS Children's Villages is a very well-known organization with a credible image it is a way for us to use their brand together with our own, which has a positive effect' (Apollo officer).

Travelife sustainability system

Travelife is a business-to-business sustainability certification programme supported by the European Union and the European Industry Association Tour Operator Initiative. It consists of an accreditation body directed towards tourism industry enterprises to make operations more sustainable. Businesses can purchase a subscription to the system and have their performance level independently assessed via an audit and the top performers in terms of these verified audits receive a Travelife award. Major UK and German tour operators, such as First Choice, Thompson, TUI, Thomas Cook, have subscribed to the Travelife Sustainability System as their preferred means of assessing their accommodation providers against environmental, social and economic criteria. Kuoni group was a founding member and has been involved in its development since 2004. Apollo achieved the status of being Travelife Certified as a tour operator in 2014 and they have been using the certification for hotel and accommodations among suppliers since 2009. Around 100 Apollo hotels are Travelife members and have achieved this certification. However, the certification, unlike the Suppliers' code of conduct, is not required of all suppliers.

The Travelife Sustainability system was one of the standards applicable to all Kuoni group members. A CSR official states that the creation of Travelife by a group of European tour operators reflected how 'the entire branch felt a need to use a standardized and simple way of ordering their hotels'. Among the many different alternatives such as ISO and other standards, the official states that 'Travelife stood out as a recognized standardized way of classifying hotels which made it possible to easily communicate to customers that this is the way we look at these questions'. Thus, the adoption of these standards was also driven by the need to promote to customers that the company had embraced sustainability practices in its operations, while their implementation has also resulted in modifications in standard operating procedures and the generation of new standards. The new owner group DER Turistik was already a member of Travelife.

Suppliers' code of conduct

The suppliers' code of conduct was first developed in 2008 by the Kuoni group in collaboration with external stakeholders such as experts, consultants and NGOs. It consists of six areas of sustainability (compliance with applicable law, environment, human rights and labour conditions, sexual exploitation of children and adolescents, local sourcing and benefiting communities, and monitoring and enforcement) and ratification of the policy was required by all Apollo's suppliers and monitored through the Travelife system. Apollo also contributed to the content of the *Suppliers' Code of Conduct* via the inner consultation circles for sustainability strategy making and, more actively, by Apollo's petition to add a clause on animals' rights issues in 2014. Apollo lobbied to include this topic as they perceived increasing customer and employee concern for animal welfare. According to Apollo officials, the concern was detected via customer feedback but it was also regarded as an issue raised by society at large in Sweden, and mobilized by NGOs. At the time of writing (February, 2017) the suppliers' code of conduct continued to operate under the new owner.

Statement of commitment on human rights

The *Statement of Commitment on Human Rights* establishes that the group will respect and promote human rights through leading by example in areas as labour rights (e.g. following international and national law, forbidding all forms of forced labour, freedom to terminate employment, freedom of association and right to collective bargaining), the rights of the child and due diligence. The standard is automatically transferred to Apollo's suppliers when a contract is confirmed and compliance is monitored with assistance from Travelife. The creation of the *Statement of Commitment on Human Rights* was an initiative of Apollo and Nordic partners. Apollo urged the creation of a policy document on human rights within Kuoni's steering committee, leading to the Statement being passed by Kuoni's board of directors in 2012.

Despite considerable progress in terms of the improvement of human and labour rights, Swedish NGOs reported during Autumn 2015 illegal labour conditions for hotel employees in properties used by the three largest Swedish tour operators (Apollo, Fritidsresor and Ving) in Dubai (SwedWatch and Fair Action, 2015) and Turkey (Fair Traveller, 2015). The report reveals how housekeepers, room attendants and other migrant workers at hotels used by the three tour operators in Dubai worked days as long as twelve hours with little or no overtime pay. Workers also stated that they paid for employment as well as employers holding their passports, which according to the International Labour Organization is a sign of forced labour. These practices violate local labour law and international conventions, as well as the human rights policies of the Swedish tour operators themselves.

The three Swedish tour operators replied in a joint communication stating they did not have knowledge about rights violations at the hotels where their customers were staying

(SwedWatch and Fair Action, 2015). Nevertheless, according to an Apollo officer, the company had performed a risk analysis regarding human rights in Dubai which shows that it is a high-risk destination, especially with regard to migrant workers (SwedWatch and Fair Action, 2015). The company also argued that the staff responsible for the contact with the hotels has instructions to report any breach of the code, and that no breach had been reported.

In a collective response to the publication of this report, the three tour operators acknowledge the violation of labour rights and communicated that together with the Travelife certification system (see below for further details about the certification system) they will start monitoring more hotels in Dubai (SwedWatch, 2015). They also argued that this is an issue affecting more than these three tour operators and it, therefore, requires a collective response. Furthermore, Apollo acknowledges that despite increasing public awareness and company concern over labour issues, consumer pressure for more sustainable and inclusive travel is not so significant (Swedish Radio A, 13/10/2015; Swedish Radio B, 13/10/2015).

Within the Kuoni Group the *Travelife Sustainability* system and *the Kuoni Suppliers Code of Conduct* were the only two standards applicable to all members and served as minimum requirements for the business units' work with sustainability issues. Apollo was encouraged by Kuoni to implement these policies, and Kuoni's CSR department regularly provide information and learning tools aiming to facilitate their implementation. However, according to Kuoni's CSR department, they struggled to achieve a 'consistent image' between members of the group in terms of sustainability. Kuoni did not monitor units such as Apollo and had no enforcement mechanism exerting punishment for non-compliance. Yet, Apollo's reliance upon Kuoni as a daughter unit means that they felt required to address these sustainability issues: 'it is not as if something would happen if we wouldn't work with sustainability and implement these standards, since they are informal requirements. However, disregarding these issues is not an alternative, it simply would not be possible' (Apollo officer).

Aware of the requirement to respond to the mother company's demands on sustainability strategy, an official stated: 'The central board of Kuoni have certain targets which they want the units to fulfil, so it is a matter of complying with their desire' (Apollo). Apollo also considered it was important to fulfil the expectations of Kuoni as Apollo also 'want to be able to impact the direction of the work that is centrally managed at Kuoni'. According to the Apollo official, the implementation of these standards has led to a steady development of awareness around issues of sustainability among Apollo employees. However, field participation of representatives from Apollo's destination areas in the strategizing of Apollo's sustainability is less visible. Local regulations as well as ideas picked up from destination personnel are mediated to Apollo's central board. Yet there are no established mechanisms to channel the flow of local demands. In the following the theoretical framework used to analyse the case is introduced.

Institutional theory

Institutional theory provides a useful framework to analyse the extent of integration of sustainability practices into corporations. While use of this theory is relatively limited in tourism (Adu-Ampong, 2017; Zapata & Hall, 2012), it has been valuable in examining sustainable practices (Van Wijk, Van der Duim, Lamers, & Sumba, 2015), including CSR reporting (de Grosbois, 2016). The following elaborates the concepts of institutional isomorphic pressures, organizational responses to institutional pressures and processes of organizational learning that are then used to frame our case under the prism of the concept of inclusive tourism.

Institutional theories focus on the pursuit of legitimacy aside from economic efficiency, with the resulting organizational conformity arising due to social norms and rituals (Meyer & Rowan, 1977). In their pursuit of legitimacy, organizations modify themselves to be compatible with the characteristics (organizational structures, beliefs and discourses) of their institutional environments. As a consequence, organizations from the same field will often be structurally similar as they respond to similar institutional pressures (cognitive, normative and coercive), resulting in a process of isomorphism (Scott, 2008).

Coercive isomorphism refers to the conformity to certain practices as a result of rules, laws or other coercive mechanisms, economic and regulatory sanctions. Yet, under conditions of uncertainty in a relatively unregulated organizational field, as in the case of sustainability in the travel industry (Gössling et al., 2015), normative and cognitive aspects of the institutional environment become more salient. Normative isomorphism comes, for example, from unquestioned adherence to industry standards but also prevalent values and preferences in a market or a community. While, cognitive isomorphism (or mimesis) refers to the unconscious reproduction of standards, practices or structures following those who appear to be successful in the organizational field.

However, organizations within the same field do not always show similar sustainability strategies and practices (Hall et al., 2016; Scott, 2008; Zapata & Hall, 2012) despite being exposed to common institutional pressures. More recent developments in institutional theory show how institutional forces can also lead to heterogeneity in a sector rather than isomorphic homogeneity, given that organizations differ in their receptivity to pressures (Hoffman, 2001). For example, the power of the department or individual promoting CSR and sustainability practices is an internal aspect that may explain different responses. Delmas and Toffel (2008) also showed how organizations channel institutional pressures through different sub-units, which frame pressures according to their routines. For example, legal departments frame them in terms of risk and liability, while financial departments do it in terms of costs and revenue. The consequence being that sustainability could be differentially framed within the same organization as a competitiveness strategy, as regulatory pressure, or as an ethical responsibility (Bansal & Roth, 2000). Other internal organizational features such as the role of leadership values (Egri & Herman, 2000), managerial attitudes (Cordano & Frieze, 2000; Sharma, 2000), and historical environmental performance can also influence how managers perceive stakeholder pressures and their response (Prakash, 2000), and the visibility of the firm. Therefore, differences in adoption of sustainability tourism practices reflect not only different levels of institutional pressures but also differences in organizational characteristics, since internal organizational dynamics act as moderating factors that magnify or diminish the influence of institutional pressures.

Oliver (1991) also suggests that organizations respond to their institutional environments in different ways, varying from compliance, compromise, avoidance, defiance and manipulation (Table 2). One of the possible responses is what has been termed as 'decoupling' (Meyer & Rowan, 1977), which refers to the process whereby

Table 2. Strategic responses to institutional pressures.

Strategies	Tactics	Examples
Acquiesce	Habit	Follow taken-for-granted institutional norms and practices
	Imitation	Copy and mimic institutional models
	Compliance	Obey rules and accept norms and practices
Compromise	Balance	Balance the expectations of multiple actors and stakeholders
	Pacification	Placate and accommodate institutional actors and elements
	Bargain	Negotiate with institutional constituents and stakeholders
Avoid	Conceal	Disguise nonconformity
	Buffer	Loosen institutional attachments
	Escape	Change goals, activities or domains
Defy	Dismiss	Ignore explicit institutional norms, mores and values
	Challenge	Contest institutional rules and requirements
	Attack	Assault the sources of institutional pressure
Manipulate	Co-option	Cooperate with influential constituents and stakeholders
	Influence	Seek to shape institutional values, rules and criteria
	Control	Seek to dominate institutional constituents and processes

Source: After Oliver (1991).

organizations 'that adopt particular structures or procedures may opt to respond in a ceremonial manner, making changes in their formal structures to signal conformity but then buffering internal units, allowing them to operate independent of these pressures' (Scott, 2008: 171). The term has been used to refer to implementation gaps in sustainability standards (Bromley & Powell, 2012; Jamali, 2010). Yet, beyond the decoupling explanation, CSR and sustainability reports and codes of conduct, although taken initially as ceremonial conformity, can turn performative and become real (Barley & Zhang, 2012). Ceremonially adopted rules can lead to change over time and recouple formal and informal structures (Egels-Zandén, 2014); as a result of reflection and negotiations that convince internal organizational actors of their appropriateness independent of instrumental considerations (Dashwood, 2012). Internal and external debates of sustainability and responsibility may, therefore, also create conditions for future change through organizational learning (Dashwood, 2012, 2014), an issue that may be critical for inclusion of inclusive tourism in CSR discourses.

Discussion

In this section, we will analyse and discuss the case of Apollo Sweden and its sustainability work informed by the theoretical framework presented above with the aim to understand what mass tourism corporations do in practice for an inclusive tourism, why their CSR and sustainability agenda is shaped as it is and the challenges they face in being more inclusive. In order to do that, we explain how institutional pressures (mimetic, coercive and normative isomorphism) shape tour operators' sustainability practices and the organizational responses to these pressures.

Institutional pressures for a more inclusive tourism

Mimetic isomorphism
In terms of mimetic isomorphism, Apollo's sustainability work follows international conventions, standards and codes of conduct promoted by international agencies such *UN Global Compact, Universal Declaration of Human Rights*, and the *UN Guiding Principles on*

Business and Human Rights. These standards and codes have turned into 'rational myths' (Meyer & Rowan, 1977), taken for granted and uncontested norms and solutions (Brunsson & Jacobsson, 2000) to the problem of integrating sustainability into business practices (Jamali, 2010). Unlike the diverse range of tourism industry codes and certification systems, these international standards have achieved worldwide recognition and are mimetically reproduced by large corporations. From that perspective, Travelife has turned into a norm for the certification of sustainability practices among European tour operators and their suppliers. Such initiatives help to harmonize the fragmented efforts of individual actors (Schwartz et al., 2008), and become uncontested norms as a taken for granted solution to problems of non-compliance with codes of conduct, as elaborated below.

Coercive isomorphism
Despite sustainability in tourism destinations being under-regulated (Tepelus, 2005), there are a number of coercive forces that determine Apollo's sustainability agenda. The Kuoni group has created a CSR system based on two compulsory components: the Kuoni *Suppliers Code of Conduct* and the Travelife certification system. These two components are the minimum requirement from the parent corporation, and are defined as 'recipes' by the Kuoni CSR manager with the flexibility to be translated into the different national contexts through strategies of compromise, such as negotiation (Oliver, 1991). These two components, therefore, provide consistency and cohesion to the group, helping to integrate the diversity of practices in different locations. Subsequently, the *Supplier's Code of Conduct* turned into a compulsory commitment for Apollo's suppliers. Yet in practice only 100 supplier hotels are monitored for some of the standards in the code by the Travelife certification system. In addition, these codes and conduct and certification systems rarely include local stakeholders in their design; which reflects in the poor inclusion of local voices and marginalized groups in their design.

Normative isomorphism
Apollo's sustainability agenda is also shaped by shifts in societal debate and the emergence of salient issues (Bansal & Roth, 2000), many of them promoted by NGOs, while others proceed from customer suggestions. NGOs in Sweden such as Shyst Resande (2015) or SwedWatch (Fair Trade Center and SwedWatch, 2008; SwedWatch and Fair Action, 2015) have triggered changes via publicizing research reports and conferences, and have nudged tour operators to bring new practices into their operations. This reveals that, in the absence of stronger regulations in destinations, the existence of strong pressures and/or stakeholders act as institutional factors in generating situations that encourage operators to integrate new values and norms remains crucial. Marginalized groups at destinations that are the focus of inclusive initiatives may be disadvantaged as a stakeholder in the development of company CSR agendas because they do not have a strong direct or indirect presence in the process.

The clause on animal rights in the *Suppliers' Code of Conduct*, the statement of commitment to human rights and the acknowledgement of ECPAT by the Apollo Nordic group illustrate how values and demands from stakeholders and what is perceived to exist in the generating markets travel to the daughter firm influencing the Apollo's sustainability agenda (Van Huijstee & Glasbergen, 2010). Partnering with NGOs is also an example of normative pressures. The importance of brand and legitimacy, and the potential to use this relationship to differentiate from competitors, is positively related to compliance in previous studies of CSR firms and NGOs (Hendry, 2006).

Industry associations such as the Tour Operator Initiative, to which Kuoni belongs to and which is responsible for the Travelife System; and other corporate collaborative platforms such as the one created by the three large tour operators in Sweden, also perform as a source of pressure by creating new standards, intensifying close scrutiny among competitors and transferring information about best practices. The high field cohesion (Bansal & Roth, 2000) in the tour operators' field, sometimes sparked by NGOs as explained above, also served to pressure Apollo to introduce sustainability standards and practices. Standards and norms *per se*, such as the Travelife System, are also pressing other tour operator firms to adopt them via normative isomorphism. This normative pressure turns into a coercive pressure for many hotel suppliers that have to work with the certification systems if that is stipulated in their contracts (although currently only for a few), and into a cognitive pressure prompting others to imitate the behaviour of successful pioneers.

Filtering institutional pressures

There are a number of organizational features of Apollo that further explain how the institutional pressures presented above are filtered to the organization, shaping how these pressures are internally translated. Size is one of them. Apollo's sustainability work only began after acquisition by Kuoni. Therefore, belonging to a large MNC can amplify the institutional pressures to work towards particular forms of tourism due to their visibility.

Another organizational feature is strategic positioning. In Apollo Sweden the CSR and Sustainability work is allocated within the Communication and PR department. As a result, CSR and sustainability work is often, although not only, framed in terms of brand management and risk management, reflecting Delmas and Toffel's (2008) finding that the subunit through which institutional pressures are channelled will affect the framing of CSR and sustainability issues. The department has limited human resources, as is usually the case for sustainability in firms, and competes internally for resources. One could speculate that firm crises such as the Dubai report are actually 'good' for CSR units, since they show the critical nature of this organizational function in terms of firm legitimacy, and might work to attract resources (as when Apollo decided to put more resources into monitoring hotels through the Travelife system).

Finally, a firm's historical sustainability performance influences how managers perceive stakeholders' pressures and how to respond to them. This means that managers in firms whose reputation has suffered, such as in the case of the Dubai Report in 2015, may be more sensitive to sustainability issues than those in other companies (Prakash, 2000).

Organizational responses to institutional pressures for a more inclusive tourism

Compliance with institutional pressures coming from the parent company and the travel market are not, however, the only two organizational responses shown by Apollo in its sustainability work. Apollo's sustainability work demonstrates how there is much room for buffering, bargaining, negotiation and influencing the parent organization, following Oliver's (1991) organizational responses (Table 1).

Buffering/decoupling

As shown by the Dubai scandal, suppliers' codes of conduct can be loosely coupled to changes in the hotel suppliers' employment practices. This episode reveals how codes of conduct risk becoming a form of symbolic compliance since they are not necessarily monitored through independent audits, creating the illusion of a staged inclusivity (Figure 1). In their website Apollo invites travellers interested in sustainability to choose a Travelife certified hotel transferring the responsibility for more inclusive tourism to the consumer and to the hotelier. Even if Travelife has come to unify a diverse range of certification systems in the sector, and are based on web-based self-assessments, individual audits are still necessary to monitor compliance with standards (Schwartz et al., 2008). However, the certification of a given supplier is not necessarily a guarantee of total compliance and the risk of further loosely coupled structures remains, as demonstrated by the research conducted by Fair Travel in Travelife certified hotels used by Swedish tour operators in Turkey (Schyst Resande, 2015). By revealing to the public the violation of labour rights by these suppliers, the NGOs evidenced the exploitative character (Figure 1) of the tour operator's sustainability work. Monitoring compliance with sustainability standards in order to move towards more fully inclusive practices may initially require the allocation of more resources. Yet given that the tour operator sector already operates with very low profit margins, experiences high competition, is budget oriented, and does not have customers motivated by sustainability preferences, this creates considerable challenges in absorbing the costs of monitoring performance (Schwartz et al., 2008). Business would, therefore, require a clear financial return to embark on such a course or face potential brand harm if they do not.

Since the risk for buffering is high in a lowly regulated sector with few specific resources allocated to monitoring gaps between voluntary standards and practices, the role of NGOs and the media in exposing non-implementation or fulfilment of standards is crucial. When the incongruences between the suppliers' code of conduct and the labour conditions of the hotels in Dubai were publicly revealed by the SwedWatch and Fair Travel report, the Swedish tour operators' reaction was to act together, making use of the collaborative platform they have created in Sweden to discuss issues of sustainability and social responsibility, to manage the reputation crisis collectively (Prakash & Potoski, 2007). Such an approach aims to 'pacify' (Oliver, 1991) institutional pressure and helps to manage brand crisis and regain lost legitimacy. Furthermore, as certification systems have gained credibility in the organizational field they have become a 'rational myth' (Meyer & Rowan, 1977) with respect to sustainable tourism, and recognized as the most trustful means to restate legitimacy.

Negotiating and influencing central CSR and sustainability work

Beyond decoupling, the Apollo case shows how the process of creation and implementation of CSR and sustainability is far from simple compliance to top-down policies. Negotiating, influencing, balancing, pacifying and co-opting tactics (Oliver, 1991) were displayed by Apollo and help explain why its sustainability agenda looks the way it does. Negotiations were ongoing for the design and implementation of the various components of Apollo's CSR policy. The statements on human rights and the ECPAT Code were introduced to the Kuoni group's CSR strategy via the Nordic partners (as a result of normative pressures as elaborated previously), and then turned into the norm and spread out to the rest of the group via Kuoni. Even in the case of the two components coming top-down from Kuoni (suppliers' code of conduct and Travelife) Apollo included new standards (Travelife) and added a clause on animals' rights issues in 2014 (also stemming from normative societal pressures as previously explained), which were incorporated into the general standards applied to all Kuoni daughter firms. This shows how firms in MNCs can also contribute to create new rules (Dashwood, 2012) and have the ability to influence (Oliver, 1991) the CSR agenda. CSR policy making in MNCs can, therefore, be a negotiated process influenced by subsidiaries' local practices. The case at hand represents a transition between unilateral inclusive policies towards a broader participation of stakeholders and institutional constituents. These windows of opportunity for subsidiaries to shape central CSR agendas are especially significant during agenda formation. Corporate CSR and sustainability work are the result of the history of a given organization and practices accumulate historically in layers when some of them fade away but others remain, even if the original pressure to introduce them has ceased (D'Aummno, Succi, & Alexander, 2000). However, the extent to which Apollo's CSR agenda will remain under their new owners remains to be seen.

The firm's efforts to anticipate sustainability standards and create new ones within the parent company also represent an organizational strategy to translate these standards locally (Sweden) (what Oliver (1991) refers to as balancing and pacifying the expectations of multiple constituents) by introducing measures, such as the animals' rights clause, that are perceived as relevant by the local market, but which may then be regarded as appropriate by the wider organization. Finally, partnering with NGOs with a good reputation such as SOS Children's Villages responds to a manipulative strategy whereby the firm intents to co-opt the NGO (Oliver, 1991), importing this influential constituent and thereby gaining social legitimacy; while the NGO also tries to influence and manage the firm's social responsibility agenda and gain necessary economic resources for their operations. This relationship may also offer insights as to how issues and mechanisms related to inclusivity may arise in company CSR agendas.

Organizational learning: collaborative platforms, compromise and sense-making
The creation of collaborative platforms can be interpreted in different ways. Partnership is a classical strategy to influence institutional constituents: manage crisis and reputation (Prakash & Potoski, 2007), negotiate with NGOs and governments, anticipate future regulation and influence public opinion. Yet, there is also an interesting aspect of organizational learning attached to these collaborations. These platforms turn into spaces for external dialogue and the scanning of best practices. Since Apollo is one of the largest and more visible firms in Sweden, they help define social responsibility and are a role model (Dashwood, 2014). Such firms, therefore, potentially contribute to creation and dissemination of norms, standards and rules about how a more inclusive tourism could be performed by mass tourism corporations.

Internally, debate around issues of sustainability also generates opportunities for 'sense-making' (Weick, 1995), finding a compromise between the institutional pressures and the internal practices within the firm. Apollo, by including a new clause into Kuoni's suppliers' code of conduct or modifying some of the Travelife's standards, tried to make sense and contextualize these general standards, coming from a top-down CSR policy, into Swedish society. Similarly, the creation within Kuoni of the inner CSR circles can be interpreted in terms of a strategy to enrol both external and internal actors (NGOs, governmental organizations, subsidiaries, employees, trade unions and different departments) into the sustainability work of the firm. In a context of scarce resources characteristic of the tour operator sector, internal and external collaborative strategies seem to be crucial both to convince or 'influence' (Oliver, 1991) external and internal actors of the criticality of CSR work and to gain the necessary resources and legitimacy to act. However, these collaborative networks, as often occurs with sustainability work, perform multiple roles: they can be used by NGOs and others to introduce changes in industry operations to facilitate sustainable tourism and they can also be a platform to define new norms and standards to be followed by others; but they can also be used by the industry to gain legitimacy and manage brand risk more effectively.

Operating in complex organizational fields, balancing interests
Tour operators operate in complex institutional environments, made of a multitude of constituents (parent corporations, generating markets, destination authorities, employees and NGOs) in changing, sometimes volatile, contexts with high levels of uncertainty. Apollo turned into a definer of social responsibility in tourism in Sweden. Its sustainability work reflects internal negotiations with the parent company to shape the CSR agenda and adapt it, although sometimes superficially, to the local context. It reflects how Apollo had to balance (Oliver, 1991) the interests, values and practices both in the society where its operations are embedded as a generating market, and the parent company's demands. It also shows how societal values and expectations travel from the customers to the MNC headquarters via national firms.

Yet, local voices from the destinations appear underrepresented in the internal processes for defining the CSR agenda leading towards staged inclusivity rather than fully inclusive practices, as often is the case in the planning process of certification systems (Haaland & Aas, 2010). In practice, their relative exclusion from the CSR organization charter means that there are no institutional elements for destination actors to shape a tour operator's agenda outside of the immediate local tourism industry suppliers and NGOs. Hence, other than coercive forces stemming from (often weak) regulations and laws as well as observing initiatives by destination partners, there is no formal mechanism for the flow of ideas from local actors back to Apollo. Thus, despite various sustainability measures taken by Kuoni and Apollo, these large tour operators remain far off from practicing fully inclusive tourism, since marginalized groups engaged in the production of services, as shown by the Dubai scandal, are excluded from the CSR agenda making. This latter aspect reinforces that the gap between the MNC headquarters and their shareholders and the destinations and the suppliers' employees is large since the interests of local production actors are not represented in the definition of rules that are centrally defined but locally implemented (Medina, 2005).

Certain issues are also more significant or salient than others (Bansal & Roth, 2000) for different organizational constituents. For example, as a result of the work of NGOs and government agencies, sexual and child abuse are salient issues in Swedish society, while issues relative to labour conditions, as in the case of Dubai, are not so controversial. In other words, the issues that become integrated with notions of inclusivity on CSR agendas depend on what is significant for constituents. In their specific spatial and institutional context and from the operator's perspective, the most significant constituent is the consumer.

A positive interpretation could be that not all salient issues can turn salient at once. As noted in the garment and footwear industry (Egels-Zandén, 2014), issues of child and forced labour (considered in Western societies as unacceptable) have been the first ones to be complied with. However, perhaps more realistically is the need to recognize that corporations usually interpret or argue that they have a legal responsibility to maximize returns to shareholders (Bakan, 2005; Stout, 2013), otherwise referred to as shareholder value exclusivity or primacy. While this approach does not preclude the adoption of more inclusive approaches to tourism, it does make it more difficult if such measures are not perceived as contributing towards a business bottom line. This is especially problematic for marginalized groups with tour operators who have the capacity to shift capacity between destinations when their activities are not generating sufficient return on investment or when they are subject to pressures that will affect returns in the future.

Conclusions

MNCs and daughter firms play a major role in sustainability work, as was the case of Apollo after their acquisition by Kuoni, including inclusive tourism which can be regarded as a significant element of the social and equity dimensions of sustainability. Although Apollo may be regarded as 'inclusive tourism light', it should be noted that in international terms their adoption of standards, compacts and codes with respect to human rights, children's rights and responsible business actions put them at the forefront of what many tourism corporations actually do with respect to inclusivity.

Notions of inclusive tourism are usually framed as part of CSR strategies and activities. This case study, therefore, sheds significant light on the processes by which inclusive tourism issues may become part of the CSR and sustainability agenda of large transnational tourism businesses. Critically, this research also suggests that the incorporation of inclusive tourism concerns within the CSR agenda-setting process is primarily a response to customer concerns, the activities of NGOs, or because of negative publicity. Regardless, these may affect brand reputation and consumer behaviour.

As the case illustrates, despite top-down coercive and normative pressures affecting tour operators within large international businesses, sub-units such as Apollo are not passive receivers of these pressures. Instead, issues of agency, negotiation and institutional entrepreneurship (Hardy & Maguire, 2008) have to be taken into consideration (Oliver, 1991; Suddaby, 2010), especially when flexible CSR and sustainability frameworks operate, and the agenda and organizational field is being shaped under structuration. In this vein, this paper calls attention towards the opportunities that daughter organizations within multinational corporations and their constituents have in shaping institutional arrangements through internal collaborative platforms and bringing concerns of inclusivity into the multinational CSR policy. This may be particularly significant in the absence of strong CSR regulatory frameworks in destinations. Yet, importantly, and not sufficiently recognized in the tourism literature, the complex set of transnational corporate and sub-contractual arrangements that typify large tour operators, provide substantial difficulties in achieving inclusivity given that the operational supply chain may mean contract businesses are several times removed from head office decision-making. In such situations, it is much easier for tour operators to engage with NGOs and governmental stakeholders rather than the actual communities that their customers visit. To gain further inclusivity. otherwise marginalized groups, therefore, need effective stakeholder representation so as to gain a 'voice' in the set of constituent relationships of large tourism operators. Furthermore, as possibly the case for some Apollo customers, concerns over animal rights may actually be more important than labour rights in a foreign destination. Nevertheless, suppliers' decoupling of codes of conduct from labour conditions and environmental footprints would pose a huge brand risk for tour operators given that they operate with very low profit margins, and compete in complex and price sensitive markets. A requirement for regular monitoring and increased surveillance (Lund-Thomsen & Nadvi, 2011), and the unification of disparate certification and codes of conducts are some actions that might help contribute to re-coupling sustainability policies, including inclusive tourism concerns, with tour operators and supplier practices (Egels-Zandén, 2014).

This paper highlights how sustainability policies and standards, can be loosely coupled, or decoupled, from internal practices, and have the potential to trigger further engagement with CSR (Vilanova, Lozano, & Arenas, 2009), and, therefore, potentially some aspects of inclusive tourism, by stimulating both intra- and inter-firm learning through collaborative processes among corporate competitors. These collaborative platforms are used to exchange and diffuse industry practices, and may also anticipate potential future normative pressures towards aspects of inclusive tourism through legislation, i.e. changes to corporate CSR law, or management of brand risks, i.e. breaches of human rights. Furthermore, in a context of scarce resources, internal and external collaborative arrangements serve to enrol, co-opt and influence both internal (employees, management boards, subsidiaries and different departments), and external stakeholders to access necessary knowledge, resources and legitimacy. The gaining of access to such arrangements by marginalized groups, for example via NGO activities, would greatly increase the likelihood of the adoption of inclusive tourism measures. Similarly, more collaborative relationships between tour operators and their suppliers could also potentially contribute to couple tighter sustainability policies and suppliers' practices (Egels-Zandén, 2014; Locke, Kochan, Romis, & Qin, 2007), for example by working together in the local translation of global standards and their application (Haaland & Aas, 2010).

Yet, none of these efforts can lead to profound changes in the sustainability practices of the mass tourism industry, including inclusive tourism, if the field remains underinstitutionalized. Previous research has shown how sustainability standards compliance is improved in countries with strong labour regulation (Locke et al., 2007; Toffel, Short, & Ouellet, 2015). Powerful players in the industry, such as large tour operators, have the ability to enable greater sustainability and more inclusive forms of tourism. But if more coercive institutional pressures, in the form of laws, regulations and incentives, are not enacted to accelerate this process, it risks perpetuating a limited adoption of inclusive practices in the mass tourism industry.

Disclosure statement

No potential conflict of interest was reported by the authors.

References

Adu-Ampong, E. A. (2017). Divided we stand: Institutional collaboration in tourism planning and development in the central region of Ghana. *Current Issues in Tourism, 20*, 295–314.

Alegre, J., & Sard, M. (2015). When demand drops and prices rise. Tourist packages in the Balearic Islands during the economic crisis. *Tourism Management, 46*, 375–385.

Apollo (2016a). Financial information. Retrieved October 28, 2016, from http://www.apollo.se/om-apollo/om-foretaget/finansiell-information

Apollo (2016b). En bättre resa [A better travelling]. Retrieved October 29, 2016, from http://www.apollo.se/om-apollo/en-battre-resa

Bakan, J. (2005). *The corporation; the pathological pursuit of profit and power*. London: Constable and Robinson.

Bansal, P., & Roth, K. (2000). Why companies go green: A model of ecological responsiveness. *Academy of Management Journal, 43*(4), 717–736.

Bartley, T., & Zhang, L. (2012). *Opening the 'black box': Transnational private certification of labor standards in China* (RCCPB Working Paper No. 18). Bloomington, IN: Research Center for Chinese Politics and Business, Indiana University.

Bricker, K., & Black, R. (2016). Framework for understanding sustainability in the context of tourism operators. In S. McCool & K. Bosak (Eds.), *Reframing sustainable tourism* (pp. 81–99). Dordrecht: Springer.

Bromley, P., & Powell, W. W. (2012). From smoke and mirrors to walking the talk: Decoupling in the contemporary world. *The Academy of Management Annals, 6*, 483–530.

Bruni, A., Cassia, F., & Magno, F. (2017). Marketing performance measurement in hotels, travel agencies and tour operators: A study of current practices. *Current Issues in Tourism, 20*(4), 339–345.

Brunsson, N. & Jacobsson, B. (2000). *A world of standards*. Oxford: Oxford University Press.

Budeanu, A. (2007). *Facilitating transitions to sustainable tourism. The role of the tour operator*. Lund: International Institute for Industrial Environmental Economics, Lund University.

Budeanu, A. (2009). Environmental supply chain management in tourism: The case of large tour operators. *Journal of Cleaner Production, 17*(16), 1385–1392.

Cordano, M., & Frieze, I. H. (2000). Pollution reduction preferences of US environmental managers: Applying Ajzen's theory of planned behaviour. *Academy of Management Journal, 43*, 627–641.

Cvelbar, L. K., Dwyer, L., Koman, M., & Mihalič, T. (2016). Drivers of destination competitiveness in tourism a global investigation. *Journal of Travel Research, 55*, 1041–1050.

D'Aummno, T., Succi, M., & Alexander, J. A. (2000). The role of institutional and market forces in divergent organizational change. *Administrative Science Quarterly, 45*, 679–703.

Dashwood, H. S. (2012). CSR norms and organizational learning in the mining sector. *Corporate Governance, 12*(1), 118–138.

Dashwood, H. S. (2014). Sustainable development and industry self-regulation: Developments in the global mining sector. *Business & Society, 53*(4), 551–582.

de Grosbois, D. (2016). Corporate social responsibility reporting in the cruise tourism industry: A performance evaluation using a new institutional theory based model. *Journal of Sustainable Tourism, 24*(2), 245–269.

de Sausmarez, N. (2013). Challenges to Kenyan tourism since 2008: Crisis management from the Kenyan tour operator perspective. *Current Issues in Tourism, 16*, 792–809.

Delmas, M. A., & Toffel, W. M. (2008). Organizational responses to environmental demands: Opening the black box. *Strategic Management Journal, 29*, 1027–1055.

Dieke, P. U. (2013). Tourism in sub-Saharan Africa: Production–consumption nexus. *Current Issues in Tourism, 16*, 623–626.

Egels-Zandén, N. (2014). Revisiting supplier compliance with MNC Codes of Conduct: Recoupling policy and practice at Chinese toy suppliers. *Journal of Business Ethics, 119*, 59–75

Egri, C., & Herman, S. (2000). Leadership in the North American environmental sector: Values, leadership styles and contexts of environmental leaders and their organizations. *Academy of Management Journal, 43*, 44–63.

Erskine, L. M., & Meyer, D. (2012). Influenced and influential: The role of tour operators and development organisations in tourism and poverty reduction in Ecuador. *Journal of Sustainable Tourism, 20*(3), 339–357.

Fair Trade Center & Swed Watch (2008). *En exkluderande resa. En granskning av turismens effecter I Thailand och Brasilien* [An exclusive travel. An evaluation of the tourism's effects in Thailand and Brazil] (SwedWatch Report 24). Retrieved from http://www.fairtradecenter.se/sites/default/files/FTC%20och%20SW%20rapport%20om%20turism%20081029.pdf

Fair Traveller (2015). *Travelife's broken promises to hotel workers. A study of labour rights at hotels in Turkey contracted by Apollo (Kuoni), Fritidsresor (TUI) and Ving (Thomas Cook)*. Retrieved from http://www.schystresande.se/schyst-resandes-material

Flyvbjerg, B. (2001). *Making social science matter: Why social inquiry fails and how it can succeed again*. Cambridge: Cambridge University Press.

Gössling, S., Hall, C. M., & Scott, D. (2015). *Tourism and water*. Bristol: Channel View.

Haaland, H., & Aas, Ø. (2010). Eco-tourism certification - Does it make a difference? A comparison of systems from Australia, Costa Rica and Sweden. *Scandinavian Journal of Hospitality and Tourism. Journal of Sustainable Tourism, 10*(3), 375–385.

Hall, C. M. (2008). *Tourism planning*. Harlow: Pearson.

Hall, C. M., Dayal, N., Majstorović, D., Mills, H., Paul-Andrews, L., Wallace, C., & Truong, V. D. (2016). Accommodation consumers and providers' attitudes, behaviours and practices for sustainability: A systematic review. *Sustainability, 8*(7), 625.

Hall, C. M., & Gössling, S. (Eds.). (2016). *Food tourism and regional development: Networks, products and trajectories*, Abingdon: Routledge.

Hall, C. M., Gössling S., & Scott, D. (Eds.) (2015). *The Routledge handbook of tourism and sustainability*. Abingdon: Routledge.

Hall, D. R., & Brown, F. (2006). *Tourism and welfare: Ethics, responsibility and sustained well-being*. Wallingford: CABI.

Hendry, J. (2006). Taking aim at business: What factors lead environmental non-governmental organizations to target particular firms?. *Business and Society, 45*, 47–85.

Hardy, C., & Maguire, S. (2008). Institutional entrepreneurship. In R., Greenwood, C., Oliver, R. Suddaby, & K. Sahlin-Andersson (Eds.), *The SAGE handbook of organizational institutionalism* (pp. 198–217). Thousand Oaks, CA: Sage.

Hoffman, A. J. (2001). Linking organizational and field-level analyses – The diffusion of corporate environmental practice. *Organization and Environment, 14*, 133–156.

Jamali, D. (2010). MNCs and international accountability standards through an institutional lens: Evidence of symbolic conformity or decoupling. *Journal of Business Ethics, 95*, 617–640.

Kuoni (2014). *The Kuoni Travel holding Ltd. corporate responsibility charter.* Kuoni Travel Holding Ltd.

Kuoni (2016). *Corporate social responsibility at Kuoni.* Retrieved October 29, 2016, from http://cr.kuoni.com/corp-responsibility/sustainability-at-kuoni/organisation

Locke, R., Kochan, T., Romis, M., & Qin, F. (2007). Beyond corporate codes of conduct: Work organization and labour standards at Nike's suppliers. *International Labour Review, 146*(1–2), 21–40.

Lund-Thomsen, P., & Nadvi, K. (2011). Clusters, chains and compliance: Corporate social responsibility and governance in football manufacturing in South Asia. *Journal of Business Ethics, 93*, 201–222.

Medina, L. K. (2005). Ecotourism and certification: Confronting the principles and pragmatics of socially responsible tourism. *Journal of Sustainable Tourism, 13*, 281–295

Meyer, J. W., & Rowan, B. (1977). Institutionalized organization: Formal structure as myth and ceremony. *American Journal of Sociology, 83*, 340–363.

Oliver, C. (1991). Strategic responses to institutional processes, *The Academy of Management Review, 16*(1), 145–179.

Prakash, A. (2000). Responsible care: An assessment. *Business and Society, 39*, 183–209.

Prakash, A., & Potoski, M. (2007). Collective action through voluntary environmental programs: A club theory perspective. *Policy Studies Journal, 35*, 773–792.

Saarinen, J., Rogerson, C. M., & Hall, C. M. (2017). Geographies of tourism development and planning. *Tourism Geographies, 19*(3), 307–317

Scheyvens, R., & Biddulph, R. (2017). Inclusive tourism development, *Tourism Geographies*. doi:10.1080/14616688.2017.1381985

Schwartz, K., Tapper, R., & Font, X. (2008). A sustainable supply chain management framework for tour operators, *Journal of Sustainable Tourism, 16*(3), 298–314.

Schyst Resande. (2008). *Kartläggning av Sveriges Researrangörer* [Mapping Swedish tour operators]. Stockholm: Schyst Resande.

Scott, R. W. (2008). *Institutions and organizations: Ideas and interests.* Thousand Oaks, CA: Sage.

Sharma, S. (2000). Managerial interpretations and organizational context as predictors of corporate choice of environmental strategy. *Academy of Management Journal, 43*, 681–697.

Shyst Resande. (2015). Travelifes broken promises to hotel workers. A study of labour rights at hotels in Turkey contracted by Apollo (Kuoni), Fritidsresor (TUI) and Ving (Thomas Cook). Retrieved from http://www.schystresande.se/schyst-resandes-material

Stout, L. A. (2013). The toxic side effects of shareholder primacy. *University of Pennsylvania Law Review, 161*(7), 2003–2023.

Strand, R., Freeman, R. E., & Hockerts, K. (2015). Corporate social responsibility and sustainability in Scandinavia: An overview. *Journal of Business Ethics, 127*, 1–15.

Suddaby, R. (2010). Challenges for institutional theory, *Journal of Management Inquiry, 19*(1), 14–20.

Swedish Radio. (2015a, October 13). A. 'Vi har brustit' [We have failed]. Retrieved from http://sverigesradio.se/sida/artikel.aspx?programid=83&artikel=6277270

Swedish Radio. (2015b, October 13). B 'Kan inte byta job eftersom laggen i Dubai inte tillåter det' [I can't change job since law in Dubai does not allow it]. Retrieved from http://sverigesradio.se/sida/artikel.aspx?programid=83&artikel=6277144

SwedWatch and Fair Action (2015). *Shattered dreams. Migrant workers and rights violations in the Dubai tourism sector* (Report No. 75). Stockholm: SwedWatch. Retrieved from http://www.swedwatch.org/sites/default/files/tmp/75_dubai_lowres_new.pdf

Tepelus, C. (2005). Aiming for sustainability in the tour operating business. *Journal of Cleaner Production, 13*, 99–107.

Toffel, M. W., Short, J. L., & Ouellet, M. (2015). Codes in context: How states, markets, and civil society shape adherence to global labor standards. *Regulation & Governance, 9*(3), 205–223.

Tveteraas, S., Asche, F., & Lien, K. (2014). European tour operators' market power when renting hotel rooms in Northern Norway. *Tourism Economics, 20*(3), 579–594.

Van Huijstee, M., & Glasbergen, P. (2010). NGOs moving business: An analysis of contrasting strategies. *Business & Society, 49*(4), 591–618.

Van Wijk, J., Van der Duim, R., Lamers, M., & Sumba, D. (2015). The emergence of institutional innovations in tourism: The evolution of the African Wildlife Foundation's tourism conservation enterprises. *Journal of Sustainable Tourism, 23*(1), 104–125.

Vilanova, M., Lozano, J. M., & Arenas, D. (2009). Exploring the nature of the relationship between CSR and competitiveness. *Journal of Business Ethics, 87*(1), 57–69.
Weick, K. E. (1995). *Sensemaking in organizations*. London: Sage.
Zapata, M. J., & Hall, C. M. (2012). Public–private collaboration in the tourism sector: Balancing legitimacy and effectiveness in local tourism partnerships. The Spanish case. *Journal of Policy Research in Tourism, Leisure and Events, 4*(1), 61–83.

Social enterprise and inclusive tourism. Five cases in Siem Reap, Cambodia

Robin Biddulph

ABSTRACT
In recent decades, social enterprise has emerged from a variety of traditions and contexts to occupy a prominent position in relation to social change. Proponents argue that people with a business orientation are uniquely equipped to identify social problems, develop solutions and to scale these up. Muhammad Yunus and the non-collateralized loans of the Grameen Bank are held to exemplify this potential. Meanwhile, mass tourism destinations are increasingly found in less developed countries, placing relatively wealthy tourists in close proximity to poor people. One response to this has been a proliferation of social enterprises within the tourism industry. This paper investigates the potentials and limitations of social entrepreneurship to achieve inclusive tourism through an analysis of five established and highly regarded social enterprises in Siem Reap. The enterprises have created worthwhile new opportunities for poor and marginalized people and contributed substantially to revitalizing elements of Cambodian culture. Beyond these significant successes, their capacity to generate broader inclusiveness in either the tourism sector or the Cambodian economy, generally, appears limited. Continued social benefits are, furthermore, contingent on the commercial success of the enterprises, in a sector which is highly competitive and volatile, with even successful, well-run businesses never entirely secure.

Introduction

In recent decades, social enterprise has been vigorously promoted around the world (Defourny & Nyssens, 2010; Kerlin, 2010). Many proponents see social entrepreneurs as persistent, creative innovators who can address social problems in ways that achieve scale and reach superior to traditional business, state or third sectors (Bornstein & Davis, 2010; Dees, 1998; Drayton & Budinich, 2010). However, there are also concerns that rather than a natural 'partnership' between business and social goals, there are often tensions and trade-offs necessary which can undermine the social value of an enterprise (Alter, 2007).

This article explores the potential of the emerging social enterprise sector to enhance the tourism sector's potential to deliver more inclusive development. Following the achievement of peace in the late 1990s, Siem Reap province in Cambodia has been host to a tourism boom which has transformed the provincial town and been a major driver of national economic growth. Meanwhile, Siem Reap has remained a relatively poor province overall, even by Cambodian standards (Mao, DeLacy, & Grunfeld, 2013; Sharpley & McGrath, 2017). Siem Reap is also host to a concentration of social enterprises. In March 2015, 29 of the 73 social enterprises registered with the umbrella group, Social Enterprise Cambodia, were based in Siem Reap (SEC, 2015). Many of these were newly established, but a small number of them had been trading for several years and some had won global industry awards, and were beginning to achieve scale and stability. The coincidence of an extended, lucrative tourism boom in Siem Reap and significant socio-economic marginalization provide an excellent context in which to explore the potentials of established social enterprises to contribute to inclusiveness in the tourism sector and beyond.

This article, therefore, examines the most established social enterprises in different sectors of Siem Reap's tourism industry, featuring a hotel, a restaurant, a handicrafts company, a performing arts company and a tour company. It particularly focuses on elements of inclusive tourism identified by the enterprises themselves as important to their missions, namely enabling poor and marginalized people to obtain decent work in the tourism sector; enabling self-representation by Cambodians on terms that they find dignified and appropriate; widening access to decision-making in the tourism sector; and re-drawing the tourism map on terms that are beneficial to the newly included people and places (Scheyvens & Biddulph, 2017).

Social enterprise as an emerging sector

In recent decades, there has been a surge of enthusiasm for ways in which the private sector generally can contribute to achieving development goals. Businesses have been encouraged to take a proactive role in international development and to become a 'consciously engaged agent of development' (Blowfield, 2012, p. 415). Driven in part by the global financial crisis and the subsequent tightening up of public development budgets, along with the scale of global development and ecological challenges, the private sector has increasingly been viewed as a source of funds and knowhow for social development (Dees, 2008). This shift towards a larger role for business is vigorously contested from a variety of ideological and practical positions (e.g. Edwards, 2008; Eikenberry & Kluver, 2004; Peck, 2013). Specific national factors likewise shaped the emergence of social enterprise: in the United States, the withdrawal of federal funding for voluntary organizations spurred them to generate their own revenue, in Europe, Italy moved early to create enabling legislation in 1991 for these new hybrids (Defourny & Nyssens, 2010), whilst in the UK, the policies of the Blair government in the UK provided a different impetus by according social enterprises a central role in the restructuring of the welfare state (e.g. Palmås, 2003, 2013; Teasdale, Lyon, & Baldock, 2013).

In addition to these practical, contextual differences, there were also markedly different ideological roots. In broad brush terms, European social movements have had more of an emphasis on governance and accountability to beneficiaries which is traced back to nineteenth-century cooperative movements (Defourny & Nyssens, 2010). In the United States, meanwhile, emphasis has been placed on the role of heroic Schumpeterian entrepreneurs bringing private sector virtues to bear in the struggle for social change, with foundations such as Ashoka, Skoll and Schwab providing training and finance to those seeking to realize this vision (Kerlin, 2006, p. 255).

Arguably, the US entrepreneur-driven model has dominated the practitioner discourse, supported by cases of small enterprises which have scaled up to reach millions of clients, such as Grameen Bank (Dees, 2007), Waste Concern in Bangladesh (Azmat, 2013), and Drishtee and Naandi in India (Desa & Koch, 2014). Elsewhere, the literature cautions that these may be special cases and that social enterprises have neither scaled up nor addressed root causes of poverty any more effectively than other organizations (Sayer, 2005, p. 19). European authors have suggested that scaling may more realistically be achieved through recruiting public support and leveraging action by political authorities rather than solely through growing a successful business (Gawell, 2006; Lyne, 2008; Palmås, 2011).

Authors charting the global spread of social enterprise beyond North America and Europe have likewise called for close attention to specific contexts (Defourny & Kim, 2011; Defourny & Nyssens, 2008), with an analysis of seven different regions suggesting social enterprise development in Southeast Asia 'appears to be in an emerging stage motivated by the innovative efforts of isolated social entrepreneurs who are working without established networks and stable sources of support' (Kerlin, 2010, p. 177).

Given that tourism is an industry which has long been associated with a potential for social and economic development (e.g. Ashley, Roe, & Goodwin, 2001; de Kadt, 1979; Scheyvens, 2011), the literature on social enterprise within tourism is surprisingly sparse. Mdee and Emmott (2008) looked at businesses offering volunteer tourism packages and made a case for certification for such social enterprises; Alegre and Berbegal-Mirabent (2016) looked at 'social innovation' in two businesses that switched from manufacturing to hospitality in Barcelona – also looking to identify success factors. The only published article attempting more general comments on social enterprise in the tourism sector was a study of 11 successful cases (von der Weppen & Cochrane, 2012). That article identified the enterprises as successes on the basis that they had received industry awards for responsible tourism. It categorized them using a typology developed by Alter (2007) and concluded that the 'most likely success factors are strong leadership, clear market orientation and organisational culture, which balances financial with social/environmental aims'. Whilst von der Weppen and Cochrane used a case study method, their findings are presented and discussed in aggregate form, and therefore, some of the usual benefits of case studies in revealing how cause and effect operate in specific contexts are lost. The use of award-winning as the indicator of success also pre-empted discussion of the nature and extent of social impacts and successes.

The current article, therefore, complements the existing literature on social entrepreneurship in tourism by providing a contextualized account of five social enterprises, where the social missions, business challenges and social impacts of each business are discussed in relation to each other. By explicitly discussing the current and envisioned social impacts of the enterprises in terms of inclusive tourism, it also contributes to the emerging literature on the concept of inclusive tourism (see other articles in this Special Issue). By focusing on the way in which a commercial sector is developing social objectives, it also contrasts with the existing literature on social enterprise in Cambodia which focuses on the way in which the NGO sector is seeking to commercialize its operations in order to survive (Khieng, 2014; Khieng & Dahles, 2015) and with the more environmentally oriented literature on eco-tourism (e.g. Neth, 2008).

In order to realize the aim of investigating the potential of social enterprises to deliver inclusive tourism, the following research questions are addressed:

- To what extent do the case study social enterprises contribute to elements of inclusive tourism?
- To what extent can those contributions be attributed to the fact that these initiatives are social enterprises?
- What do the insights about the specific cases of established social enterprises in Siem Reap suggest about the wider possibilities of social enterprise to contribute to inclusive tourism?

First, however, the method for the study is described and its strengths and limitations explained, then findings are presented in the form of descriptions of the five case study enterprises including their stories, their social impact up to December 2016 and their future plans and the challenges they face in implementing those.

Method

In order to get an overview of the Social Enterprises in Siem Reap, I consulted an online database created by the Phnom-Penh-based group Social Enterprise Cambodia who had attempted to survey all social enterprises in Cambodia and had identified a total of 73 of which 29 were in Siem Reap (Social Enterprise Cambodia, 2015). In a scoping visit in late 2015 (when in Cambodia conducting research for a separate project on tourism and rural livelihoods), I interviewed five social entrepreneurs in Siem Reap as well as the head of Social Enterprise Cambodia. On the basis of the publically available documentation and these interviews, I then selected what appeared to be the most well-established and successful social enterprises in five different sectors of the tourism industry, namely handicraft production, tourist performances, hotel, restaurant and tour companies. Four of the five enterprises responded positively to my overtures. The restaurant I contacted did not respond, and therefore, I selected what appeared to be the next most established and successful.

The primary research comprised interviews with the lead entrepreneurs of four out of five of the enterprises (I communicated with the CEO of Artisans Angkor by email instead) and also a self-assessment questionnaire completed by four out of five of the enterprises. See Table 1 for dates of the interviews and questionnaire responses as well as background

Table 1. Five case study social enterprises in Siem Reap's tourism sector.

Name Business type	# Direct beneficiaries	Year story of the SE begins	Year SE formally established	Questionnaire dates (yy/mm/dd)	Interview dates (yy/mm/dd)
Artisans Angkor *Handicraft production*	1120 employees (750 of whom are artisans)	1992	1998	16/12/02	n/a
PHARE Circus *Performing arts*	931 enrolled students	1993	2013	16/11/24	15/11/28
Soria Moria *Hotel*	35 employees	1999	2007	16/12/06	16/11/10 16/11/16 16/12/06
ABOUTAsia Tours *Tour company*	53,000 pupils in 110 schools	2006	2006	–	15/12/01 16/12/05
Haven *Training restaurant*	14 apprentices per annum	2008	2011	16/12/01	16/12/02

Source: Author's interview notes and enterprise web-sites.

details on the enterprises. Where there were gaps or anomalies, follow-up questions were posed by email. I interviewed the lead entrepreneurs (two Cambodians and two expatriates) in English and transcribed the audio recordings.

The self-assessment questionnaire was intended to provide descriptive data on the enterprises and consisted of multiple-choice questions in three parts: part 1 on the nature and structure of the enterprise including any dependency on external funding or loans; part 2 on the future vision for the enterprise, especially in relation to its social mission and the possibilities for scaling it up; part 3 on the relevance of the social enterprise to various elements of inclusive tourism. The interviews provided more in-depth information and consisted of four parts: the entrepreneur's personal background and identity; the social enterprise that they run; their general ideas on social enterprises; their specific perspectives on social enterprises in Siem Reap. Informed by the self-assessment questionnaire, the social objectives of the enterprises were categorized according to Scheyvens and Biddulph's 'elements of inclusive tourism' (2017, pp. 6–7), with the four elements covered becoming the categories of analysis. Transcripts were re-read during and on completion of the analysis and also during major revisions of the article.

The research is part of a larger study of social enterprises in Southeast Asia and Scandinavia, which included interviews with the leaders of half a dozen smaller social enterprises in Siem Reap who also provided additional information both about the five case study enterprises and about the context in which they are operating.

The choice to sample four elements gives a better understanding of their overall inclusiveness, but at the cost of more sustained investigation of any one of the elements.

Description of cases

The five cases are presented individually with the story of the enterprise, an account of the social benefits it has delivered from its inception up until the time of writing (December 2016) and a summary of current plans for the enterprise and the key challenges that it faces. These descriptions provide the foundations for the analysis of their contributions to inclusive tourism which follows.

Artisans Angkor

Story of the enterprise

Artisans Angkor is a handicrafts production and retail enterprise which has grown out of a French development assistance project. The project began in 1992 before peace was consolidated but in anticipation of a tourism revival. A vocational training centre funded through grants, the Chantiers-Ecoles de Formation Professionnelle (CEFP), established a programme to train young Cambodians in traditional skills to produce arts and craft skills. During 1998–2001, a European Union project called REPLIC transformed the project from a training programme into a semi-public company which provided employment to trained artisans. The enterprise has been fully self-funding since at least 2008 (Bolster & Brimble, 2008, p. 290), and the workers are formally constituted as an association which owns a 20% share in the business.

Social impacts

Artisans Angkor's principal social benefit is that it now provides employment with competitive wages as well as social and health insurance to 750 artisans distributed across 48 workshops mainly in rural areas of Siem Reap, making it the largest private sector employer in the province. Recruitment is specifically targeted at marginalized rural people, and at least 5% of the workforce is people with disabilities. In addition to salaries and health benefits, Artisans Angkor seeks to cultivate a feeling of pride in its employees in relation to their role in enabling a post-conflict cultural revival and showcasing of traditional Cambodian crafts, including participating in the restoration of the Angkorian temples (Artisans Angkor, 2017).

Future plans and challenges

According to their Chief Executive Officer, Artisans Angkor has four areas where they are seeking to make further improvement: historical and artistic knowledge of staff; increasing staff sense of belonging; promoting the workshops as a cultural destination in order to promote Angkorian traditional arts; becoming the high-end brand leader for local customers and thereby contributing to Khmer cultural heritage (personal communication, Vincent Drouillard, 6 June 2017).

Phare performing social enterprise (PPSE)

Story of the enterprise

The main activity of the Phare Performing Social Enterprise (PPSE) is the Phare Circus which, after the temples, is now reckoned to be Siem Reap's second most popular tourist attraction (Sharpley & McGrath, 2017, p. 95). This funds a social programme of performing and visual arts training which has been growing since its inception in 1993 and has its roots in the refugee camps established on the Thai–Cambodian border in the 1980s. Following their repatriation in 1993 to Battambang province in north-west Cambodia, nine former refugees who had studied fine arts on the border jointly founded an NGO called Phare Ponleu Selpak Association (PPSA). Over the past two decades, this NGO has grown to a scale, where, in 2015, it had 101 employees and a budget of 1,286,169 USD.

In 2013, PPSA established the PPSE with the following three aims:

(1) Create meaningful employment opportunities for Cambodian artists.
(2) Create financially sustainable social businesses that provide a reliable income streams for Phare Ponleu Selpak.
(3) Revitalize the arts sector in Cambodia and promote Cambodian art locally and internationally.

PPSE is a Cambodian Private Limited Company whose ownership shares are as follows: PPSA (71%), a social investor called Grameen Crédit Agricole Microfinance Foundation (15%), and private investors (14%). The NGO has a French chief executive and its senior management is mixed Cambodian and expatriate. The social enterprise, meanwhile, is headed by a Cambodian, Mr Huot Dara, who had worked briefly with Phare as a young volunteer interpreter in 2001 and over a decade later was recruited by them:

> They reached out to me in 2012 asking me to help lead a social enterprise in their quest for self-sustainability. Now, I had no idea what social enterprise was. I had to make a search, an internet search. I had to read a lot to really understand what it was all about. I was in the corporate world and I had no idea that this movement, something new, is going on in the world that is quite interesting. ... Now we started the social enterprise, the first performance here, under the rain, under the sky, was in February 2013. (Interview, Huot Dara, 28 November 2015)

The ownership structure, with the NGO owning 71% of the business, was made possible by a change of heart from one of the business's first investors who had intended to loan them 250,000 USD for their big top:

> When she came to see us in Siem Reap we were still performing outdoors. After her experience – she saw Eclipse, the show – she was emotional. The next day she had a change of mind, she doesn't give a loan, she gives a donation instead. So the donation went to PHARE Ponleu Selpak the school. Now the school owns an asset, and the school used the asset to contribute to the start-up of the company, valued at 250 000 dollars, and that translates to 71% of the share of the company. (Interview, Huot Dara, 28 November 2015)

In order to secure its long-term future, however, it was decided that PPSE needed its own land, the purchase of which resulted in a debt of over one million USD. At present, then, PPSE's revenues are devoted to paying off the loan for the land. However, the social enterprise still contributed 156,890 USD to the NGO in 2015 derived about equally from two sources. First, 10% of the social enterprise's revenues are paid in royalties to the school, and second, donations are collected from audiences after each performance.

Social impacts to December 2016

According to its 2015 Annual Report, Phare had 931 direct beneficiaries, being students enrolled in its Visual and Applied Arts School, its Performing Arts School and its kindergarten. Additionally, there were 12,300 indirect beneficiaries, who were members of the community who experienced this revived culture by attending performances by Phare students. This is in line with its mission to provide 'a nurturing and creative environment where young people can access quality arts training, education and social support' and vision, which is stated in terms of PPSE's passionate belief 'in the power of the arts as a tool for human development and social change'.

Future plans and challenges

As the head of the social enterprise, Huot Dara sees his mission as being to guarantee the financial security of the NGO by repaying the loans for the permanent site, which he anticipates 'will be a lot of hard work in the next five to ten years' (Interview, 28 November 2015). Another challenge, alongside clearing its debts, is that of taxation. While Dara is proud that the company shoulders its tax-paying responsibilities, and is fully transparent and accountable in its financial affairs, he regrets the absence of a separate category of business registration for social businesses whereby they might receive a lighter tax burden. Currently, Phare pays 10% VAT, 10% performance tax and a 1% minimum profit tax, which, once debts are repaid, will be replaced by a 20% corporate tax on profits.

Soria Moria Hotel

History of the enterprise

Soria Moria is a 38-room boutique hotel managed by its staff who also own 51% of the business. The enterprise was originally established by a Norwegian couple who had arrived in Cambodia during the late 1990s. Kristin was a tourism student who established another hotel in town called Earthwalkers, which was a socially responsible business, specializing in educational tours. Ken who was to become Kristin's partner in establishing Soria Moria was, at that stage, a long-term guest at Earthwalkers as he was both travelling and looking for opportunities to set up social enterprises, or in other ways to give back to society having left his own successful career.

In 2007, having sold Earthwalkers, Kristin established Soria Moria with Ken. This was to be a socially responsible boutique hotel with a 10-year lease on a 38-room property located centrally just east of the Siem Reap river. Many of the key staff, including the current leadership group of Soria Moria, were originally recruited to Earthwalkers as entry-level staff from rural areas.

In 2009, Kristin and Ken decided to return to Europe. They had discussed selling Soria Moria but were worried that potential buyers would not stay loyal to the founding ideas of responsible tourism and social enterprise. They, therefore, decided to hand over ownership and management of the hotel to the staff, and initiated a process to facilitate this. A social investor, Insitor, provided a loan to the business and also advised on the legal form for the staff to register as the owners the business as a limited company. After two years of training and handover Kristin and Ken moved to Norway in 2015 at which point Roeun Samnieng and four other staff members took over as the management committee of the hotel, with Samnieng legally responsible. During 2013–2016, an exchange scheme was run between Soria Moria in Siem Reap and a hotel group in Norway, enabling senior management from Soria Moria to gain experience of hotel management in a European context.

Social impacts to December 2016

In accordance with its responsible tourism orientation, Soria Moria has undertaken a wide variety of initiatives and collaborations supporting social and environmental objectives. In the lobby of the hotel, various fair trade and environmentally friendly products are sold on behalf of NGOs or social enterprises. On the wall are brochures which provide guests with information about a range of socially responsible tourism products. Outside the hotel are a row of White Bicycles, part of a cycle hire initiative set up by Ken and now run by Samnieng, which has channelled funds for sponsoring local students through university; the White Bicycle initiative alone had had financed accommodation and tuition fees enabling 10 Cambodians to obtain university degrees. On Wednesdays, tapas evenings were held as a means to offer opportunities for hospitality trainees to gain work experience in the Soria Moria restaurant.

However, the core social impacts relate to the employees of the hotel. Young rural people without formal training or work experience were trained in a range of functions, were promoted within the hotel to take on management roles, and in many cases were sponsored to either attend vocational training courses or university degree courses.

Finally, by handing over the business to the workforce and enabling them to fulfil the roles of managers and owners, Soria Moria has created a potential template for a shift in power relations in the tourism industry. A Cambodian-owned hotel is nothing unusual in Siem Reap, but a hotel managed by people who grew up in the countryside with no business background, no senior government connections and no family wealth, and a hotel owned by its staff, have represented a radical departure from established ways of doing business.

Future plans and challenges

In late 2016, it became clear that the radical promise of Soria Moria as a model worker-owned hotel in the tourist sector would not be fulfilled. Since the handover to the staff, and for a variety of reasons, the profits of the hotel have declined. Meanwhile, the landlord has been unwilling to fund needed renovation and has also been looking to raise the rent when the current lease expires in 2017. As a result, the personnel have made the decision not to continue the business. They discussed the possibility of continuing to trade in another location, including the possibilities of downsizing and/or changing their ownership structure but have decided against these. They see the decision to cease trading as a temporary rather than permanent cessation of the concept of Soria Moria, although if they were to resume trading, they do not expect to use the worker–owner model:

> It is hard to have too many owners, because everyone is an owner now – it is hard, they don't listen, even though they have a manager talking, they have a manager but they want to demand their own civil rights or whatever. (Interview, Ms Sem Sokha, 14 November 2016)

The current challenges for the business, therefore, relate to maximizing profitability and staff retention during the final year of trading as well as ensuring that all staff are able to transfer to good alternative employments.[1]

ABOUTAsia tours

Story of the enterprise

ABOUTAsia Tours is a tour company founded in 2006 with the specific aim of funding educational programmes in Siem Reap province. As such, in this study, it shares with the other social enterprises a fundamental motivation and orientation towards a social mission, but differs from the others in the degree to which the social mission and business mission are kept separate in the day-to-day running of the enterprise and even, to some degree, in the marketing.

Andy Booth, the founder of ABOUTAsia, traces his motivations to establish the company back to his rural childhood where educational opportunities at school set him on a path to Oxford University and then a successful career in Options trading. The target market for the business is high end tourists:

> Explore thriving jungles with world-class naturalists, dine at our private countryside villa, sip sunset drinks on ancient Angkorian waterways and be guided by leading academics to the temples with our range of exclusive experiences. (ABOUTAsia tours website)

After 10 years, ABOUTAsia is a successful and growing business which has won multiple awards for its tours. Its educational programmes provide support to state schools to enable them to deliver the officially mandated state curriculum. This includes providing school materials, and some construction and maintenance services to, and also the provision of English teachers and teaching materials for 50 English classes per day (ABOUTAsia schools homepage). In addition to the main activities, ABOUTAsia Schools are also starting to build and fund community learning centres which can be hubs for extracurricular activities for children as well as for adult education activities.

Social impacts to December 2016

The ABOUTAsia school programme provides material support to 110 schools, with the assistance varying dependent on regular assessments of the schools' needs. As at late 2016, ABOUTAsia was employing 20 teachers to give approximately 50 English language lessons per day in schools supported by the programme. ABOUTAsia has opened two community learning centres which, unlike its previous activities, are focused on complementing the state curriculum rather than gap filling within it. For children, they include a focus on art and sports, and they are also founded with the ambition of supporting adult education.

Future plans and challenges

While ABOUTAsia tour company continues to be a successful brand, attracting customers and winning awards, Andy Booth is unequivocal in saying that the main challenges relate to generating substantial and sustainable profits. So whilst the schools programme is the raison d'etre for the social enterprise, 95% of his time is focused on the business side:

> We've just been renamed again as Condé Nast top travel specialists for the country, we've just been taken on by Wendy Perrin's WOW List, and things like that, which basically from the business side says this company is at the leading edge of travel. But it doesn't mean it makes money. (Interview with Andy Booth 5 December 2016)

In this respect, he points to the challenges of a commercial market which is very competitive, especially amongst wholesale travel agents who even at the luxury end of the market are concerned to minimize costs and (unlike the end customer) tend not to be interested in whether or not a tour company generates social benefits.

Haven, training restaurant

The story of the enterprise

During 2008, the co-founders of Haven, Sara and Paul Wallimann, spent seven months working in a Cambodian orphanage where they taught English to 12–16 year olds. It became clear to them during this time that the orphanage directors did not have a clear idea of what would happen to the residents of the orphanage once they left. Sara and Paul were familiar with the strong tradition of apprenticeships in Switzerland and inspired by this tradition they decided to establish a social enterprise which would provide apprenticeships to young adults like the graduates of the orphanage where they had worked. In order to secure the capital for this, when they returned home from their travels, they formed an association, largely from their own personal networks, with 50 members.

The association, called Dragonfly, had membership fees, which covered the administrative costs of the association, and donations, which contributed to a project fund. One of the rules of the association was that only projects that could become self-sustainable after a certain time were to be supported. Each project is, therefore, required to replenish the project fund will then be used as start-up money for further projects in Cambodia.

Sara and Paul thus returned to Cambodia in April 2011 with a budget of 100,000 USD to finance the opening of the Haven restaurant and the first two years' running costs following its opening in December 2011. Neither Sara nor Paul had ambitions to open a restaurant but they each had some relevant skills. Paul had served an apprenticeship as a baker and had worked as a food hygiene inspector and teacher, and had also worked in marketing. Sara had 15 years of experience in public relations and marketing. Another member of the association, Steffi, was an accountant who came out to help two months before the restaurant opened and remained as a third Managing Partner alongside the two co-founders.

Two key recruitments were a chef and a 'house mother'. The chef had a grandmother who had worked as a cook in an orphanage and he liked the idea of doing similar work. The house mother was to provide a suitably homely environment in the house that was rented for the apprentices. She was a woman who had been working long hours in a hotel and saw little of her own three children. Haven afforded her an improved salary and allowed her children to live with her, which also contributed to the family environment they sought to cultivate in the trainees' house and in the restaurant. At the back of the restaurant is a classroom so that the trainees have theoretical lessons to complement their work experience.

The Managing Partners did not take any salary from the restaurant until it had started to break even. At their first property, they had a five-year lease, but the landlord then demanded a 400% increase in the rent, which led them to establish themselves in a new, larger property outside the centre of Siem Reap. Shortly after moving into their new site, the property adjacent to them became available. In order to avoid having a potentially noisy, disruptive neighbour (a quad bike tour company had bid for the land), they decided to purchase that land and to invest in a bakery and a herb garden on it.

The restaurant business has been very successful with the restaurant fully booked in advance during the high season, and therefore even with the unexpected acquisition of an extra business they are on course to become self-sufficient and to replenish the Dragonfly project fund.

Social impacts to December 2016

> *We are not here to change Cambodia, we are not here to save Cambodia. But we can improve, for a certain amount of young adults, their future. And that is what we are doing. (Interview with Paul Wallimann, 2 December 2016)*

At present, Haven employs 14 apprentices, who have graduated from local orphanages or similar institutions, for 16 months each, as well as 18 regular staff (some of whom are ex-trainees). The 14 apprentices constitute two shifts. They have been very successful in going on to well-paid jobs in high-end hotels and restaurants in Siem Reap.

The restaurant also seeks to source food and other materials from organizations and projects which produce in environmentally and socially beneficial ways.

Future plans and challenges
Haven as a business is very successful with Paul confident that its revenues can cover its costs, including the new bakery, and return the capital to the association. Furthermore, the association provides Haven with a degree of security which means that it can withstand unexpected shocks, much better than if it were reliant on commercial sources of financing. In these circumstances, one might expect the management team at Haven to feel extremely confident about the future. To a large extent they do, however, they do also feel a sense of insecurity, which relates to the general vulnerability of the tourism industry to disease and security-related scares, and is heightened by the awareness of the damage done to the tourism industry in Thailand as a result of civil unrest in recent years.

Analysis – established social enterprises and elements of inclusive tourism

In the analysis, four elements of inclusive tourism are selected from Scheyvens and Biddulph's (2017) menu of seven, on the basis that these best match the social objectives of identified by the lead entrepreneurs of the five case study enterprises: (1) overcoming barriers to disadvantaged groups to access tourism as producers; (2) facilitating self-representation by those who are marginalized or oppressed, so their stories can be told and their culture represented in ways that are meaningful to them; (3) widening the range of people who contribute to decision-making about the development of tourism; (4) changing the tourism map to involve new people and places.

Widening access to the production of tourism – ethical and beneficial?
One element of inclusive tourism is the engagement of relatively marginalized people in the production of tourism. Scheyvens and Biddulph demand attention to both who is included, and the terms of that inclusion. Three of the social enterprises were oriented towards engaging relatively marginalized people, though on different scales, at various levels and with different groups in mind. Artisans Angkor has created employment opportunities for 750 rural people, and also includes a 5% quota of positions for people with disabilities. Haven has an apprentice scheme which at any given time provides opportunities for 14 apprentices to enable them to make the transition from institutionalized life in orphanages to becoming regular members of the workforce. Soria Moria, meanwhile, has recruited staff from rural areas, trained them in hotel work and sponsored some of them through undergraduate and graduate studies.

Artisans Angkor is the largest of these social enterprises, employing 1120 people, including 750 artisans; this compares with the calculation of the Department of Tourism that 6400 people are employed in the tourism handicrafts value chain in Siem Reap (Mao et al., 2013, p. 123). Over time, as the tourism market has expanded, so has the amount of handicrafts that are produced overseas; Schultz (2002) noted this emerging trend in the late 1990s, whilst by 2013, an estimated 80% of souvenirs sold in Siem Reap were international imports (Mao et al., 2013, p. 124). As such, Artisans Angkor is enabling poor people who would not have the capital, access to raw materials or the marketing capacity to establish themselves and compete with these cheap imports to find a secure foothold as tourism producers. Measured only in salary, artisans working for Artisans Angkor do not appear to be much better off than other artisans working in Siem Reap. Workers interviewed in their workshop were earning about 5 USD per day (tied to their productivity) which matches the 150 USD per month which Mao et al. (2013, p. 123) found to be the average monthly wage for an experienced sculptor in Siem Reap. However, in addition, they were provided with health insurance, social insurance, and security and stability of employment, which are not readily available in the small private workshops in and around Siem Reap. Artisans Angkor is thus creating a large quantity of jobs that would not otherwise have been available to rural people in Siem Reap, and these are jobs with relatively favourable terms and conditions.

The core contributions of Haven and Soria Moria are perhaps more transformational for individuals, but are at a smaller scale. Ms Sem Sokha now a senior manager at Soria Moria who has spent six months on a work exchange in a hotel in Norway recalls her first interview for a cleaning job which was in Khmer because she could not speak English. She speaks of her pride now at the fact that she is a woman but can support her parents, especially since her father lost his sight, and talks of her great uncle's awe at her advancement.

> *What does your daughter eat? Because she is so smart. Why is she so different?" And then my mum says "We eat prahok, she eats prahok" and he would say "But she's so different compared to people in the village" and when I have been to Norway he starts to say to my mother, "Your daughter is strange, where does it come from?" And then they say to me that I have a different brain you know. And I say no, I have the same. My mum is laughing all the time. (Interview Ms Sem Sokha 14 November 2016)*

Comparable transformations are affected by Haven, as entry-level kitchen workers are able to obtain work in the best paid hotels and restaurants in the city at the end of their 15-month apprenticeships.

Supporting self-representation

The emphasis within inclusive tourism on 'self-representation in ways which people find dignified and appropriate' (Scheyvens & Biddulph, 2017) is in contrast to forms of tourism where tour operators and other tourism actors shape the representation of host communities and the interaction (or lack of interaction) with local people in ways that are demeaning. While extreme forms of exploitative representation are easy to diagnose, e.g. in forms of slum or poverty tourism which proceed without the consent of residents (Frenzel & Koens, 2012), its absence is much more difficult to identify with confidence. Tourism, like any product, relies on a coincidence of supply and demand. Notions of 'traditional hospitality' may be used to camouflage underlying inequalities of wealth and power, and it may be in the interests of all actors, hosts and guests, to maintain such notions. As MacCannell (2008) has argued, wherever relations are commoditized, there will always, inescapably, be an element of staging involved.

In such a context, firm judgements about what might be considered 'self-representation' in the context of cultural preservation and artistic production and performance are difficult. In the case of the Phare circus, there is a degree of artistic freedom for the performers who are involved in designing their own repertoire of shows. These, furthermore, involve improvising on contemporary issues and technology and are therefore not simply a slavish reproduction of past artistic practices. More fundamentally, the performers at Phare are the adult graduates of the performing arts schools, and therefore have a degree of choice and self-determination quite different from those at competing tourist performances, such as those notoriously staged in Cambodian orphanages (Guiney & Mostafanezhad, 2015; Reas, 2013).

Artisans Angkor's workshops, like Phare circus performances, combine rehabilitation of cultural traditions with the commodification of art for the tourist market. While the artisans are clearly benefiting from decent work, that work is much less clearly an instance of self-expression. For the most part, what the artisans are doing is faithfully copying the templates that their teachers in the workshops provide for them:

> At the Banteay Srei Rachana and Artisans d'Angkor workshops subject choice is primarily market driven, based on specific commissions and is largely drawn from pre-Angkorian and Angkorian masterpieces. Designs are finalized on a computer using image manipulation software which is adjusted according to the size of the sandstone block to be carved upon. (Polkinghorne, 2009, p. 11)

The French humanitarian assistance to rehabilitate Khmer culture after the ravages of genocide and war during the 1970s and 1980s was a specific post-conflict intervention, which also has echoes of French colonial attempts to preserve Cambodian art and crafts in the face of the modern influences (Edwards, 2007, pp. 148–158). The ironies inherent in colonial cultural preservation projects endure; the buyers for these products which are marketed as 'essentially Cambodian' are largely western, with national and regional tourists far less likely to buy them (Winter, 2014, p. 305).

However, notwithstanding the presence of a Western aesthetic and a Western market to frame these cultural representations, the activities of Artisans Angkor do enable the artisans to connect with elements of their own culture that they would recognize from both the walls of the Angkorian temples, and from their everyday lives. Meanwhile, commissions that Artisans Angkor have undertaken include restoration of sculptures at the Angkor Wat temples and pieces for the Royal Palace; the enterprise is thus engaged in work that is symbolically connected with the representation of the nation. What this means for individual artisans and whether they find this a dignified and appropriate form of self-expression would require more in-depth research than was possible in this context.

Widening participation in decision-making

Both Soria Moria, where workers own 51% of the business, and Artisans Angkor, where an employee share scheme gives the workers a 20% share in the business, represent schemes to strengthen the position of workers within the businesses where they are employed. The Artisans Angkor scheme is focused on benefit sharing and corporate solidarity, whereas in the case of Soria Moria, there has been an explicit attempt to challenge existing power relations, enabling the hotel to function as a worker cooperative in the short term, but also with the intention of proving this as a model which might be replicated elsewhere in

Siem Reap and beyond. By late 2016, however, these ambitions for Soria Moria had been set aside and plans were being made to cease trading. Nevertheless, for the five years from the departure of the Norwegian entrepreneurs in 2011, the workers, none of whom had a university education or a background in business before they were recruited by Soria Moria, successfully ran a 38-room boutique hotel in central Siem Reap. As such, the initiative may serve as an inspiration for similar initiatives, and as a source of lessons learned.

It would require a more in-depth case study to draw authoritiative lessons from the Soria Moria experiment with worker ownership. However, the interview findings suggest some tentative observations. One is that the model of worker–ownership and management was not the original plan. It was inspired by the wish (shared by both the Norwegian entrepreneurs and the senior Cambodian management) to preserve the responsible tourism ethos of the hotel when the founders left. If conceived as a worker cooperative from the beginning, it may have had stronger foundations. Second, and relatedly, the two managers interviewed for this research were clearly high-achieving and highly motivated individuals. However, when asked about their future ambitions, one wanted to lead an NGO, and the other to get a senior management role in one of the large international hotels in Siem Reap. A hotel run as a social enterprise effectively requires a hotel manager, an NGO manager and a business manager. Soria Moria's leadership arguably contained only two of these three and as such perhaps illustrates the scale of the management challenge of establishing such an undertaking sustainably. Finally, a significant factor rendering the hotel unviable was the steeply rising rent. Social investors wishing to establish viable hotel co-operatives may need to seriously consider investing not only in the people but also in the property.

Re-drawing the tourism map in inclusive ways

Some of the key inclusive tourism initiatives in developed countries have involved deliberate attempts to redraw the tourism map, specifically taking tourists away from town centres and the sites that destination marketers usually place in the fore, and instead finding opportunities for interaction and enjoyment in the less celebrated areas of cities and regions. In the context of a tourism boom town such as Siem Reap where tourism is dominant and expanding, this search for new attractions and complementary activities is part of the expected pattern of development and is thus not, in itself, necessarily to be interpreted as inclusive. None of the case study enterprises was primarily focused on opening up new areas for tourism activities, though some influence in that direction come from ABOUTAsia tours establishing a lodge in a rural village, and also conducting research and devising new routes so that its clients can explore the temples without the presence of other tourists (Dattani, 2013), and through Phare circus providing a shop window for its schools in Battambang and therefore possibly awaking more tourist interest in that province.

The Siem Reap day-time tourism map is dominated by the temple complex, which is mainly concentrated in two districts immediately north of the provincial town. Many hotels and tour companies offer 'village tours' and 'rural experiences,' which potentially widen tourism benefits. However, in practice, these are often in peri-urban areas of the provincial town, or very close to the main temple routes. In this context, the social enterprises have geographically expanded the *benefits* of tourism, especially the large-scale, more dispersed impacts relating to the 48 rural workshops established by Artisans Angkor and the 110 schools assisted by ABOUTAsia tours.

Nevertheless, these activities and benefits are still concentrated in the districts within Siem Reap province that are closest to the temples. These are substantial contributions to extending the tourism's reach and making it more inclusive. However, these are not the scale-able innovations which some social enterprise proponents have hoped for (Dees, 2007, p. 26); they do not promise to yield benefits for the half a dozen districts in Siem Reap that are remote from the temples, or the 23 provinces in Cambodia that are not hosts to the tourism boom.

Concluding discussion

By viewing established social enterprises in Siem Reap through an inclusive tourism lens – asking who is included, on what terms and with what significance (Scheyvens & Biddulph, this issue), these five cases in Siem Reap provide examples of how social enterprises in the tourism sector can be socially inclusive and, to some degree, empowering. They show marginalized people becoming established producers in the tourism sector, whether this is the 750 artisans employed by Artisans Angkor or the 35 people with rural backgrounds employed at Soria Moria. In the short term, employees experience terms and conditions which compare favourably with those elsewhere, inside and outside the tourism sector. In the long term, they are able to develop career paths, as evidenced by the graduates of the Haven apprentice programme gaining employment in high-end restaurants and hotels through Siem Reap and the graduates of the Phare performing arts school providing artistic direction to the Phare circus which is now a leading attraction in Siem Reap. Meanwhile, benefits of tourism have been extended beyond the tourism sector, as, for example, with the 50 daily English language classes sponsored by ABOUTAsia and the 110 state schools receiving equipment from them. As earlier research in Siem Reap has shown, opportunities for individuals from one family or village can set up path dependencies which positively influence the opportunities of relatives and neighbours for years and even generations (Biddulph, 2015).

The ways in which these enterprises have contributed to inclusive tourism are quite different to the trajectories suggested by the more Schumpeterian strands of the social enterprise literature. They are not characterized by an entrepreneur who has (like Mohamed Yunus with Grameen) identified a social problem, developed an innovative solution and then scaled it up (c.f. Dees, 2007, p. 26). They are, rather, conventional tourism businesses (a tour company, a hotel, a restaurant, a souvenir production and retail company, and a performing arts company) which have integrated a social mission into their business model in different ways. The two largest, and arguably most established, of the five cases in this study, Phare and Artisans Angkor, have both received a huge subsidy in the form of substantial, long-term aid projects dating back to the 1980s and 1990s. Their strong market positions are largely attributable to decades of human resource development and product development delivered through humanitarian assistance, before the decision to commercialize. While this partly intersects with the commercialization of the NGO sector documented by Khieng and Dahles (2015, p. 237), there are important distinctions. First, the successful tourism social enterprises in this study, including those that were previously aid dependent, employ experienced private sector managers at senior levels in their organizations. Second, their customers are tourists and not their beneficiaries, and therefore, the harmonizing of commercial success and social accountability that Khieng and Dahles celebrate in commercializing NGOs is not part of the narratives of success in this study.

The three businesses which do more closely resemble the entrepreneur-centred model are rooted in the experiences of foreign travellers in the 2000s who saw opportunities to address social needs. In this respect, Haven, which (in the European tradition of co-operatives and governance-orientation) is financed through an association of 50 sympathetic supporters in Switzerland, has a degree of security not afforded to those at Soria Moria and ABOUTAsia. This might be interpreted as a cautionary note regarding the potential of entrepreneur-driven owner-operated social enterprises in tourism boom towns. What seems realistic in the early stages of a tourism boom may quickly become unrealistic as margins tighten and competition intensifies. While ABOUTAsia's enduring success demonstrates that social enterprises without aid subsidies and social investors are possible, the support that the other businesses have received in order to become established commercially should not be overlooked when the potential of social enterprise in the tourism sector is evaluated. This relates to two further cautionary notes which may be drawn from this study in relation to, first, regulatory environments and, second, the contingency of social benefits on business results.

The social enterprise literature stresses the importance of a 'supportive infrastructure' (Dees, 2007, p. 29; Kerlin, 2010, p. 177; Khieng & Dahles, 2015), but in Cambodia, the only options are to register as an NGO or, as in these five cases, a fully-fledged business with no tax benefits or concessions to incentivize the social orientation of the businesses. Furthermore, a major challenge that most social entrepreneurs in Siem Reap reported was the inconsistency with which tax regulations were implemented. While it is possible to advocate for a more favourable and more consistently implemented regulatory environment (and there are moves afoot in this direction with the Ministry of Commerce in Phnom Penh), it is also necessary to draw a more sober conclusion. It is in the nature of a developing country that it is not 'Denmark' but 'Djibouti' (Pritchett & Woolcock, 2004) and therefore likely to be plagued by poorly functioning and unpredictable institutions, a situation which the tourism sector is unlikely to be immune from. A social enterprise which seeks to publish honest accounts and pay taxes in full will struggle to survive in direct competition with businesses which do not feel obliged to play by the same rules and which make informal payments in order to avoid their obligations.

As a number of the entrepreneurs in this study stressed, tourism is a highly volatile and vulnerable sector. The social benefits of these enterprises are contingent on the success of the businesses, which are in turn contingent on the overall success of the sector. The social enterprises in this study have demonstrated a variety of ways to make tourism more inclusive. Their potential to provide social security that can withstand the ups and downs of business cycles is, however, more limited. This point is often overlooked by social enterprise proponents when they compare social enterprises favourably with state institutions and government programmes (Dees, 2007). At the time of writing, notwithstanding their substantial social contributions, there is nothing to suggest that these enterprises can either fundamentally transform the tourism sector, or that their business models can radically change social security and inclusion in wider society beyond the tourism sector.

Note

1. While this article was under review, I learned that Soria Moria would continue trading at new premises with new ownership (so no longer an owner cooperative model) but retaining the responsible tourism orientation and the commitment to support local social enterprises and NGOs (personal communication, Mr Rouen Samnieng, 29 September 2017).

Acknowledgements

I would like to thank the lead entrepreneurs of these five social enterprises for taking the time out of their busy work schedules to share the experiences and information on which this article is based. Thanks also to three anonymous reviewers for critical, constructive comments and to Special Issue editor Professor Regina Scheyvens and Tourism Geographies editor Professor Alan Lew for professional oversight of an exemplary process.

Disclosure statement

No potential conflict of interest was reported by the author.

Funding

Svenska Forskningsrådet Formas [grant number 2015-1540].

References

Alegre, I., & Berbegal-Mirabent, J. (2016). Social innovation success factors: Hospitality and tourism social enterprises. *International Journal of Contemporary Hospitality Management, 28*(6), 1155–1176.
Alter, K. (2007). Social *enterprise typology*. Retrieved from http://www.4lenses.org/setypology
Artisans Angkor. (2017). *Restoration of Angkor*. Retrieved from http://www.artisansdangkor.com/projects-22-restoration-of-angkor-site.php
Ashley, C., Roe, D., & Goodwin, H. (2001). Pro-poor tourism strategies: Making tourism work for the poor. London: Siem Reap.
Azmat, F. (2013). Sustainable development in developing countries: The role of social entrepreneurs. *International Journal of Public Administration, 36*(5), 293–304.
Biddulph, R. (2015). Limits to mass tourism's effects in rural peripheries. *Annals of Tourism Research, 50*(0), 98–112.
Blowfield, M. (2012). Business and development: Making sense of business as a development agent. *Corporate Governance: The International Journal of Business in Society, 12*(4), 414–426.
Bolster, P., & Brimble, P. (2008). Cambodia: Corporate social responsibility and the Cambodia Business Initiative in Rural Development (C-BIRD). *The Social and Ecological Market Economy – a Model for Asian Development? 287*, 287–299.
Bornstein, D., & Davis, S. (2010). *Social entrepreneurship: What everyone needs to know*. Oxford: Oxford University Press.

Dattani, M. (2013 March 14). *Angkor: The road less travelled. National Geographic Traveller*. Retrieved from http://www.natgeotraveller.co.uk/destinations/asia/cambodia/angkor-the-road-less-travelled/
de Kadt, E. (1979). *Tourism: Passport to development* ? New York, NY: Oxford University Press.
Dees, J. G. (1998). The meaning of "social entrepreneurship." Comments and suggestions contributed from the Social Entrepreneurship Founders Working Group. Retrieved from http://faculty.fuqua.duke.edu/centers/case/files/dees-SE.pdf
Dees, J. G. (2007). Taking social entrepreneurship seriously. *Society, 44*(3), 24–31.
Dees, J. G. (2008). Philanthropy and enterprise: Harnessing the power of business and social entrepreneurship for development. *Innovations: Technology, Governance, Globalization, 3*(3), 119–132.
Defourny, J., & Kim, S. Y. (2011). Emerging models of social enterprise in Eastern Asia: A cross–country analysis. *Social Enterprise Journal, 7*(1), 86–111.
Defourny, J., & Nyssens, M. (2008). Social enterprise in Europe: Recent trends and developments. *Social Enterprise Journal, 4*(3), 202–228.
Defourny, J., & Nyssens, M. (2010). Conceptions of social enterprise and social entrepreneurship in Europe and the United States: Convergences and divergences. *Journal of Social Entrepreneurship, 1*(1), 32–53.
Desa, G., & Koch, J. L. (2014). Scaling social impact: Building sustainable social ventures at the base-of-the-pyramid. *Journal of Social Entrepreneurship, 5*(2), 146–174.
Drayton, B., & Budinich, V. (2010). Can entrepreneurs save the world? A new alliance for global change. *Harvard Business Review, 88*(9), 56–64.
Edwards, M. (2008). *Just another emperor? The myths and realities of philanthrocapitalism*. New York, NY: Demos: A Network for Ideas and Action, The Young Foundation.
Edwards, P. (2007). *Cambodge: The Cultivation of a Nation, 1860-1945*. Honolulu, HI: University of Hawaii Press.
Eikenberry, A. M., & Kluver, J. D. (2004). The marketization of the nonprofit sector: Civil society at risk ? *Public Administration Review, 64*(2), 132–140.
Frenzel, F., & Koens, K. (2012). Slum tourism: Developments in a young field of interdisciplinary tourism research. *Tourism Geographies, 14*(2), 195–212.
Gawell, M. (2006). *Activist entrepreneurship: Attac'ing norms and articulating disclosive stories* (PhD). Stockholm University, Stockholm.
Guiney, T., & Mostafanezhad, M. (2015). The political economy of orphanage tourism in Cambodia. *Tourist Studies, 15*(2), 132–155.
Kerlin, J. A. (2006). Social enterprise in the United States and Europe: Understanding and learning from the differences. *VOLUNTAS: International Journal of Voluntary and Nonprofit Organizations, 17*(3), 246–262.
Kerlin, J. A. (2010). A comparative analysis of the global emergence of social enterprise. *VOLUNTAS: International Journal of Voluntary and Nonprofit Organizations, 21*(2), 162–179.
Khieng, S. (2014). Funding mobilization strategies of nongovernmental organizations in Cambodia. *VOLUNTAS: International Journal of Voluntary and Nonprofit Organizations, 25*(6), 1441–1464.
Khieng, S., & Dahles, H. (2015). Commercialization in the non-profit sector: The emergence of social enterprise in Cambodia. *Journal of Social Entrepreneurship, 6*(2), 218–243.
Lyne, I. (2008). How can social enterprise really tackle social exclusion? A comparative study of children's welfare in the United Kingdom and Cambodia. *Education, Knowledge and Economy, 2*(3), 175–190.
MacCannell, D. (2008). Why it never really was about authenticity. *Society, 45*(4), 334–337.
Mao, N., DeLacy, T., & Grunfeld, H. (2013). Local livelihoods and the tourism value chain: A case study in Siem Reap-Angkor Region, Cambodia. *International Journal of Environmental and Rural Development, 4*(2), 120–126.
Mdee, A., & Emmott, R. (2008). Social enterprise with international impact: The case for Fair Trade certification of volunteer tourism. *Education, Knowledge and Economy, 2*(3), 191–201.
Neth, B. (2008). *Ecotourism as a tool for sustainable rural community development and natural resources management in the Tonle Sap Biosphere Reserve* (PhD). University of Kassel, Kassel.

Palmås, K. (2003). *Den Barmhärtiga Entreprenören: Från privatisering till socialt företagande* [The compassionate entrepreneur: From privatisation to social enterprise]. Stockholm: Agora.
Palmås, K. (2011). *Prometheus eller Narcissus: Entreprenören som samhällsomvärvare* [Prometheus or Narcisuss: The entrepreneur as social revolutionary]. Stockholm: Korpen Koloni Förlag.
Palmås, K. (2013). Varför vi misslyckats: Tio års diskussion om socialt entreprenörskap. In L. Trägårdh, P. Selle, L. S. Henriksen, & H. Hallin (Eds.), *Civilsamhället klämt mellan stat och kapital* [Civil society caught between the state and capital (and book title is "Why we have failed: discussing ten years of social entrepreneurship")] (pp. 256–266). Stockholm: SNS.
Peck, J. (2013). Excavating the Pilbara: A Polanyian exploration. *Geographical Research, 51*(3), 227–242.
Polkinghorne, M. (2009). The artists of Angkor: Contemporary and medieval stone workshops in Cambodia. *The Asian Arts Society of Australia, 18*(4), 10–12.
Pritchett, L., & Woolcock, M. (2004). Solutions when the solution is the problem: Arraying the disarray in development. *World Development, 32*(2), 191–212.
Reas, J. P. (2013). Boy, have we got a vacation for you': Orphanage tourism in Cambodia and the commodification and objectification of the orphaned child. *Thammasat Review, 16*, 121–140.
Sayer, J. (2005). Guest editor's introduction: Do more good, do less harm: development and the private sector. *Development in Practice, 15*(3-4), 251–268.
Scheyvens, R. (2011). *Tourism and poverty*. London: Routledge.
Scheyvens, R., & Biddulph, R. (2017). Inclusive tourism development. *Tourism Geographies*. Advance online publication. doi:10.1080/14616688.2017.1381985
Schultz, K. (2002). Traditional arts and crafts for the future. *Museum International, 54*(1–2), 56–63.
Social Enterprise Cambodia. (2015). Social Enterprise Cambodia. Retrieved from http://socialenterprisecambodia.org
Sharpley, R., & McGrath, P. (2017). 7 Tourism in Cambodia: Opportunities and Challenges. In K. Brickell & S. Springer (Eds.), *The handbook of contemporary Cambodia* (pp. 87–98). Abingdon: Routledge.
Social Enterprise Cambodia. (2015). Find a social enterprise. Retrieved from http://socialenterprisecambodia.org/find-social-enterprise/
Teasdale, S., Lyon, F., & Baldock, R. (2013). Playing with numbers: A methodological critique of the social enterprise growth myth. *Journal of Social Entrepreneurship, 4*(2), 113–131.
Winter, T. (2014). 15 Postconflict heritage in Asia. In P. Basu & W. Modest (Eds.), *Museums, heritage and international development* (pp. 295–307). Abingdon: Routledge.
von der Weppen, J., & Cochrane, J. (2012). Social enterprises in tourism: An exploratory study of operational models and success factors. *Journal of Sustainable Tourism, 20*(3), 497–511.

Too precarious to be inclusive? Hotel maid employment in Spain

Ernest Cañada

ABSTRACT

Hoteliers have steadily been able to reduce costs and increase employees' workload as a result of mass unemployment sparked by the financial crisis, beginning in 2008, and associated legislative reforms by the Spanish government. Outsourcing has been hotels' main instrument in this drive. Hotel chambermaids are among the groups most affected by this phenomenon. This article analyses the impacts of outsourcing on hotel maids' working conditions, while questioning the possibilities for achieving inclusive tourism given the current outsourcing trend. It is based on 44 in-depth interviews with a range of informants, including 24 hotel maids who have experienced the process of outsourcing, in major Spanish tourism destinations. This study aims to understand the changes these workers have experienced and perceived in their working conditions. The research results highlight a marked deterioration in hotel maids' working conditions in recent years, most notably involving (a) a reduction in their salary and the loss of professional categories, (b) work overload, (c) greater uncertainty in the duration of employment, timetables and work schedule, (d) de-professionalisation, (e) segmentation, division and an increase in competition between hotel staff, (f) the accentuation of health problems and (g) a decrease in the capacity of representation and the defence of workers' collective interests.

1. Introduction

There is a clear tension between the notion that tourism can be 'inclusive' in the sense of offering economic development and political empowerment, on the one hand, and the sector's tendency for competition and deregulation, on the other. As neo-liberalism has implied the erosion of working conditions, terms of inclusion for the workforce have deteriorated. This article examines the situation of Spanish hotel chambermaids[1] over the past decade in order to identify trends in their employment, while asking whether there is evidence that tourism is, or can be, an inclusive, empowering source of employment.

The financial crisis of 2007–2009 has precipitated increased unemployment and poverty in much of Europe (Eurostat, 2015). This has been followed by significant transformations in labour policies and labour management that have led to an increase in inequalities, particularly in southern Europe and among women (Leschke & Jepsen, 2012; Otobe, 2011), similar to those which have occurred during previous economic downturns (Fallon & Lucas, 2002). The crisis has been interpreted as a necessary adjustment for the conservation of the capitalist system, which allows the conditions of capital reproduction to be preserved. Critical scholars have pointed to the complexity of this multi-clausal process (Subasat, 2016) and its implications for urban transformation (Holgersen, 2015), whose specific impacts on tourism work we aim to explore in this article.

We focus our attention on the case of Spain, given the relevance which tourism has acquired for the country's economy since the 1960s (Murray, 2015). By 2015, the tourism sector accounted for 11.7% of Spain's GDP and 11.85% of employment (Exceltur, 2016). In this year, the country boasted a total of 414,590 hotel workers, an exceptionally feminised group as is also the case elsewhere in the world (Obadić & Marić, 2009). The prominence of tourism in Spain's economy is even greater in many coastal areas, such as the Balearic Islands, where tourism represents 44.8% of local GDP and 32% of employment (Exceltur, 2014). Moreover, Spain provides a case which exemplifies transformations in the workplace brought about by the financial crisis. Coupled with the scale of the Spanish tourism sector, the country is especially useful for understanding the ability of mass tourism to be more inclusive, or less so, from the perspective of those who work in this sector.

Particular attention is paid to hotel chambermaids or housekeepers (known as *camareras de piso* in Spanish), devoted to cleaning rooms and common areas in hotels. In Spain, hotel employees are not statistically sorted by occupation in the national Labour Force Survey (LFS). However, both experts and chambermaids themselves concur that hotels maids comprise between 25% and 30%t of hotel staff. Thus, they constitute approximately 100,000 workers in Spain, out of a total of over 300,000 employees registered in the hotel sector according to the LFS (Encuesta de Población Activa) (EPA, 2016). This group has been particularly impacted by outsourcing in hotels after the Spanish Government's labour reform of 2012. This reform, apparently formulated in response to the financial crisis and mass unemployment, entails a radical change in the way in which work is organised. Its main goal is the primacy of company agreements over collective sectoral agreements, resulting in the outsourcing of departments that are crucial to the functioning of hotels.

---

[1] This article uses the terms hotel chambermaids, hotel maids and hotel housekeepers interchangeably as synonyms designating professionals who perform the tasks of general cleaning and making beds in hotels.

Furthermore, this article considers what kind of role 'work' has in inclusive tourism, and to what extent the transformations that have taken place in working conditions lead towards greater inclusivity. We use the concept of 'decent work' formulated by the International Labour Organisation (ILO) through its Director General, Juan Somavía, during the organisation's 87th International Labour Conference (ILO, 1999). The concept of decent work intimately concerns ILO's four strategic objectives: employment, social protection, workers' rights and social dialogue. Closely tied to these issues, hotel workers' struggles against outsourcing and the 'precarisation' of labour conditions directly align with three of the key elements of 'inclusive tourism' as defined by Regina Scheyvens and Robin Biddulph (2017). These authors propose a more complex understanding of inclusive tourism, one which better integrates a range of different factors. It moves beyond a strictly defined vision conceived solely in terms of 'inclusive growth' (Bakker & Messerli, 2016; Hampton, Jeyacheya, & Long, 2017) which has, to date, dominated what little literature exists around this concept. First, their understanding of inclusive tourism concerns the challenge of dominant power relationships in the tourism industry. Second, it deals with the promotion of the self-representation of marginalised groups, in this case hotel maids, in order to represent their experience based on their own narratives. Third, by broadening the range of actors who can make decisions regarding tourism, this conception of inclusive tourism defends the role of trade unions and women's groups as collective spaces of organisation. In this last regard, outsourcing policies attempt to put to an end to the participation of such organisations in tourism's decision-making processes.

Diverse international instruments recognise the relevance of adequate working conditions for progress towards sustainable tourism. Foremost amongst these is the International Social Tourism Organisation's (ISTO) Montreal Declaration, which states in article 6 that:

> The tourism sector must create jobs and at the same time guarantee the fundamental rights of the people who work in this sector. (ISTO, 1996)

The theoretical framework on which we focus our research is based on studies of critical geography and on critical interdisciplinary analyses. These have focused on how the conditions of capitalist accumulation devalue work (Brenner, 2003), as well as the fact that tourism is understood to be one of the main agents of capitalist accumulation (Britton, 1991; Mosedale, 2011, 2016). Simultaneously, tourism is also considered one of its spatial-temporal solutions, following David Harvey's (2003, 2014) theoretical approach, which has been deployed in the field of tourism by different authors (Fetcher & Neves, 2012; Fletcher, 2011; Yrigoy, 2014). Tourism work, however, has not been sufficiently analysed from this perspective, as described below.

2. Work in the geography of tourism

The production processes of the economic and social landscape are an essential part of human geography (Harvey, 2006 [1982]). The role of capital, its institutions and the social resistances it causes under different regimes of accumulation, have been highlighted by a range of sources (Brenner & Theodore, 2002; Harvey, 2012). Nonetheless, as Andrew Herod has explained, in the geography of capital there is a tendency to ignore, or to simply neglect, the role of work and of the working class in the production of the economic geography of capitalism (Herod, 1997). Thus, although work has been approached in human geography by various authors (Castree, Coe, Ward, & Samers, 2004; Herod, 2001; Herod & Aguiar, 2006; Massey, 1995), this issue continues to be poorly studied by our discipline, much in the same way that the spatial issue has also been insufficiently dealt with in studies on work (Herod). Yet by conceptualising capitalism as a spatial system, according to Herod (2001), it is possible to identify how workers produce their own geographies, even if these are imposed upon them under certain conditions. Thereby, the spatial focus can contribute to exploring the conceptualisation of the world of work. In fact, the tourism proletariat could be understood as one of the highest expressions of neoliberal capitalism and its spatial logics, coinciding with the focus of Aguiar and Herod (2006) for the case of domestic and cleaning work. In this regard, there has been some discussion as to the need and potential for greater collaboration between the geography of work and other social sciences, such as history or studies on labour relations, in order to contribute greater richness and complexity to such analyses (Ellem & McGrath-Champ, 2012).

Looking specifically at tourism in the early 1990s, Britton (1991) criticised the fact that the geography of tourism was characterised by a weak link to economic geography and that it lacked solid theoretical foundations. It is worth noting that, since this time, notable progress has been made in these areas (Ioannides & Debbage, 1998; Mosedale, 2011, 2016). However, despite such progress, the labour issue continues to occupy a marginal space in the economic geography of tourism (Bianchi, 2011). Similarly, different reviews of existing literature on tourism work have identified a lack of attention and neglect with which labour issues are approached in this sphere, unlike other issues, despite the fundamental importance of personal service to tourism operations (Ballantyne, Packer, & Axelsen, 2009; Baum, Kralj, Robinson, & Solnet, 2016; Ladkin, 2011; Solnet, Baum, Robinson, & Lockstone-Binney, 2015). Research on tourism work tends to be directed towards resolving problems of human resource management, rather than a concern for tourism work in itself within a more complex context analysis (Baum et al., 2016). As a result, the situation of tourism workers and their marginalisation in decision-making has not been analysed in sufficient depth. Meanwhile, Zampoukos and Ioannides (2011), while questioning the superficiality of studies on tourism work, highlight how the vast majority of people employed in tourism are badly paid, have low professional qualifications, are hired on temporary and part-time contracts, experience high turnover, and have scarce chances of developing a professional career. The fact that a significant portion of these workers in the lowest levels of the industry are women and immigrants suggests that they are being associated with the unpaid work of housewives performed within the home, thereby perpetuating labour divisions based on gender and nationality. Hence, it is proposed that the issue of work should be placed at the centre of the analysis of the geography of tourism.

In this context, it seems evident that crucial critical research on tourism work needs to move forward and further develop its analysis based on an assessment of the quality of employment generated by the tourism sector. Two complementary theoretical–conceptual instruments may be of special use to this end: the concept of 'decent work', proposed by ILO (1999), and that of 'inclusive tourism'. The former makes it possible to analyse the quality of the work involved in tourism, while the latter gauges its integration in the operation of the industry.

3. The work of hotel maids: the state of the issue

International studies on the work of hotel maids reveal the practical social invisibility of this group (Hunter & Watson, 2006). In most countries, most housekeeping employees are women, many of whom are immigrants from low-income countries (Dyer, McDowell, & Batnitzky, 2010). The 'feminisation' of this type of work has also been associated with strong gender discrimination that is expressed in lower wages and a lack of professional recognition (Ferreira & Ramos, 2016), as well as such workers' limited capacity to influence the trade union agenda. Within this context, the construction of their identities as a group of workers entails a complex interaction between their gender, class, race and ethnicity (Adib & Guerrier, 2003).

Moreover, tourism's seasonality has contributed to hotel companies traditionally adopting flexible hiring mechanisms. This has had significant consequences for the quality of tourism employment (Adler & Adler, 2003; Castellanos & Pedreño, 2006). In the context of increased labour flexibility, many companies have resorted to these forms of recruitment, with a growing imposition of seasonal and part-time work, outsourcing part of the workforce and the increased intensity of work. Overall, this has resulted in a deterioration of working conditions and increasing precariousness (Puech, 2004; Seifert & Messing, 2006). Similarly, during times of high occupancy, it is normal for established work schedules to be exceeded, rendering employees' work-life balance especially complicated (Dyer, McDowell, & Batnitzky, 2011; McNamara et al., 2011).

Hotel maids are often a divided and disunited group. In part, this is due to the diverse forms of recruitment that coexist within the same workforce. It is also tied to issues of origin and nationality, upon which compartmentalised relationships of solidarity have been built between workers. These divisions serve as a basis for accentuating their high levels of exploitation and reducing their capabilities for resistance (McDowell, Batnitzky, & Dyer, 2007; Puech, 2007).

Working conditions in hotels' housekeeping departments have given rise to higher rates of accidents and serious injuries than other jobs in the service industry. This is demonstrative of a clear deterioration in the health of hotel maids as a result of the way in which they have to work (Buchanan et al., 2010; Burgel, White, Gillen, & Krause, 2010; DaRos, 2011; Hsieh, Apostolopoulos, & Sönmez, 2013; Krause & Scherzer, 2005; Krause, Rugulies, & Maslach, 2010; Liladrie, 2010; McNamara, Bohle, & Quinlan, 2011; Sanon, 2013, 2014; Scherzer, Rugulies, & Krause, 2005). Alongside the relationships between hotel maids' specific tasks and health problems, scholars also highlight the psychosocial impacts on workers' health wrought by the high effort–reward imbalance caused by the organisation of their work (Burgel et al., 2010).

In Spain, most hotel housekeepers and hotel maids are women. A significant proportion are immigrants from Southern America, Morocco and eastern Europe, among others. Furthermore, it has been noted that they receive very low salaries and are subject to extremely vulnerable employment conditions (Albarracín, 2013). Mass unemployment in Spain, with rates reaching 26.1% of the active population in 2013 (Banyuls & Recio, 2015) and labour reforms in 2010 and 2012, have enabled hoteliers to carry out a series of labour adjustments with a strong impact on working conditions and the lives of housekeeping department staff (Cañada, 2015).

4. Outsourcing: Impacts on labour conditions

Of the different processes identified above, the outsourcing of housekeeping departments stands out due to the strong influence it has had on making working conditions precarious. Outsourcing consists of hiring services from a third company, which takes charge of the workers and takes over the management of a certain process. Outsourcing processes have been characterised in different studies as a mechanism for reducing business costs, with a significant impact on working conditions. In particular, outsourcing has been shown to lead to a decrease in salaries (Basualdo & Morales, 2014; Dube & Kaplan, 2010; Moreno, Godino, & Recio, 2014; Munro, 2012; Petersen, Hjelmar, Vrangbeak, & La Cour, 2011); the loss of social benefits (Basualdo & Morales, 2014; Dube & Kaplan, 2010); the intensification of work (Holgate, Hebson, & McBride, 2006; Moreno et al., 2014; Munro, 2012; Petersen et al., 2011); the loss of workers' autonomy (Munro, 2012); a decrease in job security (Petersen et al., 2011); negative effects on workers' health, including increased stress and burnout (Basualdo & Morales, 2014; Petersen et al., 2011); loss of quality in customer service and in the service provided (Lethbridge, 2012; Munro, 2012; Petersen et al., 2011); a decline in unionisation (Dube & Kaplan, 2010); and negative effect on the forms of union organisation and collective bargaining capabilities. In tandem, outsourcing also acts as a powerful disciplinary factor among hired staff (Basualdo & Morales, 2014). Thus, outsourcing has been associated with a general loss in both job and service quality across the board (Castillo, 2005; Moreno et al., 2014 Warhust et al., 2012).

In the specific field of the hotel industry, the relevance of fixed-term workers' recruitment and their outsourcing in staff management is evident, given that these have become the most common forms of recruitment (Davidson, McPhail, & Barry, 2011). As in other sectors, a number of other issues have also been identified, such as legislation offering workers poor protection, low wages, difficult access to training and career development (Soltani & Wilkinson, 2010) and scant attachment to their place of work and profession (Hall, 2000). In addition, a higher incidence of such 'precarisation' processes is evident amongst woman workers (Davidson et al., 2011; Soltani & Wilkinson, 2010).

5. Methodology

The methodology used in this study is based on a thorough literature review of the role of work in tourism, particularly the specific work of hotel maids and housekeepers, and outsourcing, the phenomenon which most directly affects the precariousness of their work. In addition to this literature review, the study is based on 44 in-depth interviews, including interviews with 24 hotel maids whose contractual statuses differ considerably (see Table 1).

The present article is based on the aforementioned 24 interviews, specifically with workers who have experienced outsourcing in the Spanish cities of Barcelona (5), Tarragona (5), Madrid (4), Seville (4), Valencia (2), Cáceres (1), Tenerife (1), Cádiz (1) and A Coruña (1). All of these workers were contracted as hotel chamber maids by 'multiservice' companies. In some cases, these workers were fired by hotels before being contracted by the multiservice companies which took over responsibility for the hotels' housekeeping departments. In other cases, the workers were directly hired by multiservice companies to perform housekeeping duties within the hotels. Six of the workers interviewed are

Table 1. In-depth interviews.

Interviewed people	Number	Sex	Municipality	Country of birth	Occupation	Union affiliation
Outsourced workers	24	Women: 24 Men: 0	Barcelona: 5 Tarragona: 5 Madrid: 4 Sevilla: 4 Valencia: 2 Cáceres: 1 Tenerife: 1 Cádiz: 1 A Coruña: 1	Spain: 18 Colombia: 1 Cuba: 1 Ecuador: 2 Russia: 1 Morocco: 1	Chamber maid: 24	CCOO: 4 UGT: 1 None: 19
Key Informants	20	Women: 8 Men: 12	Barcelona: 5 Madrid: 7 Mallorca: 5 Málaga: 2 Sevilla: 1	Spain: 20	Union Leader: 16 Lawyer: 1 Doctor: 1 Labour inspector: 1 Social worker: 1	CCOO: 10 UGT: 6 None: 4

originally from countries other than Spain (Colombia, Ecuador, Cuba, Russia and Morocco). With only one exception, all the remaining housekeepers were not unionised. Nonetheless, 14 were engaged in different social groups to defend their labour rights. These emerging groups were recently created via the social networks which enable housekeepers from different areas and workplaces to meet one another. In the case of Seville, the women interviewed are members of CAPISE, the Association of Hotel Maids in Seville.

Low levels of union affiliation among outsourced maids are widespread, a fact confirmed by union leaders of Spain's principle unions in the hotel sector. The workers selected by this article are part of a broader research study, involving interviews with 100 workers. Interviewed workers were first contacted through union organisations and social networks. Those interviewed first provided the contact details of other outsourced workers for the purposes of this research. Interviews were carried out outside of their workplaces, principally in workers' homes, in bars or in local trade unions' premises. The duration of each interview varied between 45 and 60 minutes. All the interviews were recorded, enabling transcripts to be created and analysed. Selection criteria employed for the purposes of this study aimed at understanding common perceived problems in working conditions, rather than local or territorial specificities.

The interviews were carried out in a semi-structured manner, which made it possible to identify the career path of each worker and their socio-economic and family context. It also enabled us to explore and reconstruct their labour experiences, paying special attention to the following aspects: types of tasks carried out; working conditions; forms of recruitment; effects on health; changes experienced and perceived; group dynamics; identification of elements of dissatisfaction; relations with the company, trade union and work colleagues; the effect of work on their everyday lives; and the characteristics and experiences of outsourcing processes.

Other actors were also interviewed, including trade union leaders (16), both from CCOO, the Workers' Commissions [Comisiones Obreras] and UGT, the General Worker's Union [Unión General de Trabajadores]. Other interviewees included a lawyer (1), a doctor (1), a labour inspector (1) and a social worker (1). Interviews with these actors were also semi-structured, although they focused on the participants' knowledge, derived from their field of expertise, of the labour situation in hotels and, specifically, the phenomenon of outsourcing.

In a context marked by strong power inequalities, this research is theoretically and methodologically grounded in the conviction that in order to analyse changes in workers' working conditions, it is necessary to consider workers' own perceptions. The changes experienced and perceived by workers allow us to develop a detailed picture of the phenomena being studied and their complexity.

5. Context: outsourcing in the Spanish hotel industry

In Spain, outsourcing processes in hotels' key departments were enabled by a 2012 labour reform, spearheaded by the ruling Spanish People's Party (PP – Partido Popular) government through 'Royal Decree – Law 3/2012 of 10 February on urgent measures for labour market reform'. This labour reform is the last of 53 modifications of labour regulations carried out since 1984 (Aragón, 2012). At its core, this reform is concerned with controlling inflation by reducing prices and wages. Thus, it further intensifies the trend of making labour relations more flexible, a trend that is well underway in Spain (Bañuls & Recio, 2015). Alongside its concern with conditions for recruitment, dismissal and unemployment benefits, this 2012 reform places special emphasis on a key point shared with previous reforms, namely: the desire to transform the structure of collective bargaining on working conditions by facilitating more individualised bargaining at the company level, where the power of workers is far weaker. This has led to drastically fewer workers in the private sector being covered by a collective agreement. For instance, coverage fell from 89% to 76% between 2011 and 2012 alone, thereby increasing the fragmentation of labour relations (Banyuls & Recio, 2015, pp. 55–56).

Outsourcing in Spain has been regulated since the Statute of Workers' Rights (Estatuto de los Trabajadores) was passed on 10 March 1980 (MESS, 2015). This law marked the first regulation governing labour relations in Spain after the end of the dictatorship of Francisco Franco and the approval of the new Constitution in 1978, and substituted the Law on Labour Relations (08/04/1976), and part of the Employment Ordinance for the Hospitality Industry (28/02/1974). Outsourcing was permitted as long as a series of employers' responsibilities were fulfilled (article 42 of the Statute) (MESS, 2015). However, outsourcing remained rare because companies had to pay the same amount to both outsourced workers and to those workers who were recruited directly (articles 81, 82 and 83) (MESS, 2015). In other words, the minimum standards established by collective bargaining took precedence over other agreements and prevented companies from paying lower wages to outsourced labour.

With the labour reform of 2012, the conditions that discouraged the spread of outsourcing in hotels in much of Spain were modified. By allowing company agreements to take priority over collective agreements, outsourcing became attractive as a source of cheap labour. The modifications promoted in the 2012 labour reform are reflected in the new text of the Statute of Workers' Rights, amended by a Royal Decree issued on 23 October 2015 (article 84.2) (MESS, 2015).

5.1. Different visions of the same strategy

Most business sector representatives consider that outsourcing is simply a cost reduction strategy (Hinojosa, 2016, p. 20; Hosteltur, 2016, p. 14). The assessment of outsourcing by professional associations, trade union organisations and tourism workers themselves does not coincide with that of employers' associations. Nor are they in agreement with the view that housekeeping work should not be considered a core activity in the hotel industry. The interest in decreasing labour costs is identified as one of the main reasons for this view, albeit not the sole reason for such arguments.

The Spanish Association of Head Housekeepers in Hotels and Other Organisations (*Asociación Española de Gobernantas de Hotel y Otras Entidades*) (ASEGO) identified hoteliers' intention to take advantage of the financial crisis as a means of reducing labour costs and tackling staff management challenges:

> Question: What do you think this move towards outsourcing is due to?
> Reply: To cost, to cost purely and simply. To not wanting to have staff tied to the company, to wanting to reduce the size of the workforce, and also due to the problems [the hoteliers' experience] with unions. Evidently, if a hotel has a smaller workforce, it also has fewer union representatives. (Interview 1, woman, head housekeeper, Madrid)

Although the phenomenon of multiservice companies has existed for years, the type of outsourcing that has been taking place in recent years in the hotel industry is a novelty for trade union organisations, both due to its intensity and the fact that it is now affecting processes or departments that are considered 'core' to the functioning of hotels:

> Outsourcing activities that are not considered core parts of a business' activity have been practiced for a very long time, since the 1970s, beginning in industry, but then spreading to any other type of activity. What is the current novelty? That mass outsourcing of some activities in the service sector is taking place because of the recently implemented labour reforms in Europe, which make it possible to decrease labour costs in order to promote a business of service provision interposed between the main activity and the subsidiary one. (Interview 2, union leader, man, Madrid)

From this perspective, hoteliers' interest in outsourcing responds mainly to the possibility of reducing labour costs:

> The main reason why outsourcing takes place is the savings this affords companies in terms of wages, social security fees, days off, holidays and sick leave, amongst others. Besides this, hotels threaten not to renew contracts with multiservice companies if they don't take on more tasks and responsibilities than the ones they have already been contracted to perform. (Interview 3, hotel maid, unionist, Tenerife)

The spread of this model of outsourcing in housekeeping departments in many hotels has had multiple consequences for a 'labour group' that was already experiencing a strong deterioration in their working conditions. To a certain extent, it has contributed to making these conditions even more precarious. Many workers describe this change as a traumatic process that has degraded their work and hence their living conditions (Cañada, 2016).

6. Results: impacts of outsourcing

The information provided by different reports and statements by union leaders confirms that outsourcing in hotels is considered to have produced multiple negative impacts on workers. Through in-depth interviews with outsourced workers, seven of the effects produced have been identified and described here.

Through the information provided by different reports and statements by union leaders outsourcing in hotels has been considered to have produced multiple negative impacts on workers. Through in-depth interviews with outsourced workers, seven of the effects produced have been identified and characterised.

(a) *Salary reduction and loss of professional category*

One of the effects felt most keenly by workers hired through multiservice companies is the decrease in their wages. By moving from a hospitality agreement to a cleaning or company agreement, wages may fall by 30%–40%. In many cases, the workers interviewed went from earning between EUR 1100 and 1200 per month, depending on the provisions of the collective hospitality agreement in their province, to receiving a much lower wage. In some instances, this could even be around the minimum wage of EUR 655 per month. In other cases, payment by external companies is provided on a 'per room' basis, with great variations according to the type of company and the area of work. Overall, this entails a clear decrease in the final wage received by workers. In many of the interviews conducted, workers reported the price received per room is around EUR 2.5. However, in some cases it is as low as EUR 1.13.

Failing to apply the sectoral agreement also entails the loss of certain benefits, such as paying workers 40% more for working on a bank holiday or for working at night. Another benefit that workers are losing, which had functioned to complement their wages, is hotels' obligation to guarantee workers both breakfast and lunch during their shifts. Now, in outsourced hotels it is increasingly common for the company not to assume this commitment. Another frequent problem, reported by many of the outsourced female workers interviewed, is that multiservice companies attempt to trick them out of receiving the full-agreed sum which corresponds to their salary (Cañada, 2016, pp. 98–100).

This change is also reflected in the loss of professional categories recognised in workers' contracts, which decline in status from 'hotel maid' to categories like 'cleaner', 'ironer' or 'labourer'. In the case of head housekeepers and other middle management jobs, a similar trend is evident, both in terms of their wages and the recognition of their professional status. In fact, in order to supplement their low wages, they also have to take up cleaning rooms.

The wage drop experienced by this group of workers has an especially great effect given the context of overall unemployment in Spain in recent years. Before the financial crisis, the wages of many of these female workers might have been just one more family wage. However, with the decline in employment in other sectors, such as construction, theirs may become the only wage coming into their household. Thus, the repercussions of decreasing their wages are even more serious, given their family's greater dependence on this source of income.

(b) *Work overload*

Since the crisis, the vast majority of hotels in Spain have experienced the general trend of an increased workload. Mass unemployment and the possibilities afforded by the latest labour reforms act as disciplinary mechanisms which favour the intensification of work. In the hotel industry, it has become common practice to assign workers a certain number of rooms and set tasks for each working day, which are generally impossible to fulfil without rushing all day long and which multiservice companies have steadily continued to increase. According to the workers interviewed for this study, many workers recruited as fixed-term and part-time employees, whether outsourced or not, are increasingly faced with abusive situations which require them to work for more hours than they are supposed to without additional pay (Cañada, 2016).

As multiservice companies compete with each other to make the best offers to hotels, they often try to reduce the size of their workforce or to increase the number of rooms which each worker has to clean. In addition, when hotels increase their demands on these multiservice companies, both in terms of quality and by requiring them to perform new tasks, this does not result in such companies increasing the staff number of staff they employ in order to meet this extended workload. Instead, a work overload tends to affect their workers.

Meanwhile, the reduction in the number of 'valets' has also impacted the 'overload' of work for hotel maids. As a professional category, valets are mainly men devoted to taking in and removing furniture from rooms, taking away laundry, replenishing rooms with clean bedding, cleaning windows and other tasks which help to alleviate the burden on chambermaids when their work accumulates. Many multiservice companies lack experience in the hotel sector, as do many of the hotel maids that they recruit. This means an increase in the work of coordination and supervision performed by head housekeepers:

> Sometimes sheets coming from the laundry service are dirty, so the maids have to go back [...] and look for another set of sheets, clean sheets, without hairs, without tears, without spots, and this means a loss of time. This happens because nobody controls outsourced services. Before, the head housekeeper was controlling all this. (Interview 1, woman, head housekeeper, Madrid)

(c) *Greater uncertainty in the duration of employment, timetables and work schedule*

Recruiting through multiservice companies means that workers permanently live in a state of insecurity in terms of the real duration of their employment, regardless of the timescale indicated by their contracts. An issue identified among fixed-term workers is the fact that most feel obliged to accept changes in their timetables or days off, depending on the needs of the company, for fear of not having their contract renewed or simply not being called again. This leads to a state of insecurity that makes it difficult to balance their work and personal lives, especially in the case of women with young children. In housekeeping departments, it is already customary for workers to have to rush in order to finish the number of rooms assigned to them. With outsourcing, this trend is increased and it becomes normal for workers to not have the breaks they are due, including going without meal times.

Some workers claim that companies' discretionary power to change timetables or days off has become a way of imposing certain tasks and workloads, while having workers at their disposal at all times, depending on their interests. It even appears that this way of managing shifts has become a way of rewarding or sanctioning workers, with a clear disciplinary intention. Thus, it is common for many workers to report not knowing what their work timetable is at the start of the week, which makes balancing their personal and family life much more complicated. The difficulties of balancing work and domestic/family life has a 'cascading' effect on the whole family structure, in that it is fundamentally based on women's work.

(d) *De-professionalisation*

The fact that multiservice companies compete with each other to obtain contracts to manage hotel services means that they put pressure on working conditions in a way that ultimately affects the quality of the service performed. The increase in workload, and the fact that work must be carried out within a stipulated timeframe, which is generally insufficient for the task at hand, means that there is ever more pressure on workers. This makes it difficult for them to do their work well, both with regard to the job of cleaning as well as offering personalised customer service. In turn, since there is greater staff turnover in different workplaces, job insecurity abounds. Workers find it extremely difficult to build a career in these conditions. As a result, workers end up reducing emotional ties to their profession and their workplace. The consequence of this new way of organising work is a loss in the quality of services, since it is ultimately impossible for workers to carry out all the tasks they are assigned to a high standard or to cope with the daily pressure they are under, despite superhuman effort.

Furthermore, on many occasions the multiservice companies which have taken over the management of housekeeping departments do not have sufficient experience or are ill-prepared to take on such work in hotels. One of the great deficiencies identified is related to poor investment in staff training by the multiservice companies that hire workers. An added problem is that multiservice companies on the whole are not exclusively devoted to cleaning hotel rooms, but rather cover many sectors. Moreover, the people employed do not necessarily know enough about the characteristics of hotel work, which may lead to a loss in the quality of this service. This is compounded by high staff turnover, as many workers frequently leave their jobs in response to the conditions they are subjected to by multiservice companies. In turn, this brings about the loss of trained professionals in the sector. Yet, staff turnover is not limited to workers hired by multiservice companies, but rather to the turnover of the companies contracted by hotels, with the changes in staff that this also involves.

Growing pressure to save on costs, induced by competition between multiservice companies and the wages that a hotel assigns to an outsourcing company, affects the tools and cleaning materials available to workers. In some cases, it is reported that there is less control and exigency in changes of bedding. This is one of the many ways in which multiservice companies seek to save on costs. The difficulty which workers face in adequately performing their jobs may also affect professionalism in the sector overall. On the one hand, older workers find it more difficult to carry out their work adequately and, on the other, there are also more obstacles to training younger workers. These obstacles are generated by the pace of work, the atmosphere of tension and competition between fixed-term workers and permanent contract or permanent season contract workers, or even issues like the workers' country of birth. As women start retiring from these jobs, the workers replacing them in these conditions have barely been given the training necessary to be able to carry out their work adequately and, in turn, to acquire healthy work habits that will help to prevent occupational hazards and illness.

Thus, poor working conditions ultimately result in the deterioration of customer service. Many workers interviewed in this study reported that there is a loss in the quality of room cleanliness, especially when guests remain in the hotel over an extended period and chambermaids have to prioritise rooms from which guests are checking out. There is also a perceived lower ability to control lost property and even guest security regarding their belongings. The disassociation of staff from the establishment where they work also facilitates greater neglect of the hotel's infrastructure or furniture. Finally, this also affects the image of hotels, especially in more upscale establishments. Ultimately, the loss of service quality and 'de-professionalisation' may affect the future of the tourism industry in a particular location. The progressive de-professionalisation of hotel chambermaids as a group reduces their ability to influence the organisation of their work or to defend their interests. It also reduces the terms by which they can feel included in an increasingly fragmented and exclusive labour structure.

(e) *Segmentation, division and increase in competition between hotel staff*

For fear of outsourcing, a profound segmentation is taking place between workers of certain contractual conditions and those who are subcontracted. Recruitment through different companies within the same hotel weakens the nexus and mutual support between workers. In the specific case of middle management, such as head housekeepers, this trend places them in a very complicated situation, between the demands of the external company and those of the hotel. Various interviewed workers identified the change that has occurred, and how they are no longer viewed in the same way by their former colleagues, claiming that now 'workers stick to their own [group]'. This situation also seems to be affecting the capacity to coordinate departments within the same hotel. This situation is especially highlighted by the housekeepers interviewed, who suffer most intensely the effects of this lack of coordination caused by outsourcing.

In the late 1990s and early 2000s, increasing numbers of immigrant workers from countries with a lower average income than Spain arrived and assumed the lowest-level places in the Spanish job market (Garrido, Miyar, & Muñoz, 2010). Subsequently, when the crisis began, it was these immigrant workers, especially women, who were left in the worst conditions (Colectivo IOE, 2012; Muñoz, 2012). As the crisis occurred and multiservice companies began to mushroom, with practically no union representation or structures of social cohesion, solidarity between workers in many workplaces has had to be organised according to country of origin, thus exacerbating internal divisions. Spanish nationals interviewed in a hotel in Barcelona, where they are the minority, described with special anger their relationship with other housekeepers of Dominican and Moroccan origin.

(f) *Accentuation of health problems*

The intensification of work and rise in conditions of insecurity increase risks to hotel maids' health, both physical and mental. An initial manifestation is tiredness and constant exhaustion, which makes everyday life outside the hotel very difficult. Also commonplace are bruises on workers' legs because of the blows they receive while rushing to perform the tasks assigned to them. Pain in the upper and lower back, neck, shoulders and arms is also commonplace as chambermaids must constantly repeat the same movements, compounded by bad posture which is difficult to avoid given the intense pace of their work. Many also suffer from problems in their knees, usually the right knee, which they use to move beds without having to bend down. According to several interviewees, it is normal for hotel chambermaids who have worked in the sector for many years to have had surgery for ailments like hernias or carpal tunnel syndrome. The findings of several research initiatives, carried out in other contexts, confirm these assertions (Buchanan et al., 2010; Burgel et al., 2010; DaRos, 2011; Hsieh et al., 2013; Krause & Scherzer, 2005; Krause et al., 2010; Liladrie, 2010; McNamara et al., 2011; Sanon, 2013, 2014; Scherzer et al., 2005).

Cleaning products can also be hazardous to workers' health. While hotels in recent years have had tighter controls placed on the type of products used, many hotel chambermaids report a variety of situations that lead to these mechanisms not being particularly effective. On the one hand, workers themselves perceive that the strongest products available, and therefore the most toxic and dangerous ones for their health, are the most efficient for cleaning. As such, they continue to use these products since they feel it will help them save time. Some also report that these products are generally still used in some hotels, although at times they are used 'secretly'. On the other hand, it is common for the use of protective equipment, such as gloves or masks, to be limited. Workers themselves are often reluctant to use these items as it is extremely uncomfortable for these to be worn and taken off continually. Given their fast pace of work, many prefer not to use protective items altogether. According to most interviewed workers, moreover, such protective materials are often not available in sufficient quantities in hotels and outsourcing companies.

This way of working, coupled with chronic tiredness, pain, the feeling of never being able to finish their work on time, and some cases of abuse by head housekeepers or supervisors, means that stress and anxiety have become an ever-present feature of hotel chambermaids' lives. Many suffer from insomnia. In fact, in many workplaces it is not unusual to see workers crying because of the anguish and powerlessness they feel. In time, such situations can lead to depression.

Tiredness, pain and stress have made it quite normal for workers to have to take medicine to be able to handle their workday. The phrase, 'I have ibuprofen for breakfast' has become somewhat customary. The fact that workers have been taking this type of medication continuously for many years, combined with the excesses of self-medication, can also impact their health in other ways. Evidence exists of a causal relationship between job insecurity and the deterioration of workers' health, a phenomenon repeatedly highlighted by scholars studying other professional sectors (Benach, Vives, Tarafa, Delclos, & Muntaner, 2016). The case of the outsourced floor maids studied appears to reinforce this causal relationship within the field of tourism and particularly in the hotel sector.

(g) *Decrease in the capacity of representation and defence of collective interests*

Multiservice companies also hinder workers' ability to unite in defence of their interests, as well as the very possibility of union organisation more broadly. This heightened defencelessness also results in increased pressure which, on occasion, can lead to harassment and abuse of workers in a bid to force them to comply with their assigned workload. Union organisations view the recent labour reform and the specific phenomenon of outsourcing as a direct attack on workers' fundamental rights and on themselves as unions. This employers' offensive on union organisations comes at a time when they are in a weak position, beset by widespread critical opinions from diverse ideological and political standpoints concerning their role and legitimacy. At the same time, outsourcing has directly reduced workers' ability to choose their representatives.

6. Conclusions: decent work for inclusive tourism

The financial crisis and the way in which it has been handled by Spanish and European public authorities has led to a worsening of working conditions for all workers. This is particularly evident in the service sector and in tourism, one of the main activities in which the economies of southern Europe have specialised (Banyuls & Recio, 2015). This deterioration most significantly affects vulnerable sectors that occupy the lowest positions in the occupational structure, with a particularly marked impact on woman workers. Through management instruments like outsourcing and subcontracting, an intense process of 'precarisation' has been produced, which remains hidden under the macro figures which celebrate the growth of Spanish tourism.

The case of outsourced hotel chambermaids in Spain showcases the effects of recent policies intended to increase labour flexibility, which different scholars have analysed at length (Puech, 2004; Seifert & Messing, 2006). Tourism experts have usually linked flexibility to the seasonal nature of tourism (Adler & Adler, 2003; Castellanos & Pedreño, 2006). However, the research on outsourced maids in Spain highlights that flexibility strategies are increasingly disconnected from the seasonal factor, since they are deployed as corporate strategy to reduce labour costs. Indeed, the process of 'flexibilisation' is also taking place in urban destinations such as Barcelona or Madrid, which are far less affected by seasonality than seaside resorts. The outsourcing process exacerbates enduring issues of the division and segmentation of the labour force, with notable effects on its capacity for resistance and the defence of workers' interests (McDowell et al., 2007; Puech, 2007). It also increases the number of hours worked without a fixed schedule, thus heightening the difficulties of combining work and family life, as highlighted by several scholars (McDowell et al., 2007).

Another issue highlighted in the literature, and confirmed by the chambermaids interviewed for this study, is the clear relationship between forms of work organisation and health problems (Buchanan et al., 2010; Burgel et al., 2010; DaRos, 2011; Hsieh et al., 2013; Krause & Scherzer, 2005; Krause et al., 2010; Liladrie, 2010; McNamara et al., 2011; Sanon, 2013, 2014; Scherzer et al., 2005).

Outsourcing means that work in hotels, particularly in housekeeping departments, is becoming further distanced from the concept of 'decent work' formulated by the ILO. The way in which the outsourcing process of housekeeping departments is mainly taking place in hotels in Spain clearly violates and reduces the various facets of 'decent work' as discussed above.

- Wages paid through multiservice companies are clearly not sufficient for workers to be able to maintain decent living conditions. This is true both when these companies pay wages stipulated by their own company agreement, as well as when their payments are based on cleaning agreements or on multiple payment systems for work

performed by employees. The salaries which hotel maids receive under these conditions are evidently on the threshold of the phenomenon of 'working poverty'.
- Employment is ever more insecure, with the question of when and how to renew or recall workers left to the discretion of the company. Workers, therefore, feel coerced into accepting impositions on their timetables, work days, or days off. This, in turn, makes it increasingly difficult for them to balance their work with their private lives.
- Deterioration in workers' physical and mental health is accentuated in the context of outsourcing. This deterioration has already generated a problem of social alarm due to the way in which workers are being affected by ill-health.
- The forms of recruitment used in the sector, and the difficulty most workers face in reaching the age of retirement in a good condition, represents a clear deterioration in the conditions of social protection. These phenomena are evidently reducing guaranteed social protection conditions.
- Finally, outsourcing affects freedom of association in two ways. First, by acting in a discriminatory manner against workers who aim to unionise themselves in multiservice companies. Second, by reducing trade unions' capacity for collective bargaining. This makes it impossible to foster social dialogue, one of the basic aspects of decent work. This, in turn, has clear implications for workers' and unions' ability to exercise their basic democratic rights.

Because of the serious impacts which outsourcing policies have had on work in hotels' housekeeping departments, there has been an intense reaction by trade unions and different women's organisations. There have been frequent demonstrations at workplaces and complaints on social networks. This has led to growing media attention, resulting in a public debate on the situation of this group of workers. Moreover, political statements have been made by governments of cities which are leading tourism centres, the parliaments of Spain's autonomous communities, and the national Congress of Deputies calling for outsourcing to be better regulated. These calls have also been in favour of repealing Spain's 2012 labour reform (Cañada, 2016). In these ways, hotel maids have managed to make the problem of their working conditions visible within the context of the growth of tourism in Spain, both in terms of the number of tourist arrivals and in terms of investments and corporate profit. Chambermaids have made strong claims in four key areas: the need to improve their working conditions; the demand for public recognition of their work; the vindication of their collective organisations as spaces of participation; and the willingness to commit to quality tourism services. The impacts of this transformation have yet to be explored, particularly its impact on spaces where these workers are concentrated in vulnerable situations which can hardly be regarded as 'inclusive'. The implications of 'non-inclusive' work on urban spaces which specialise in tourism remains a key issue for future research.

Furthermore, the experience of hotel maids in Spain reveals the barriers which exist to our moving towards inclusive tourism (Scheyvens & Biddulph, 2017). Specifically, the fact that a group of workers central to this industry are witnessing how the quality of their work is deteriorating, their benefits are being reduced to the extent that they are increasingly on the threshold of poverty, and they are losing influence in decision-making on hotel operations. Their case reveals that inclusive tourism must take into account class and gender dimensions. In spite of international declarations by multilateral organisations and civil society on the need for decent working conditions in the tourism sector, the importance of such conditions is often overlooked. A class and gender sensitive approach provides an indispensable dimension to inclusive tourism, as a proposal for a fairer and more equitable development model. The case study of hotel chambermaids in Spain illustrates the critical plight of a considerable proportion of tourism industry workers. It points to the strong challenge faced by a truly inclusive tourism framework – that is, the challenge of one integrating working conditions into its analysis.

At the same time, the demands of woman workers themselves may be understood as a call for more inclusive tourism. Their struggle against outsourcing and in defence of their labour rights entails a challenge to the power relations which exist in the industry. It involves a call for new legislative frameworks and respect for collective bargaining between business people and trade unions as a way of ensuring fairer labour relations. With their demands, especially actively voiced in social networks, they also want to make themselves visible and to lay claim to the dignity and value of their work for the operation of hotels. This means acknowledging their self-representation and their demand to be recognised not only as cleaners, but rather as workers able to provide personalised customer service in line with the highest standards of the housekeeping profession. Finally, their struggle also entails a vindication of the role of workers organised collectively and freely, able to participate in decision-making on how the tourism industry operates. Thereby, inclusive tourism provides us with a horizon of hope and can become a useful analytical instrument for assessing to what extent a certain activity, company or destination actually comes close to being 'inclusive' or not. Moreover, inclusive tourism offers us a new way of approaching the social conflicts present in tourism activity.

The problem not only lies in specific 'bad' practices, which it is necessary to redress, but rather in a model of labour management that is based on making tourism employment more precarious. For societies that aim to be democratic, this is a phenomenon they simply cannot allow. Indeed, improved tourism quality must be understood as a better integration of tourism activities within the environment, an environment which includes workers. Given its commitment to quality, sustainable and inclusive tourism is not possible if action is not taken in defence of decent work. As such, the development of inclusive tourism necessarily depends on the improvement of tourism workers' working conditions. This entails both the need to strengthen labour rights, while simultaneously undoing the pitfalls of increasing de-regulation.

Acknowledgments

I would like to express my gratitude for the suggestions and review of this text by Ivan Murray and Macià Blàzquez (University of the Balearic Islands), Regina Scheyvens (Massey University), Robin Biddulph and María José Zapata (University of Gothenburg) and by anonymous reviewers of the journal Tourism Geographies, all of whom contributed to enhancing the quality of this article.

Disclosure statement

No potential conflict of interest was reported by the author.

Funding

The present article was written within the framework of the project entitled "Crisis y reestructuración del litoral turístico español" [Crisis and restructuring of the Spanish tourist coast] (CSO2015 & 64468-P), managed by GIST-UIB and funded by the Ministry of Economy and Competitiveness of the Government of Spain [Convocatoria 2015, Modalidad 1: Proyectos de I+D del Programa Estatal de Fomento de la Investigación Científica y Técnica de Excelencia, Subprograma Estatal de Generación del Conocimiento].

References

Adib, A., & Guerrier, Y. (2003). The interlocking of gender with nationality, race, ethnicity and class: The narratives of women in hotel work. *Gender, Work and Organization, 10*(3), 413–432.

Adler, P., & Adler, P. (2003). Seasonality and flexible labor in resorts: Organizations, employees, and local labor markets. *Sociological Spectrum, 23*(1), 59–89.

Aguiar, L. M., & Herod, A. (Eds.). (2006). *The dirty work of neoliberalism: Cleaners in the global economy*. Oxford: Blackwell.

Albarracín, D. (2013). Las trabajadoras de los establecimientos hoteleros. Trayectorias en el túnel silencioso de la subordinación [The workers of hotel establishments. Trajectories in the silent tunnel of subordination]. *Sociología del Trabajo, 77*, 27–4 5.

Aragón, J. (2012). *Las reformas laborales en España y su repercusión en materia de empleo. 52 reformas desde la aprobación del estatuto de los trabajadores en 1980* [Labor reforms in Spain and their impact on employment. 52 reforms since the approval of the workers' statute in 1980]. Madrid: Fundación 1o de May o.

Bakker, M., & Messerli, H. R. (2016). Inclusive growth versus pro-poor growth: Implications for tourism development. *Tourism and Hospitality Research, 17*(4), 384–391.

Ballantyne, R., Packer, J., & Axelsen, M. (2009). Trends in tourism research. *Annals of Tourism Research, 36*, 149–152.

Basualdo, M., & Morales, D. (2014). *La terciarización laboral. Orígenes, impacto y claves para su análisis en América Latina* [Labor outsourcing. Origins, imapcts and keys for its analysis in Latin America]. Buenos Aires: Siglo XXI Editores.

Baum, T., Kralj, A., Robinson, R., & Solnet, D. (2016). Tourism workforce research: A review, taxonomy and agenda. *Annals of Tourism Research, 60*, 1–22.

Bañuls, J., & Recio, A. (2015). La crisis dentro de la crisis. España bajo el neoliberalismo conservador [The crisis within the crisis. Sapin under conservative neoliberalism]. In S. Lehndorff (Ed.), *El triunfo de las ideas fracasadas. Modelos del capitalismo europeo en la crisis [The triumph of failed ideas. Models of European capitalism in the crisis]* (pp. 39–69). Madrid: Fuhem Ecosocial – Los Libros de la Catarat a.

Benach, J., Vives, A., Tarafa, G., Delclos, C., & Muntaner, C. (2016). What should we know about precarious employment and health in 2025? Framing the agenda for the next decade of research. *International Journal of Epidemiology, 45*(1), 232–238.

Bianchi, R. V. (2011). Tourism, capitalism and Marxist political economy. In J. Mosedale (Ed.), *Political economy of tourism: A critical perspective* (pp. 17–37). London: Routledge.

Brenner, C. (2003). Labour flexibility and regional development: The role of labour market intermediaries. *Regional Studies, 37*(6/7), 621–633.

Brenner, N., & Theodore, N. (2002). *Spaces of neoliberalism: Urban restructuring in North America and Western Europe*. Oxford: Blackwell.

Britton, S. (1991). Tourism, capital, and place: Towards a critical geography of tourism. *Environment and Planning D: Society and Space, 9*, 451–478.

Buchanan, S., Vossenas, P., Krause, N., Moriarty, J., Frumin, E., Shimek, J. A. M., ... Punnett, L. (2010). Occupational injury disparities in the US hotel industry. *American Journal of Industrial Medicine, 53*(2), 116–125.

Burgel, B., White, M., Gillen, M., & Krause, N. (2010). Psychosocial work factors and shoulder pain in hotel room cleaners. *American Journal of Industrial Medicine, 53*(7), 743–756.

Castellanos, M. L., & Pedreño, A. (2006). Los nuevos braceros del ocio. Sonrisas, cuerpos flexibles e identidad de empresa en el sector turístico [The new workers of leisure. Smiles, flexible bodies and company identity in the tourism sector]. Madrid: Mino y Dávila Editore s.

Castillo, J. J. (2005). Contra los estragos de la subcontratación. Trabajo decenteAgainst the ravages of outsourcing decent job. *Sociología del Trabajo, 54*, 3–27.

Castree, N., Coe, N. M., Ward, K., & Samers, M. (2004). *Spaces of work: Global capitalism and geographies of labour*. London: SAGE.

Cañada, E. (2015). *Las que limpian los hoteles. Historias ocultas de precariedad laboral [The ones that clean the hotels. Hidden stories of job insecurity]*. Barcelona: Icaria Editoria l.

Cañada, E. (2016). *Externalización del trabajo en hoteles. Impactos sobre los departamentos de pisos [Outsourcing in hotels. Impacts on apartment departments]*. Barcelona: Alba Sud Editori al.

Colectivo, I. O. E. (2012). *Impactos de la crisis sobre la población inmigrante [Impacts of the crisis on the migrant population]*. Madrid: Colectivo IOE / Organización Internacional para las Migraciones (O IM).

DaRos, J. (2011). *Preventing workplace injuries commonly sustained by hotel guestroom attendants* (UNLV Theses/ Dissertations/Professional Papers/Capstones Paper 1097). Las Vegas: University of Nevada.

Davidson, M., McPhail, R., & Barry, S. (2011). Hospitality HRM: Past, present and the future. *International Journal of Contemporary Hospitality Management, 23*(4), 498–516.

Dube, A., & Kaplan, E. (2010). Does outsourcing reduce wages in the low-wage service occupations? Evidence from janitors and guards. *Industrial and Labor Relations Review, 63*(2), 287–306.

Dyer, S., McDowell, K., & Batnitzky, A. (2010). The impact of migration on the gendering of service work: The case of a West London hotel. *Gender, Work & Organization, 17*(16), 635–657.

Dyer, S., McDowell, K., & Batnitzky, A. (2011). Migrant work, precarious work-life balance: What the experiences of migrant workers in the service sector in Greater London tell us about the adult worker model. *Gender, Place & Culture: A Journal of Feminist Geography, 18*(5), 685–700.

EPA. (2016). Active Population Survey 2016. Retrieved from www.ine.es/dyngs/INEbase/es/categoria.htm?c=Estadistica_P&cid=1254735976594

Ellem, B., & McGrath-Champ, S. (2012). Labor geography and labor history: Insights and outcomes from a decade of cross-disciplinary dialogue. *Labor History, 53*(3), 355–372.

Eurostat (2015). *Employment statistics*. Luxembourg: Eurostat

Exceltur (2014). *Estudio de Impacto Económico del Turismo: IMPACTUR [Study of the economic impact of tourism]*. Madrid: Author.

Exceltur (2016). *Valoración turística y empresarial de 2015 y perspectivas para 2016. Informe Perspectivas Turísticas*, 55 [Tourism and business valuation of 2015 and perspectives for 2016]. Madrid: Aut hor.

Fallon, P., & Lucas, R. (2002). The impact of financial crises on labor markets, household incomes, and poverty: A review of evidence. *The World Bank Research Observer, 17*(1), 21–45.

Ferreira, C. R., & Ramos, J. (2016). Pay gap by gender in the tourism industry of Brazil. *Tourism Management, 52*, 440–450.

Fletcher, R. (2011). Sustaining tourism, sustaining capitalism? The tourism industry's role in global capitalist expansion. *Tourism Geographies, 13*(3), 443–461.

Fletcher, R., & Neves, K. (2012). Contradictions in tourism. the promise and pitfalls of ecotourism as a manifold capitalism fix. *Environment and Society: Advances in Research, 3*, 60–77.

Garrido, L. J., Miyar, M., & Muñoz, J. (2010). La dinámica laboral de los inmigrantes en el cambio de fase del ciclo económico [The labor dinamycs of immigrants in the phase change of the economic cycle]. *Presupuesto y Gasto Public, 61*, 201–221.

Hall, R. (2000). Outsourcing, contracting-out and labour hire: implications for human resource development in Australian organizations. *Asia Pacific Journal of Human Resources, 38*(2), 23–41.

Hampton, M., Jeyacheya, J., & Long, P. H. (2017 preview). Can tourism promote inclusive growth? Supply chains, ownership and employment in Ha Long Bay, Vietnam. *The Journal of Development Studies.* Advance online publication. doi:10.1080/00220388.2017.1296572

Harvey, D. (2003). *The new imperialism.* Oxford: Oxford University Press.

Harvey, D. (2006). *Limits to capital.* London: Verso.

Harvey, D. (2012). *Rebel cities: From the right to the city to the urban revolution.* London: Verso.

Harvey, D. (2014). *Seventeen contradictions and the end of capitalism.* Oxford: Oxford University Press

Herod, A. (1997). From a geography of labor to a labor geography: Labor's spatial fix and the geography of capitalism. *Antipode, 29*(1), 1–31.

Herod, A. (2001). *Labor geographies: Workers and the landscapes of capitalism.* New York, NY: Guilford Press.

Herod, A., & Aguiar, L. M. (2006). Introduction: Cleaners and the Dirty Work of Neoliberalism. *Antipode,* 38(3), 425–434.

Hinojosa, V. (2016). Pablo Vila, director del Hotel Madrid Marriot Auditorium: «La externalización es una herramienta de gestión que ha salvado empresas». *Hosteltur, 20,* 20–21.

Holgate, J., Hebson, G., & McBride, A. (2006). Introduction: Cleaners and the Dirty Work of Neoliberalism. *Industrial Relations Journal,* 37(4), 310–328.

Holgersen, S. (2015). Economic crisis, (Creative) destruction, and the current urban condition. *Antipode, 47*(3), 689–707.

Hosteltur (2016). Jesús Lizarraga, Director General de Operaciones de Grupo Elosa: «Limpiar una habitación de hotel influye en su cue nta de resultados» [Jesus Lizarraga. General operations manager of the Elosa Group: «Cleaning a hotel romm influences th income statement»]. *Hosteltur, 20,* 14.

Hsieh, Y., Apostolopoulos, Y., & Sönmez, S. (2013). The world at work: Hotel cleaners. *Occupational and Environmental Medicine, 70*(5), 360–364.

Hunter, P., & Watson, D. (2006). Service unseen: The hotel room attendant at work. *International Journal of Hospitality Management, 25*(2), 297–312.

International Labour Organization. (1999). *Trabajo decente. Memoria del Director General a la 87ª reunión de la Conferencia Internacional del Trabajo [Decent job. Report of the General-Director to the 87th session of the International Labor Conference].* Geneva: Auth or.

International Social Tourism Organisation. (1996). *Declaración de Montreal - Por una visión humanista y social del Turismo [Declaration of Montreal - For a humanistic and social vision of tourism].* Montreal: OI TS.

Ioannides, D., & Debbage, K. G. (1998). *The economic geography of the tourist industry.* London: Routledge.

Krause, N., & Scherzer, T. (2005). Physical workload, work intensification, and prevalence of pain in low wage workers: Results from a participatory research project with hotel room cleaners in Las Vegas. *American Journal of Industrial Medicine, 337,* 326–337.

Krause, N., Rugulies, R., & Maslach, C. (2010). Effort–reward imbalance at work and self-rated health of Las Vegas hotel room cleaners. *American Journal of Industrial Medicine, 53*(4), 372–386.

Ladkin, A. (2011). Exploring tourism labor. *Annals of Tourism Research, 38*(3), 1135–1155.

Leschke, J., & Jepsen, M. (2012). Introduction: Crisis, policy responses and widening inequalities in the EU. *International Labour Review, 151*(4), 289–312.

Lethbridge, J. (2012). *Empty promises: The impact of outsourcing on the delivery of NHS services.* London: UNISON.

Liladrie, S. (2010). 'Do not disturb/please clean room': Hotel housekeepers in Greater Toronto. *Race & Class,* 52(1), 57–69.

Massey, D. (1995). *Spatial divisions of labor: Social structures and the geography of production.* New York, NY: Routledge.

McDowell, L., Batnitzky, A., & Dyer, S. (2007). Division, segmentation, and interpellation: the embodied labors of migrant workers in a greater london hotel. *Economic Geography, 83*(1), 1–25.

McNamara, M., Bohle, P., & Quinlan, M. (2011). Precarious employment, working hours, work-life conflict and health in hotel work. *Applied Ergonomics, 42*(2), 225–232.

Ministerio de Empleo y Seguridad Social. (2015). Real *Decreto Legislativo 2/2015, de 23 de octubre, por el que se aprueba el texto refundido de la Ley del Estatuto de los Trabajadores [Royal CDecrees Law 2/2015, of October 23, approving the revised text of the Law on the Workers' Statute]*. Texto consolidado. Madrid: Agencia Estatal Boletín Oficial del Estad o.

Moreno, S., Godino, A., & Recio, A. (2014). Servicios externalizados y condiciones laborales: De la competencia de precios a la presión de los tiempos de trabajo [Outsourced services and working conditions. From price competition to the pressure on work times]. *Sociología del Trabajo, 81*, 50–67.

Mosedale, J. (Ed.). (2011). *Political economy and tourism: A critical perspective*. New York, NY: Routledge.

Mosedale, J. (Ed.). (2016). *Neoliberalism and the political economy of tourism*. New York, NY: Routledge.

Munro, A. (2012). Thirty years of hospital cleaning in England and Scotland – An opportunity for "better" jobs? In C. Warhurst, F. Carré, P. Findlay, & C. Tilly (Eds.), *Are bad jobs inevitable? Trends, determinants and responses to job quality in the twenty-first century* (pp. 176–190). Basingstoke: Palgrave Macmillan.

Murray, I. (2015). *Capitalismo y turismo en España. Del «milagro económico» a la «gran crisis» [Capitalism and tourism in Spain. From the «economic miracle» to the «great crisis»]*. Barcelona: Alba Sud.

Muñoz, J. (2012). Evolución del empleo y del paro de las mujeres inmigrantes en el mercado de trabajo español. El impacto de la actual crisis económica [Ecolution of employment and unemployment og immigrant women in the Spanish labor market. The impact of the current crisis]. *Cuaderno de Relaciones Laborales, 30*(1), 115–137.

Obadić, A., & Marić, I. (2009). The significance of tourism as an employment generator of female labour forcé. *Ekon Misao Praksa DBK GOD, XVIII*(1), 93–114.

Otobe, N. (2011). *Global economic crisis, gender and employment: The impact and policy response* (Employment Working Paper, 74). Geneva: ILO.

Petersen, O. H., Hjelmar, U., Vrangbaek, K., & La Cour, L. (2011). *Effects of contracting out public sector tasks. A research-based review of Danish and international studies from 2000*. Copenhagen: AKF (Danish Institute of Governmental Research).

Puech, I. (2004). Le temps du remue-ménage. Conditions d'emploi et de travail de femmes de chambre [The time of the commotion. Condicions of employment and work of chambermaids]. *Sociologie du Travail, 46*(2), 150–16 7.

Puech, I. (2007). Cleaning time, protest time: Employment and working conditions for hotel maids. *Sociologie du Travail, 49*(1), 50–65.

Sanon, M. (2013). Hotel housekeeping work influences on hypertension management. *American Journal of Industrial Medicine, 56*(12), 1402–1413.

Sanon, M. (2014). Agency-hired hotel housekeepers: An at-risk group for adverse health outcomes. *Workplace Health & Safety, 62*(2), 81–85.

Scherzer, T., Rugulies, R., & Krause, N. (2005). Work-related pain and injury and barriers to workers' compensation among Las Vegas hotel room cleaners. *American Journal of Public Health, 95*(3), 483–488.

Scheyvens, R., & Biddulph, R. (2017). Inclusive tourism development. *Tourism Geographies*. Advance online publication. doi:10.1080/14616688.2017.1381985

Seifert, A., & Messing, K. (2006). Cleaning up after globalization: An ergonomic analysis of work activity of hotel cleaners. *Antipode, 38*(3), 557–578.

Solnet, D., Baum, T., Robinson, R., & Lockstone-Binney, L. (2015). What about the workers? Roles and skills for employees in hotels of the future. *Journal of Vacation Marketing, 22*(3), 212–226.

Soltani, E., & Wilkinson, A. (2010). What is happening to flexible workers in the supply chain partnerships between hotel housekeeping departments and their partner employment agencies? *International Journal of Hospitality Management, 29*(1), 108–119.

Subasat, T. (Ed.). (2016). *The great financial meltdown systemic, conjunctural or policy created?* Cheltenham: Edward Elgar.

Warhurst, C., Carré, F., Findlay, P., & Tilly, C. (Eds.), (2012). *Are bad jobs inevitable? Trends, determinants and responses to job quality in the twenty-first century*. Basingstoke: Palgrave Macmillan.

Yrigoy, I. (2014). Economies of tourism destinations. The production of tourist spaces as a spatial fix. *Tourism Geographies, 16*(4), 636–652.

Zampoukos, K., & Ioannides, D. (2011). The tourism labour conundrum: Agenda for new research in the geography of hospitality workers. *Hospitality & Society, 1*(1), 25–45.

Challenges to inclusive tourism experiences for wheelchair users at historic sites

Ayşe Nilay Evcil

ABSTRACT
Historic sites and heritage buildings are popular places to visit in many parts of the world. This paper seeks to contribute to the body of knowledge regarding the experiences of wheelchair users at heritage sites. A questionnaire was used to collect descriptive data about preferences of and barriers faced by wheelchair users in Sultanahmet Square, Istanbul. Sultanahmet Square is the most popular tourist attraction in Istanbul, and contains an open-air museum featuring the city's oldest relic. The study shows that this heritage site is not sufficiently prepared for wheelchair users who wish to participate in a day trip. The challenges they experienced arose from difficulties many designers encounter while trying to create accessible environments and meet the requirement of restoration and conservation at the same time. The obstacles can only be overcome with the support of national policies that take into account the constraints and barriers that affect each location's accessibility. To promote the development of such policies, awareness about constraints and barriers must be raised among both the designers and service providers in tourism. Universal design offers guidelines that will help lead to better design solutions.

Introduction

Leisure and recreational activities are great stress reducers and thereby play an important role in people's lives. These activities can help relieve symptoms of depression, influence careers and support overall feelings of success and satisfaction. Some are also very important for the rehabilitation (Sen & Mayfield, 2004; Taylor & Jozefowicz, 2012) and care of the elderly and people with disabilities (PWD), which helps ensure social sustainability for future generations. As stated by many theorists, PWD have the same needs and desires to participate in leisure activities as do able-bodied people (Darcy & Daruwella, 1999; Guerra, 2003; Smith, 1987; Yau, McKercher, & Packer, 2004). Shared recreational activities are opportunities to build and maintain relationships among PWD as well as in the larger society. These activities are important starting points for facilitating social inclusion between PWD and the rest of the community. However, the idea of spending enjoyable time away from home is sometimes both a dream and a nightmare for PWD, especially for wheelchair users.

Rodriguez (2014) defines leisure as active (such as taking part in sports) and passive (such as reading a book or playing sudoku) and more home-based (such as watching television or listening to music) or out and about (such as visiting an attraction, museums, art galleries or national parks). Some are social entertainment (such as attending sports events and theaters) (Rodriguez, 2014). Others can be enjoyed individually (such as painting) or in a group (such as a tour group).

A traditional view holds that recreation and leisure activities recharge an individual's battery, so performance in workplaces, homes, schools, etc., is improved. For this reason, leisure is regarded not only as spare time to fill, but also as an essential element necessary to personal development. Participation in leisure and tourism activities is considered a human right under the Universal Declaration of Human Rights (Article 24, 1948) mandated by the United Nations General Assembly. In addition, leisure also plays an important role in successful adaptation to retirement (Nimrod, 2007).

Despite the universal recognition of the necessity for leisure activities available to all, many researchers have noted travel-related constraints encountered by PWD such as site inaccessibility, entrance fees, inadequate information about tourist areas, inaccessibility in transportation and inadequate space for accommodation, such as architectural barriers inside buildings (Turco, Stumbo, & Garncarz, 1998; Yau et al., 2004).

Despite barriers, PWD continue to travel for tourism and leisure. Many researchers regard PWD along with the elderly as a new consumer niche (Card, Cole, & Humphrey, 2006; Prager, 1999; Ray & Ryder, 2003; STCRC, 2008) and have been trying to raise awareness about barriers that prevent accessible tourism (Oladokun, Ololajulo, & Oladele, 2014; Sen & Mayfield, 2004; Smith, 1987; Taylor & Jozefowicz, 2012; Yau et al., 2004). At the same time, the many challenge that arises between conservation and creating solutions to physical barriers remains an untouched area for investigation especially for sites that offer day trip tourism activities for PWD, such as heritage sites and historical places (Naniopoulos, Tsalis, & Papanikolaou, 2015).

The objective of this study is to evaluate wheelchair users' preferences and participation in leisure and recreation activities in one historic place in Turkey where many tourist attractions have been restored. Sultanahmet Square, which was named a UNESCO World Heritage Site in 1985, was selected as the case study because it is one of the oldest places in Istanbul where both locals and visitors want to visit museums, churches, mosques or a palace, either alone or with a tour, or they can simply walk around shop and eat in a restaurant. The study also aims to understand what gaps in design have been overlooked that prevent full access for wheelchair users who want to make a day trip in historic sites to enjoy activities like those described above.

The study aims to answer the following questions regarding PWD's (specifically wheelchair users) preferences in historical sites:

(1) Is there a relationship between making a day trip to historic place and its physical accessibility?
(2) Is there a relationship between source of information about an area's accessibility and willingness to visit historic places?
(3) Is there a relationship between travel companion and willingness to visit historic places?
(4) What are the relationship between accessibility and architectural items in Sultanahmet?

Literature review

One of the earliest studies to describe barriers facing PWD who travel was Smith's research in 1987. He categorized barriers for people traveling with disabilities as intrinsic, environmental and interactive (communication) (Smith, 1987). Intrinsic barriers relate to a person's physical, cognitive, or psychological state. Environmental barriers concern physical elements of the built environment, such as architectural elements and transportation constraints. Interactive barriers refer to communication barriers that interfere with the interaction of people and the society. Other researchers have noted travel-related constraints encountered by PWD such as site inaccessibility, entrance fees, inadequate information about tourist areas, inaccessibility in transportation, and inadequate space for accommodation, such as architectural barriers inside buildings (Turco et al., 1998; Yau et al., 2004). Some of the most informative studies are those in which PWD explained their travel experiences, because these studies examine people's experiences instead of researchers' evaluations (Samdahl & Jekubovich, 1997). A common thread in all of these studies is that they all generally describe constraints as being two-dimensional, relating either to the person (physical and psychological aspects, etc.) or to social and physical environments (interaction between individuals, inaccessibility, etc.).

Recently, Darcy (2004) examined both leisure constraints and social factors that travelers with disabilities often confront and must negotiate. Other researchers take the analysis a step further and try to differentiate between barriers and constraints. According to McGuire (1984), constraints affect a person's ability to fully enjoy all aspects of travel and tourism and can be overcome, while barriers are obstacles that prevent them from participating in activities in the first place.

Another topic relevant to this discussion is motivation. Despite barriers, PWD continue to travel for tourism and leisure. In two different studies, Crompton (1979) and Shi, Cole, and Chancellor (2012) used a push-and-pull model to examine the leisure travel motivations. Shi et al. showed that although mobility-impaired people shared many motives with able-bodied people, they also have unique motivations including desire for independence, to be in a natural environment, or to enjoy adventure and risk.

Besides, accessible tourism, as an emerging topic, pays attention to barriers inhibiting PWD in the tourism literature. Many researchers describe PWD and the elderly as a new consumer niche (Card et al., 2006; Prager, 1999; Ray & Ryder, 2003; STCRC, 2008) and are trying to raise awareness about barriers that prevent accessible tourism (Oladokun et al., 2014; Sen & Mayfield, 2004; Smith, 1987; Taylor & Jozefowicz, 2012; Yau et al., 2004).

Patterson (2001) observed that 'the category of constraints (in different disciplines) are quite similar. The environmental constraint is similar to the structural constraints, and the task constraint includes the psychological and emotional facet of the organism constraints' (pp. 35–36). Despite the considerable body of literature on barriers and constraints and how they affect travel behaviors, very little research has been conducted regarding the conditions at heritage sites and how they affect different types of disabilities. Few seem to be looking into what types of challenges must be resolved when working with restoration in order to guarantee accessibility.

Barriers and constraints encountered by PWD at leisure and tourist attraction sites

Leisure and tourism industries are trying to improve accessibility provisions in order to include PWD, especially since most developed countries (Australia, Canada, and European Countries) want to attract these visitors as next consumer niche (Ray & Ryder, 2003; STCRC, 2008). 'Together with family and friends, they create a potentially significant, but often ignored market' (Yau et al., 2004, p. 947). This market is new for Turkey and service providers are willing to take part in it, but weaknesses still exist, such as transportation problems, personnel without training in the needs of PWD consumers who visit tourist enterprises and unsuitable interior design of hotel rooms (Öztürk, Yaylı, & Yeşiltaş, 2008), just to name a few.

Researchers studying barriers in tourism encountered by PWD (Smith, 1987; Yau et al., 2004) often define tourism as containing at least a one-day accommodation at the destination. For this paper, we decided not to investigate overnight journeys, but instead to concentrate on the early stages of decision-making and planning activities for day trips, and then the activity stage itself where barriers and constraints are often faced by wheelchair users. Barriers and constraints facing wheelchair users fall under two main headings: decision-making stage and the activity stage. Inadequate information about an activity or tourist attraction, including specific about overall accessibility features and personal and his/her family related issues, along with economic inadequacy, can prevent individuals from deciding to undertake leisure activities at the decision-making stage. Even when adequate information and provision can be found during the decision-making stage, most PWD realize that unanticipated problems can still arise on site (Table 1).

For wheelchair users, information about the accessibility features of the visited area is of vital importance during their decision-making stage (McKercher, Packer, Yau, & Lam, 2003; Yau et al., 2004). Often, they will decide not to visit an area if not enough accessibility information is available, including areas that are well known for leisure activities. Basically, many PWD decide to stay at home because of the inadequate information. PWD, particularly wheelchair users, need to feel confident that physical arrangements have been made at their destination that will meet their special physical needs (e.g. ramps, bars, etc.) (Guerra, 2003). For these visitors, the reliability of the information provided for a visited area is equally important to the provision itself (Darcy & Daruwella, 1999;

Table 1. Barriers and constraints facing wheelchair users in leisure and recreation activities.

Decision-making stage	During the activity stage
Inadequate information about an activity or tourist attraction point • Special physical needs existence (e.g. ramps, bar) • Reliability and inaccuracy of information • Internet usage problems (illiterate of Internet usage because of age or other impairment) • Official websites problems (give poor/not any details about physical accessibility and provisions)	Accessibility problems happen on site • Unsuitable tour program • Inaccessible common facilities (e.g. public toilets, information centers, souvenirs shops, cafes, etc.)
Overall accessibility features • Transportation problems (unavailable public transport) • Parking problems • Uneven pedestrian paths • Entrances (with stairs or threshold) without ramps • Inadequate vertical and horizontal circulation (narrow corridors, narrow lift, slippery ground, etc.) • Unsuitable toilets (not usable for wheelchair dimensions) Personal and his/her family-related issues • Families' over-protective behaviors • Fear and anxiety about new environment Economic inadequacy	*Unexpected problems* • Lack of care and maintenance for equipment (e.g. elevator out of order, loss of guest wheelchair, loss of mobile ramp, locked toilet, etc.)

McKercher et al., 2003). A big constraint at this stage is difficulties encountered when trying to get the needed information. Indeed, UN Convention on the Rights of PWD urges states that all entities open to public or providing services or information should ensure full accessibility for PWD, including the Internet and other information communication technology (ICT) (UN, 2014, Article 9 and Article 21). Research shows that the Internet is the most important source for collecting information, and is preferred much more than collecting information from relatives and friends (Burnett, 1996; STCRC, 2008). 'The Internet can enable persons with disabilities to search for detailed, reliable and up-to-date information... and can also provide opportunities for the exchange of experiences amongst consumers' (Eichhorn, Miller, Michopoulou, & Buhalis, 2010, p. 6). But, it is not always possible to verify information shared on the Internet. Often, information sources cannot be checked against an official website for an area because the website does not address accessibility issues or does so poorly. Additionally, many users do not trust the websites, so they remain undecided (Buhalis & Michopoulou, 2011). Detailed information about accessibility for wheelchairs is often not even mentioned on websites or in written guides. Sen and Mayfield (2004) state that in many brochures of historic places and museums, the level of accessibility of the site is not evident. This is because no uniformity of signage or symbolic representation for the level of accessibility exists. Accurate and adequate information systems are essential for making decisions about outdoor activities. Small and Darcy (2011) underline inadequate information provision as one of the dominant themes of mobility disability complaints in tourism sector. In addition, web designs need to make provisions for individuals who have difficulty processing some types of information or are not able to use a keyboard or mouse. This is an area where all members of the tourism industry need to put more effort towards improvement.

Overall, accessibility features include both transportation- and location-related items. Many sources have documented the accessibility problems with public transport, even in developed countries (Casas, Horner, & Weber, 2009; Evcil, 2009; Hine & Mitchell, 2001; Taylor & Jozefowicz, 2012). Accessibility provisions of a building or site may include parking, pedestrian paths, entrances, vertical and horizontal circulation access and access to services and facilities (e.g. toilets) inside the building. Designing accessible spaces both inside and outside the building has a great influence on the quality of leisure activities for everyone, especially relating to the safety and enjoyment for tourists with disabilities. Fortunately, both service providers and local governments are beginning to view accessibility provisions not as obstacles to be overcome, but, rather, as marketing tools because they allow them to reach a huge new potential market (Guerra, 2003).

At the decision-making stage, the support of the family also has a big influence on a PWD's confidence about participating in a leisure activity. If the family displays overprotective behaviors, then the PWD may give up and not engage in a proposed activity. Some develop a fear of being outside the home and live in a state of anxiety about encountering new environments. To overcome these patterns, wheelchair users often prefer to have an informed partner without disabilities to accompany them, whether family members or friends, since this creates a sense of security. Additionally, each positive trip they experience motivates them to try future tourism activities (Yau et al., 2004).

In general, economic conditions are not considered to be a significant barrier to engagement in leisure and tourism activities for PWD (Nimrod, 2007), but there are two views on this aspect. Ray and Ryder (2003) referred to PWD as the next consumer niche because 'the group is large and growing and they have more money to spend than often is thought' (p. 58). This is one reason many developed countries are trying to increase tourism income and are making new provisions for the elderly and PWD. In some countries (e.g. England and Turkey), PWD are excused from paying entrance fees at cultural sites (e.g. museums and heritage sites) as well as for public transportation. On the other hand, different studies argue that economic conditions for the elderly and PWD vary from country to country, and in some cases, the economic status of these groups does create a constraint to participation in leisure activities (Gleeson, 1998). The type of leisure activity is also a consideration: playing golf or tennis, going on tours or participating in weekend retreats often require larger amounts of money, while visiting theatres, museums, gardens, walking tours or picnicking do not.

After the initial decision-making stage comes the activity stage where, once again, wheelchair users may face accessibility problems. For example, they may not be able to find a suitable tour when they visit historic buildings and sites. Or, they may find that common facilities accessible to 'normal' (fully abled) people may be inaccessible for PWD (e.g. toilets, information centers, souvenir shops, cafes, museums, etc.) (Cameron, Darcy, & Foggin, 2003). Additionally, lack of care and maintenance for equipment (e.g. elevators and/or guest wheelchairs) can also prevent visits. These unexpected situations frequently arise due to unconscious behavior on the part of service providers and staff at historic places. One way to deal with this aspect of lack of awareness is to create training programs that encourage empathy: How does a person with disabilities feel when he/she can't visit a museum because of a broken guest wheelchair? Raising awareness in society about the requirements of PWD needs to be an ongoing endeavor.

Possibilities and limitations to the creation of accessible tourism in historic places

Historic places and heritage buildings with their surrounding grounds are not only important for their architectural and historic significance, but also regarded as the masterpieces attracting tourist activities in many countries; in other words, the 'must-see places.' By educating visitors about heritage and history, they contribute to a sense of place and local identity. Surprisingly, however, most of them are still inaccessible to physically impaired people. It is clear that alteration to heritage buildings must be carefully designed to avoid damaging the historic fabric and to prevent future decay, but sensitivity to those issues should not be used as rationale for not improving their accessibility. Small accessibility adjustments that make big differences in accessibility for historic environments can be achieved while retaining the heritage values of buildings and grounds. This is exemplified by the compliance with fire and safety regulations which is required for any public building in which new and modern technical equipment is installed.

Unfortunately, challenges almost arise when conservation of a historic building and accessibility are thought about at the same time. It must be accomplished, however, because in many developed countries, historic properties are not exempt from accessibility guidelines (e.g. ADA in the USA, Equality Act in the UK and DDA in Australia), and access to these buildings and sites is a human right protected by disability acts and the Universal Declaration of Human Rights.

In 2008, ICOMOS (the International Council of Monuments and Sites), ratified a non-binding international Ename Charter in which they declared seven principles for guiding experts in technical means and methods for heritage buildings. In the first principle, the meaning of accessibility is explained in the following terms: 'Interpretation and presentation programmes should facilitate physical and intellectual access by the public to cultural heritage sites' (Ename Charter, Principle 1, 10.04.2007). Another guideline proposed by the Australian ICOMOS Burra Charter cautions that good conservation work should do as much as necessary and as little as possible.

In some cases, budget limitations affect the development of provisions to accommodate accessibility for PWD, especially at historic sites. Research shows that accessibility for all can be achieved without higher costs (Buhalis, Darcy, & Ambrose, 2012), but if that is not the case, grants or loans can help alleviate this problem. However, other problems usually arise because historic property owners are often not informed about new trends in design such as universal design. This suggests that accessibility awareness is an often overlooked but necessary step in helping historic sites come up with reasonable, affordable and effective solutions.

Another limitation in the creation of accessibility for all in historic places is related to designers' and other technical people's knowledge about recent solutions. In this sense, universal design is one of the fair approaches but, many of today's designers have had little training in it.

Universal design and its approach to tourism

Universal design was first used by architect Ron Mace and his colleagues from North Carolina State University in 1985. It is a wider approach than accessible design which promotes accessibility just for PWD. Universal design goes 'beyond technical standards that provide only minimal accessibility in compliance with regulations and extends design to increase the capacities of men, women and children of all ages and abilities' (Salmen & Ostroff, 1999, p. 3). Universal design is a way of thinking how the world meets the needs of all people without discrimination and thereby facilitates an inclusive world (Preiser & Ostroof, 2001). It is based on seven key principles to ensure an equitable environment (Center for Universal Design, 2008):

(1) Equitable use; (2) Flexibility in use; (3) Simple and intuitive use; (4) Perceptible Information; (5) Tolerance for error; (6) Low physical effort; (7) Size and space for approach and use.

In tourism research, one of the common complaints of mobility-impaired people is lack of accessibility which creates social inequality for them (Small & Darcy, 2011). The implication of universal design can create a social inclusion when the design of environment is safe, usable, and equitable for all. This is an opportunity for the tourism industry to adopt universal design principles as a starting point to embrace everybody and grant PWD their right to discover beauties of the world. Following universal design principles helps alleviate the tension that sometimes exists between the conservation and historic sites, and helps create accessibility provision (Darcy, Ambrose, Schweinberg, & Buhalis, 2010).

Methods

This study focuses on Sultanahmet Square which is located in a historic part of Istanbul and was named a UNESCO World Heritage Site in 1985. Improving accessibility at this site has presented some complicated issue because accessibility provisions sometimes conflict with the desire to conserve the site. Because of potentially unresolved issues, this study chose Sultanahmet Square to demonstrate the effects of accessibility provisions on wheelchair users' day trips to heritage site.

The target population for this study consisted of wheelchair users who are members of three different non-governmental organizations (NGO) for PWD. They were asked to fill out a questionnaire which consisted of two parts. In the first part, personal demographic data was collected and, in the second part, his/her preferences and experiences participating in leisure and recreation activities in historic places were investigated. To conduct the study, 138 wheelchair users were questioned, but due to some improperly answered questions, 13 of these respondents were excluded from the final tabulations. The results reflect 125 wheelchair users' replies to the questionnaire which assessed their experiences on Sultanahmet's current accessibility layout. The questionnaires were administered in April 2013, May 2013, and July 2015 during their groups' meetings.

In the questionnaire, respondents categorized architectural elements to evaluate accessibility, as either accessible, not accessible or partially accessible. Our 12-item wheelchair accessibility checklist is inspired by the instrument originally developed by McClain and Todd (1990), Useh, Moyo, and Munyonga (2001) and Evcil's (2009) surveys and three new

Table 2. Demographics of participants ($n = 125$).

Sample characteristics	N	%
Gender		
Male	68	54.4
Female	57	45.6
Total	125	100.0
Profession		
Student	26	20.8
Employee (white collar)	19	15.2
Laborer (blue collar)	31	24.8
Self-employment	14	11.2
Unemployed	35	28.0
Total	125	100.0
General idea about wheelchair accessibility in Sultanahmet after the last improvement		
Access totally provided	14	11.2
Access not provided	98	78.4
No idea	13	10.4
Total	125	100.0

items were added: accessible approach from sidewalk to tourist and information office, accessible approach from sidewalk to food and beverage service areas, and availability of road surface of pedestrian crossing (see Appendix for items).

Study results

The total number of respondents is 125. Of the respondents, 45.6% are male and 54.4% are female (Table 2). Ninety-eight of 125 respondents (78.4%) evaluated the Sultanahmet historic square's accessibility and rated the last improvements as 'not enough.' Only 14 respondents (11.2%) stated that the historic square is readily accessible for wheelchair users since the last improvements (Table 2).

This paper also tried to answer four research questions. To compile this part, IBM SPSS.20 program was used. Because of the categorical data received from questionnaire, Chi-square test was performed to find relationships between variables. First research question was: 'Is there a relationship between making a day trip to historic place and its physical accessibility?' The Fisher Exact test showed us that the relationship between accessibility and visiting heritage sites is significant at the 0.05 level (value = 0.99, $p < 0.05$) (Table 3). In other words, people who like to visit heritage sites in spare times are

Table 3. Relationship between historic place visiting and controlling physical accessibility in Sultanahmet.

		Historic place visiting (HPV)		
		Visiting	Not visiting	Total
Controlling	f	70	9	79
	%	88.6	11.4	100
Not controlling	f	7	39	46
	%	15.2	84.8	100

Fisher Exact test: 0.99, $p = 0.000$.

Table 4. Relationship between historic place visiting and source of information about Sultanahmet's accessibility.

		Source of information about access				
		Relatives	Friend	Internet	Not asking	Total
Visiting	f	13	40	13	11	77
	%	16.9	51.9	16.9	14.3	100
Not visiting	f	17	5	19	7	48
	%	35.4	10.4	39.6	14.6	100

Pearson Chi-square: 24.352, df = 3, $p = 0.000$.

Table 5. Relationship between historic place visiting and taking a travel companion for a day trip to Sultanahmet.

		Taking a travel companion				
		Relatives	Friends	Tour	Alone	Total
Visiting	f	22	46	8	3	79
	%	27.8	58.2	10.1	3.8	100
Not visiting	f	10	15	7	14	46
	%	21.7	32.6	15.2	30.4	100

Pearson Chi-square: 20.129, df = 3, $p = 0.000$.

also interested in the accessibility of the area (88.6%). This percentage is 15.2 for people who do not control accessibility (Table 3).

Second research question was: 'Is there a relationship between source of information about accessibility and willingness to visit historic places?' Again a relationship was found according to Chi-square analysis ($\chi^2 = 24.352$, df = 3, $p < 0.000$) (Table 4). While 51.9% of respondents who like visiting historic places use their friends as a source of information in order to check accessibility, this percentage is 10.4 for respondents who do not like visiting historic places. The Internet was not mentioned as an important source of information (16.9%) among the respondents who like visiting, whereas this percentage is 39.6 for who do not like visiting historic places (Table 4).

We also tried to find whether having someone to visit with, influenced visitors. The Chi-square test pointed a statistically significant relationship ($\chi^2 = 20.129$, df = 3, $p < 0.000$) (Table 5). The majority of wheelchair users prefer being with their friends (58.2%) when they visit historic places whereas it is 32.6% for respondents who do not visit historic places. Very few respondents (3.8%) prefer visiting alone. It is also unfavorable buying day trip tour (10.1%) among the respondents who like visiting historic places in their spare time while it is 15.2% for respondents who do not like visiting (Table 5).

Finally, the relationship between accessibility and architectural items in Sultanahmet was assessed. The respondents evaluated these 12 items according to their direct observation/experience in Sultanahmet. According to our results, people rated most items partially accessible; for example, crossing (75.2%), doors (72.8%) and cafes/restaurants' facilities (72%). Public transportation (38.4%) came first in accessibility provisions. Respondents rated sidewalks accessibility the lowest (63.2%) regarding them essentially as inaccessibility (Table 4). Added to this, ramps (55.2%), parking (43.2%) and stairs (43.2%) were also categorized as inaccessible items (Table 6).

Table 6. Relationship between accessibility provision and architectural items in Sultanahmet.

Architectural items		Access provided	Access not provided	Access partially provided	Total
1	f	28	3	94	125
	%	22.4	2.4	75.2	100
2	f	25	9	91	125
	%	20	7.2	72.8	100
3	f	21	26	78	125
	%	16.8	20.8	62.4	100
4	f	33	2	90	125
	%	26.4	1.6	72	100
5	f	13	54	58	125
	%	10.4	43.2	46.4	100
6	f	17	32	76	125
	%	13.6	25.6	60.8	100
7	f	11	69	45	125
	%	8.8	55.2	36	100
8	f	29	79	17	125
	%	23.2	63.2	13.6	100
9	f	4	54	67	125
	%	3.2	43.2	53.6	100
10	f	29	16	80	125
	%	23.2	12.8	64	100
11	f	29	18	78	125
	%	23.2	14.4	62.4	100
12	f	48	19	58	125
	%	38.4	15.2	46.4	100

Pearson Chi-square: 375.916, df = 22, $p = 0.000$.

Discussion and recommendation

This case study, conducted in Istanbul, Turkey, investigated only wheelchair users' preferences and barriers encountered in Sultanahmet Square. This might be accepted as a limitation of the study. For further research to overcome this problem, quota sampling is suggested. The second limitation might be related to the area. Since each conservation area or heritage site is unique, all obtained results cannot be generalized. But, despite this, some similarities can be derived from the results as described above.

This research explores how far recent amendments at a historic site have integrated accessibility provisions for wheelchair user's needs and preferences. There is an immediate need to find creative and inclusive design solutions in heritage sites to ensure greater social sustainability. If PWD, including wheelchair users, are to be part of the next consumer niche, dubbed by the *Wall Street* Journal as 'handicapitalism' (Prager, 1999), designers, services providers and local authorities need to provide a new conservation practices in order to ensure that people's needs and wants are met and to provide equity for everyone to visit historic places without damaging historic assets.

Relatively easy physical improvements such as changing the slope of a ramp or making a slight change in floor covering, which may not alter the character of a historic site, can mean a huge improvement for PWD (European Communities, 2014). Therefore, easy access, especially in heritage sites, is almost always effective at encouraging more participation in daily leisure activities (Rodriguez, 2014). This research showed how even basic elements of physical environments (e.g. sidewalks, ramps, stairs, parking areas) are still inaccessible.

One must keep in mind that the benefits of conservation include much more than design implementation. They also play an important role in creating social equity, by providing conditions for a more fair and balanced participation of different visitors. Therefore, no discussion on accessibility is complete without understanding accessibility needs in historic places as a civil right.

This study documents that wheelchair users want to visit heritage buildings during their spare time, but unfortunately, because of barriers they are still unable to fully enjoy the cultural and social life offered by these historic sites (Card et al., 2006; Jamaludin & Kadir, 2012). Despite the perceptible shift in both the policy and practice of improving accessibility for PWD in Turkey, creating accessibility for all people while preserving historic values remains a challenging process. Amendments are necessary for both the Turkish Disability Act (no. 5378) and the law regarding the protection of cultural and natural assets (no. 2863). Historic places and heritage sites must also be included under the definition of 'public space' (as the law no. 5378 recently stands no such stipulation regarding historic places and heritage sites exists). Guaranteeing accessibility provisions for PWD even in historic places is the law in the USA, UK, Canada, Australia and in most other developed countries. Athens' Acropolis, the historic city of Olinda in Brasil, Madrid's historic center in Spain, Denmark's Viborg historic and accessible city, etc. demonstrate ways to provide accessibility and visitability for all people in historic sites.

The availability of accurate information and details regarding accessibility in historic places creates another constraint for PWD. As the respondents stated in this study, they want and need to check the accessibility of an area before they visit. For wheelchair users who want to visit an historic place, accessibility information about the site is vital; thus, this information must be realistic, detailed, and updated frequently, preferably across a variety of formats. The results of this study show us that despite the frequency of Internet usage among Turkish people (47.4% of Turkish household use Internet in 2012, see www.tuik.gov.tr/PreHaberBultenleri.do?id=13569), wheelchair users cannot rely on the Internet to provide accurate information about accessibility features. Videos of each accessibility provision at a site would be a big help to PWD. Additionally, providing photographs or plans of key features, such as the entrance and restrooms, on the websites of tourist attractions would enable PWD to feel confident regarding the accessibility provisions (European Communities, 2014). An investigation of why wheelchair users do not rely on the Internet as a source of information about accessibility could be a topic for further research in order to determine the exact nature of what kind of information would be most helpful for them. However, it must be kept in mind that elderly wheelchair users may not be able to use the Internet as easily as younger people, and some PWD are unfamiliar with contacting tourist information offices by other means, such as phone; therefore, these constraints must also be considered when creating service provision.

Fortunately, universal design principles provide good starting point for sharing information to help all users to the greatest extent possible.

In the survey, the wheelchair users mostly preferred a travel companion even for a short trip within the city. This might be related to the need for assistance for the task of daily living as well as the lack of services available to them. The most common travel companions were friends. This finding is parallel to the study results of Var, Yesiltas, Yaylı, and Öztürk (2011) who examined PWD's travel patterns in Turkish settings. At the same time, as is true for all people, traveling with a friend or a family member may make the trip more interesting and pleasant as well. Our investigation also showed that few wheelchair users preferred buying day trip tour since disabled friendly day trips are very rare and mostly private. Accessible tourism is still new for Turkey and therefore the Turkish tourism sector is not ready (Öztürk et al., 2008) to provide different opportunities (day trip, half-day trip, long-trip, etc.) for PWD.

In Turkey, a system for auditing access is not common. Auditing regulations were approved in July of 2013 with the publication of Accessibility of Monitoring and Control Regulations (no. 28713) in the official gazette. There is an immediate need to specialized audits who have both architectural and restoration graduate backgrounds. An access action plan is also needed which can be prepared when the access audit and conservation assessment have been completed (Donnelly, 2011) as is the case in many European countries.

It is also needed to increase awareness about accessibility of PWD in historic places among designers and service providers who work in tourism. Universal design is still fairly new to the design world, so efforts by both national and international organizations such as the International Union of Architecture (UIA), which is helping to create awareness of universal design principles by giving awards to projects, are much needed and appreciated.

The results of this study remind us that designers working in the field of conservation-restoration must be encouraged to pursue skills and knowledge about creating accessibility. Local authorities, NGOs like the Chamber of Architects, and universities could start giving awards to the best accessibility design projects. They could also organize competitions both among professionals and university students to reward endeavors that achieve both conservation and physical improvements that provide accessibility for all people visiting historic sites.

Conclusion

This paper focuses on the preferences of wheelchair users and the barriers they encounter in daily leisure activities, especially at historic places. It is significant to understand wheelchair users' experiences at heritage site where access to leisure activities is still unequal.

Even though wheelchair users have been identified as the next consumer niche in tourism (Card et al., 2006; Prager, 1999; Ray & Ryder, 2003; STRC, 2008) along with other disability groups, many problems still exist and, as our results show, historic places are not fully accessible for wheelchair users, as well as a number of other user groups in society (Williams, Rattray, & Grimes, 2007). Additionally, our study found that there is a relation between accessibility and visiting heritage sites.

PWD desire activities in historic places just like able-bodied people (Allan, 2013), but the tension between conservation and achieving accessibility objectives (Darcy et al., 2010) is still restricting their accessibility at many historic sites. This is especially problematic because enjoying these experiences has been deemed a human right; historic sites must provide accessibility for the entire population regardless of abilities. Our study also showed that accessible information is also problematic for many reasons. There are 'web pages of societal and institutional services (which) are not satisfactory and accessible for the all disabled citizens' (Altinay, Saner, Bahçelerli, & Altinay, 2016, p. 89). Our results show that wheelchair users do not prefer Internet for gathering information about accessibility. Additionally, not only access to physical areas is important, but also the quality and reliability of information offered (Williams et al., 2007). Added to this, accessibility is related to choosing travel companions. In general, just like other people, the PWD in our study chose to travel with companions. While this is true, it must be acknowledged that they also must be enabled to travel independently without the need for assistance by another person if that is what they choose to do (Var et al., 2011). Our results show us that wheelchair users required the assistance of friend or family member, but we did not investigate all of the factors involved in their decision. Traveling alone or with another person is a personal choice which can have positive (greater enjoyment when visiting with a friend) or negative (needing assistance or having to cope with problems) motivators. In our case, wheelchair users chose to travel with a companion because they questioned the site's accessibility. Their choice could be the result of prejudice formed during previous experiences, but similar results were found by Var et al. (2011) in their research of travel patterns of PWD in Turkey.

The results of the study demonstrate the various level of accessibility in the physical environment of Sultanahmet Square. Wheelchair users mostly complain about the condition of sidewalks (inadequate width and improper surface), improperly designed slopes of ramps, accessibility of car parking, and unavailability of accessible utilities (e.g. platform lift) along staircases. Many studies have pointed out that 'reaching a good understanding of how to serve customers with particular access needs may not be easy for providers, especially when major architectural improvements are required' (Darcy et al., 2010, p. 310). Despite difficulties that exist, the principles of universal design are now becoming more recognized. As their use and popularity increase, more accessible tourism environments will become available to provide for the needs of all people.

Currently, many tourists with disabilities are still segregated from participating fully in day trip to historic places as a consequence of basic accessibility problems. This study focused on Sultanahmet Square in Istanbul, a place dating back to the Roman Empire. While the study is specific to Istanbul, the universal outcomes of social segregation demonstrated by our study provide insights for other developed and less developed countries. In sum, visiting historic places without any problems is still not a simple task for wheelchair users and probably social justice and equity will take times.

Acknowledgements

I would like to express my sincere thanks to the editors of the special edition and most particularly to the two anonymous reviewers for their insightful and critical comments, which greatly enhanced my paper.

Disclosure statement

No potential conflict of interest was reported by the author.

References

Adams, J., & Foster, L. (2012). *Easy access to historic buildings*. Swindon: English Heritage.
Allan, M. (2013). Disability tourism: Why do disabled people engaging in tourism activities? *European Journal of Social Sciences, 39*(3), 480–486.
Altinay, Z., Saner, T., Bahçelerli, N. M., & Altinay, F. (2016). The role of social media tools: Accessible tourism for disabled citizens. *Educational Technology and Society, 19*(1), 89–99.
Buhalis, D., Darcy, S., & Ambrose, I. (2012). *Best practice in accessible tourism: Inclusion, disability, ageing population and tourism*. Bristol: Channel View.
Buhalis, D., & Michopoulou, E. (2011). Information-enabled tourism destination marketing: Addressing the accessibility market. *Current Issues in Tourism, 14*(2), 145–168.
Burnett, J. J. (1996). What services marketers need to know about the mobility-disabled consumer. *The Journal of Services Marketing, 10*(3), 3–20.
Cameron, B., Darcy, S., & Foggin, E. (2003). *Barrier-free tourism for people with disabilities in the Asian and Pacific region* (ST/ESCAP/2316). New York, NY: United Nations.
Card, J. A., Cole, S. T., & Humphrey, A. H. (2006). A comparison of the accessibility and attitudinal barriers model: Travel providers and travelers with physical disabilities. *Asia Pacific Journal of Tourism Research, 11*(2), 161–175.
Casas, I., Horner, M., & Weber, J. (2009). A Comparison of three methods for identifying transport based exclusion: A case study of children's access to urban opportunities in Erie and Niagara counties, New York. *International Journal of Sustainable Transportation, 3*(4), 227–245.
Center for Universal Design. (2008). Retrieved October 15, 2016, from http://www.ncsu.edu/ncsu/desing/cud
Crompton, J. L. (1979). Motivations for pleasure vacation. *Annals of Tourism Research, 6*(4), 408–424.
Darcy, S. (2004). *Disabling journeys: The social relations of tourism for people with impairments in Australia–an analysis of government tourism authorities and accommodation sector practices and discourses* (Doctoral dissertation). University of Technology, Sydney, Australia. Retrieved June 1, 2013, from http://hdl.handle.net/2100/260
Darcy, S., & Daruwella, P. (1999). The trouble with travel: People with disabilities and travel. *Social Alternatives, 18*(1), 41–46.
Darcy, S., Ambrose, I., Schweinberg, S., & Buhalis, D. (2010). Chapter 19 conclusion: Universal approaches to accessible tourism. In D. Buhalis & S. Darcy (Eds.), Accessible *tourism concepts and issues*. Bristol: Channel View.
Donnelly, J. (Ed.). (2011). *Access improving the accessibility of historic buildings and places*. Dublin: National Disability Authority Government of Ireland.
Eichhorn, V., Miller, G., Michopoulou, E., & Buhalis, D. (2010). *Enabling disabled tourists? Accessibility tourism information schemes*. Paper presented at TRANSED 2010, 12th international conference on mobility and transport for elderly and disabled people, Hong Kong, China, 2–4 June 2010. Retrieved July 17, 2013, from http://epub.surrey.ac.uk/1090/1/fulltext.pdf
Evcil, A. N. (2009). Wheelchair accessibility to public buildings in Istanbul. *Disability and Rehabilitation: Assistive Technology, 4*(2), 76–85.

European Communities. (2014). *Improving information on accessible tourism for disabled people.* European Commission Office for Official Publications of the European Communities. Retrieved from https://bookshop.europa.eu

Gleeson, B. (1998). Disability and poverty. In R. Fincher & J. Nieuwenhuysen (Eds.), *Australian poverty: Then and now* (pp. 314–333). Carlton: Melbourne University Press.

Guerra, L. S. (2003). *Tourism for all: Organising trips for physically disabled customers.* Fern Barrow, Poole: MA European Tourism Management, Bournemout University.

Hine, J., & Mitchell, F. (2001). Better for everyone? Travel experiences and transport exclusion. *Urban Studies, 38*(2), 319–332.

Jamaludin, M., & Kadir, S. A. (2012). Accessibility in buildings of tourist attraction: A case studies comparison. *Procedia – Social and Behavioral Sciences, 35,* 97–104.

McClain, L., & Todd, C. (1990). Food store accessibility. *American Journal of Occupational Therapy, 44,* 487–491.

McGuire, F. (1984). A factor analytic study of leisure constraints in advance adulthood. *Leisure Sciences, 6*(3), 313–326.

McKercher, B., Packer, T., Yau, M., & Lam, P. (2003). Travel agents as facilitators or inhibitors of travel: Perception of people with disabilities. *Tourism Management, 24*(4), 465–474.

Naniopoulos, A., Tsalis, P., Papanikolaou, E. & Kalliagra, A. (2015). Accessibility improvements interventions realised in byzantine monuments of Thessaloiki, Greece. *Journal of Tourism Future, 1*(3), 254–268.

Nimrod, G. (2007). Retirees' leisure: Activities, benefits and their contribution to life satisfaction. *Leisure Studies, 26*(1), 65–80.

Oladokun, O. J., Ololajulo, J., & Oladele, O. I. (2014). Analysis of factors enhancing special needs people participation in recreation and cultural tourism activities in Osogbo Metropolis, Osun State, Nigeria. *Mediterranean Journal of Social Sciences, 5*(20), 2916–2925.

Öztürk, Y., Yaylı, A., & Yeşiltaş, M. (2008). Is the Turkish tourism industry ready for a disabled customers market? The view of hotel and travel agency managers. *Tourism Management, 29*(2), 382–389.

Patterson, T. S. (2001). Constraints: An integrated viewpoint. *Illuminaire, 7*(1), 30–38.

Prager, J. H. (1999). People with disabilities are next consumer niche. *Wall Street Journal,* B1–B2.

Preiser, W. F. E., & Ostroof, E. (2001). *Universal design handbook.* New York, NY: McGraw Hill.

Ray, N. M., & Ryder, M. E. (2003). "Ebilities" tourism: An exploratory discussion of the travel needs and motivations of the mobility-disabled. *Tourism Management, 24,* 57–72.

Rodriguez, P. R. (2014). How do disabled individuals spend their leisure time? *Disability and Health Journal, 7,* 196–205.

Salmen, J., & Ostroof, E. (1999). Part I: Architectural fundamentals universal design and accessible design 1. In D. Watson, M. J. Crasbie, J. H. Callender (Eds.), *Time saver standards.* (7th ed.) Norwalk, CT: McGraw Hill.

Samdahl, D. M., & Jekubovich, N. J. (1997). A critique of leisure constraints: Comparative analyses and understandings. *Journal of Leisure Research, 29*(4), 430–452.

Sen, L., & Mayfield, S. (2004). Accessible tourism transportation to and accessibility of historic building and other recreational areas in the city of Galveston, Texas. *Public Works Management and Policy, 8*(4), 223–234.

Shi, L., Cole, S., & Chancellor, H. C. (2012). Understanding leisure travel motivations of travellers with acquired mobility impairments. *Tourism Management, 33*(2012), 228–231.

Small, J., & Darcy, S. (2011). Chapter 1: Tourism, disability and mobility. In S. Cole & N. Morgan (Eds.), *Tourism and inequality problems and prospects.* Wallingford: CABI.

Smith, R. (1987). Leisure of disabled tourist: barriers to participation. *Annals of Tourism Research, 14*(3), 376–389.

Sustainable Tourism Cooperative Research Centre (STCRC). (2008). Accessible *tourism: Understanding and evolving aspect of Australian tourism.* Australia: Bundall Printing.

Taylor, Z., & Jozefowicz, I. (2012). Intra-urban daily mobility of disabled people for recreational and leisure purposes. *Journal of Transport Geography, 24,* 155–172.

Turco, D. M., Stumbo, N., & Garncarz, J. (1998). Tourism constraints for people with disabilities. *Parks and Recreation, 33*(9), 78–84.

United Nations. (2014). Convention on the rights of PWD, 11th session, 30 March–11 April 2014. Retrieved October 23, 2016, from www.ohchr.org/CRPD/DGCArticle12

Useh, U., Moyo, A. M., & Munyonga, E. (2001). Wheelchair accessibility of public buildings in the central business district of Harare Zimbabwe. *Disability Rehabilitation, 23*, 490–496.

Var, T., Yesiltas, M., Yaylı, A., & Öztürk, Y. (2011). A study on the travel patterns of physically disabled people. *Asia Pacific Journal of Tourism Research, 16*(6), 599–618.

Williams, R., Rattray, R., & Grimes, A. (2007). Online accessibility and information needs of disabled tourists: A three country hotel sector analysis. *Journal of Electronic Commerce Research, 8*(2), 157–171.

Yau, M. K., McKercher, B., & Packer, T. L. (2004). Traveling with disability: More than an access issue. *Annals of Tourism Research, 31*(4), 946–960.

Appendix

Questionnaire form (original in Turkish)

Section A: Please choose the appropriate one.

Gender	Male
	Female
Your occupation	Student
	Government employee (white collar worker)
	Laborer (blue collar worker)
	Self-employment
	Unemployed

Section B: Please answer the following questions

1. Please put a cross for each accessibility provision of Sultanahmet Square as ACCESSIBLE, NOT ACCESSIBLE or PARTIALLY ACCESSIBLE

	Accessible	Not accessible	Partially accessible
Access to public transport vehicles			
Access to car parking			
Ramps (kerb ramps, building entrance ramps, etc.)			
Sidewalk (width and surface)			
Level access for building entrance			
Doors (entrance)			
Accessible tools along staircases (outside)			
Access from sidewalk to tourist and information office			
Accessibility of public phones			
Accessibility of toilet provision			
Access from sidewalk to food–beverage service area			
Availability of surface of pedestrian crossing			

2. What do you think about the Sultanahmet Square's accessibility after the last improvements?
   - Wheelchair accessibility is totally provided
   - Wheelchair accessibility is not provided
   - I have no idea

3. Would you like to visit historic places in your spare time in general?

   Yes   No

4. What type of trip do you prefer in Sultanahmet Square?
   - I like traveling alone
   - I like traveling with relatives
   - I like traveling with friends
   - I like buying daily trip
5. Do you check the accessibility provisions of destination area (Sultanahmet Square) before going there?

   Yes   No

6. How do you check the accessibility provision of historic area (Sultanahmet Square)?
   - I checked the accessibility provision of the historic area by asking to my friends
   - I checked the accessibility provision of the historic area by asking to my relatives
   - I checked the accessibility provision of the historic area by using internet
   - I do not check

Stakeholder collaboration in the development of accessible tourism: A framework for Inclusion

Julie Nyanjom ⓘ, Kathy Boxall and Janine Slaven

ABSTRACT
Stakeholder collaboration is increasingly being lauded as important in the development of accessible tourism. The purpose of this study is to explore how stakeholders collaborate in the development of accessible tourism. Drawing on research conducted in Western Australia, the study utilises qualitative approaches in its exploration. The evidence from the study strongly indicates that there is minimal collaboration between stakeholders in the development of accessible tourism. The findings suggest that when there are multiple and diverse stakeholders at play, an organic, circulatory and developmental approach to stakeholder collaboration should be adopted to innovatively move towards inclusive tourism – an ideal that aspires to equal access and inclusion for all. To this end, four emergent interrelated themes are considered: control and coordination, communication, clarity of roles and responsibilities and collaboration and integration. From these themes, a framework that can be applied to encourage collaboration is proposed.

Introduction

The purpose of this study is to explore how stakeholders collaborate in the development of accessible tourism. Accessible tourism strives for the inclusion of all people in tourism activities and is intricately linked to a legal framework authorised by disability legislation. Several researchers have called for stakeholder collaboration in the development of accessible tourism (e.g. Darcy, 2011; Gillovic & McIntosh, 2015; Michopoulou, Darcy, Ambrose, & Buhalis, 2015; O'Neill & Knight, 2000). Yet, there is scarce empirical research on stakeholder involvement in accessible tourism practice. Although consensus is held amongst researchers that stakeholder collaboration is critical for tourism development (Byrd, 2007; Jamal & Getz, 1995), it is also acknowledged that a collaborative approach to tourism development is highly complex (Jamal & Getz, 1995; O'Neill & Knight, 2000; Waligo, Clarke, & Hawkins, 2013). Fundamental to the process is the deep understanding of diverse perspectives from multiple and heterogeneous stakeholders.

Tourism, in general and accessible tourism in particular, is a highly fragmented industry dependent on numerous components. Sustaining the success of accessible tourism requires the participation of a wide range of critical stakeholders (see Michopoulou and Buhalis, 2011, for a comprehensive stakeholder analysis). Whilst recognising the critical role of other principal stakeholders in the development of accessible tourism, this paper brings to focus the fundamental role of people with disabilities in the process. We argue that the development of accessible tourism would be challenging to achieve without the holistic and essential involvement of people with disabilities. This group, although most impacted by access and inclusion issues, is marginalised in society (National People with Disabilities and Carer Council, 2009; Shaw & Coles, 2004) and generally ignored by the Hospitality and Tourism (H&T) industry as a viable market segment (Darcy & Pegg, 2011; Gillovic & McIntosh, 2015; Shaw & Coles, 2004). For economic as well as socially moral reasons, people with disabilities should be the main stakeholders at the collaborative table. Disability is a dynamic and evolving construct that requires continual discussions about emergent perspectives (Shelton & Tucker, 2005; Stumbo & Pegg, 2005; Yau, McKercher, & Packer, 2004). The voices of people with disabilities are therefore critical to the process. Given their historical exclusion however, collaborative efforts that include people with disabilities need to be approached with empathy, caution and humility (Oliver & Barnes, 2012). Careful thought needs to be given to an evaluative approach that acknowledges the inherent complexities and multilayered interactions that are required with people with disabilities as substantive stakeholders in the development of accessible tourism.

In our exploration, we propose a framework that can be applied in the complex process of stakeholder involvement. Derived from the findings of our study, our framework is presented as an approach that takes into consideration the historical and social perspectives of people with disabilities, whilst at the same time being driven by an organic, circulatory and developmental approach that considers the dynamics inherent to the process of stakeholder collaboration. This framework is proposed as a step towards explaining how collaborative efforts can be enhanced in the development of accessible tourism to innovatively move the agenda towards inclusive tourism. We argue that inclusive tourism goes beyond access issues and define the term as an ideal that includes the participation of all stakeholder groups, including people with disabilities, in policy, planning and governance of the development of accessible tourism (see Scheyvens and Biddulph, 2017, for an indepth conceptualisation of the term 'Inclusive Tourism'). Our framework is also offered to initiate further discussion and debate on a topic that has to date received a dearth of empirical research.

Accessible tourism

The fundamental goal of accessible tourism is 'tourism for all'. Buhalis and Darcy (2011) define accessible tourism, and within the definition, clearly emphasise interaction between stakeholders as critical to improving access and inclusion. The definition states:

> Accessible tourism is a form of tourism that involves collaborative processes between stakeholders that enables people with access requirements, including mobility, vision, hearing and cognitive dimensions of access, to function independently and with equity and dignity through the delivery of universally designed tourism products, services and environments.... . (Buhalis & Darcy, 2011, p. 10)

The optimism implied by the above definition has yet to be achieved. People with disabilities continue to face many barriers whilst attempting to enjoy H&T services. Accessible tourism literature confirms that despite people with disabilities' growing financial affluence (Stumbo & Pegg, 2005) and their desire to utilise H&T services domestically and/or internationally (Darcy & Dickson, 2009), people with disabilities as potential guests continue to be ignored by the H&T industry (Gillovic & McIntosh, 2015; Shaw & Coles, 2004). Efforts to ensure equity and dignity have so far failed to recognise the complexities in the social situation of people with disabilities, which influence their ability to make use of H&T services. For example, discrimination towards people with disabilities continues to be systematic, systemic and entrenched in communities' ways of life (National People with Disabilities and Carer Council, 2009). Due to this exclusion, too few people with disabilities have meaningful opportunities to contribute to the process of political and policy change; yet, these changes have significant impact on their quality of life. This means that the perspectives of the fundamental group of people for whom accessible tourism exists have little input in its policy development.

The dynamics between key accessible tourism stakeholders have also posed challenges to accessible tourism development. Government agencies control access legislation, leaving reasonable adjustments to service providers and addressing discriminatory practices only after they have occurred (Gillovic & McIntosh, 2015); service providers do not view the emerging market of people with disabilities as significant (Darcy & Pegg, 2011), do not understand the needs of people with disabilities (O'Neill & Knight, 2000; Patterson, Darcy, & Mönninghoff, 2012; Poria, Reichel, & Brandt, 2011) and do not go beyond the minimum legislative requirements to ensure that people with disabilities experience quality customer service (Grady & Ohlin, 2009; Shelton & Tucker, 2005; Stumbo & Pegg, 2005; Yau et al., 2004).

Due to the fragmented nature of the H&T industry, delivering a quality experience at destination level for people with disabilities has proved complex and challenging (Michopoulou & Buhalis, 2011). A single visit to a destination includes an orchestrated chain of activities that involve many entities, including short or long distance travel, local transportation, accommodation, retail, dining and tour excursions. For a person with disabilities to achieve a quality holiday experience, all components of the journey need to be accessible. Yet, this is often not the case. The provision of accessible communication channels, especially in terms of relevance and reliability of information, poses critical challenges (Darcy, 2010; Eichhorn, Miller, Michopoulou, & Buhalis, 2008). In addition, people with disabilities' inability to fully negotiate the built environment continues to be a barrier to full participation. This is despite the focus on the built environment, which has seen progress being made environmentally, specifically in Australia, the United States and the United Kingdom, through disability legislation, with government providing an essential framework for the development process through regulation and control (Grady & Ohlin, 2009; Patterson et al., 2012; Shaw, Veitch, & Coles, 2005).

It is clear that much more needs to be done to propel accessible tourism forward. Research indicates that the development of accessible tourism will require approaches that take the industry beyond physical access issues (Shelton & Tucker, 2005; Stumbo & Pegg, 2005; Yau et al., 2004) to confront the social, political and economic perspectives of sustainable development (Darcy, Cameron, & Pegg, 2010). Further development will need a change of perspectives, to view accessible tourism as a 'social force' rather than an industry (Higgins-Desbiolles, 2006), in order to facilitate a whole-of-life approach that prioritises the quality of life of tourists with disabilities (Darcy & Dickson, 2009). Imperative to this change will be improved engagement of people with disabilities as incumbent stakeholders. Benefits can accrue if the recognition, understanding and knowledge about the long history of marginalisation and exclusion of this group are taken into account in deliberations that influence policy and decision-making. Accessible tourism is fundamentally a social construct, and the values, beliefs and ways of knowing of all stakeholders are vital to its development.

Consequently, fundamental to developing the symbiotic relationship between accessibility and tourism is the need to involve all key stakeholders in the development process with a focus on the inclusion of people with disabilities. Collaborative efforts can increase the quality of the planning process, increase engagement and ownership through education and training and enhance stakeholder trust in the management of disability legislation (Michopoulou et al., 2015; Patterson et al., 2012). Stakeholder preconceptions about disability also have considerable influence on collaborative dynamics. Exploring how stakeholders can collaborate in the development of accessible tourism must, therefore, include understandings of disability (Shaw & Coles, 2004; Shelton & Tucker, 2005).

Understanding disability

Historically, disability has been understood as an individual deficit that is bio-medical in origin and viewed as a personal tragedy for the individual concerned (Oliver & Barnes, 2012). Although the ways in which we understand disability have changed over recent years, medicalised understandings continue to dominate in some contexts today (Beresford, 2016). Such understandings are of course relevant when people with disabilities undergo medical treatment; but in the world of H&T, they are both incongruous and problematic. It may be helpful here to consider the origin of such understandings and why it is that they have prevailed. Oliver and Barnes (2012) argue that deficit-based understandings of disability can be traced to the industrial revolution in the United Kingdom, when 'able-bodied' and 'able-minded' individuals were required to work in the rapidly developing mills and factories. People with disabilities who were unable to keep pace with the new working practices were excluded from the factories and placed in institutions.

Early practices of institutionalisation did not differentiate between different types of impairment. People with intellectual disabilities, mental illness and physical or sensory impairments were often placed together in the same institutions – in Australia, for example, people with disabilities were incarcerated with convicts in the early penal colonies (Rosen, 2006). As medical and scientific knowledge developed, different arrangements were made for people with different impairment types, with state governments providing asylums for people with intellectual disabilities and mental illness and charitable organisations developing institutions for people with physical impairments (Chenoweth, 2000). However, as the numbers of people being institutionalised continued to escalate and the costs of providing institutional care spiralled, policies of deinstitutionalisation were introduced from the 1960s, with some countries (for example, the United States of America) beginning the processes of deinstitutionalisation earlier than others. In Western Australia, deinstitutionalisation took place from the 1970s, and policies of mass institutionalisation are no longer in favour in the western world. However, because deinstitutionalisation was implemented so recently, the policies and practices of institutionalisation are still part of living memory and in some contexts, the medicalised deficit-based understandings of disability, which supported those policies and practices, continue to prevail (Beresford, 2016).

It is important to note, however, that understandings of disability have changed and developed over the years. In the U.K, for example, organisations of (rather than for) people with disabilities developed their own understandings of disability, the most influential of which is that published by the Union of the Physically Impaired Against Segregation (Union of the Physically Impaired Against Segregation [UPIAS], 1976). The UPIAS definition differentiated between impairment (functional limitation) and disability (socially imposed restriction) and was used to develop the social model of disability, which firmly locates the causes of disability in the social environment rather than in the individual (Oliver & Barnes, 2012). Social model understandings of disability are perhaps most easily understood in relation to wheelchair users. A wheelchair user may have an impairment (functional limitation that limits their physical mobility) but if ramps, lifts and accessible toilets are in place, they will be less disabled than if steps block their entry to buildings, or the lack of lifts and accessible toilets further impedes their access within those buildings. Using this example, it is not difficult to see that increasing physical access to buildings and to the facilities therein directly reduces the disability (socially imposed restriction) people with impairments experience. By making hotel entrances and other facilities accessible, the H&T industry can therefore play its own role in preventing or reducing disability. Conversely, by failing to take account of the access needs of disabled guests, the industry may play a part in *exacerbating* disability (socially imposed restriction) (Boxall, Nyanjom, & Slaven, 2018). As legislation regarding accessible buildings has been implemented, service providers have been required to build or retrofit accessible spaces and rooms; yet, research evidence continues to highlight people with disabilities' dissatisfaction with the accessible facilities provided (Poria et al., 2011; Shaw & Coles, 2004).

For the H&T industry, it is therefore important to understand ways in which service providers may contribute to the socially imposed restriction experienced by people with disabilities with a range of different impairments, including sensory and intellectual impairments. We do not have the space to go into this in detail here, other than to point out that the people with the greatest knowledge of disability (socially imposed restriction) caused by H&T service providers are people with disabilities who have used these services.

Stakeholder theory

Stakeholder theory can be applied to gain an understanding of the dynamics inherent in social interactions. Numerous studies have applied the stakeholder theory in the tourism field to explore stakeholder collaboration (e.g. Byrd, 2007; Cárdenas, Byrd, & Duffy, 2015; Waligo et al., 2013). The stakeholder theory was advanced by Freeman (1984), who defined a stakeholder as 'any group or individual who can affect or is affected by the achievement of the organization's objectives' (p. 46). Freeman (1984) outlined three procedures for effective stakeholder management as: identification and legitimisation of stakeholders, relationship building processes and transaction management.

The identification and legitimisation of stakeholders necessitate involvement of all those with vested interests in tourism development, including marginalised stakeholders considered to be at the fringe, in the decision-making processes (Hart & Sharma, 2004; Shaw & Coles, 2004). Stakeholders often coexist but do not interact with each other, and this lack of involvement can be detrimental to tourism development efforts. Initiating relationship-building processes that encourage participation can invigorate development and result in positive outcomes (Freeman, 1984). Relationship management involves the clarification of roles and responsibilities (Gray, 1989), because stakeholders have varied capabilities to perform different tasks. Stakeholders do not have to be involved equally in decision-making (Byrd, 2007). It is important, however, that all interests from key stakeholders are identified and understood (Byrd, 2007; Michopoulou & Buhalis, 2011).

The stakeholder theory provides a perspective on government regulation and control and suggests that stakeholder management depends on resources, time and leadership (Byrd, 2007). The availability of these elements facilitates effective stakeholder collaboration that allows for deeper empowerment, engagement and ownership of the decision-making process, whilst limited availability of these elements tends to discourage involvement. In policy and legislation, governments often involve stakeholders by using methods such as public hearings, advisory committees and surveys. This is often at the initial stage of the project, after which involvement tends to taper-off as the project progresses to its conclusion (Vernon, Essex, Pinder, & Curry, 2005). Effective stakeholder collaboration, however, requires a holistic approach to involvement throughout the implementation process.

Stakeholder collaboration in accessible tourism

Collaboration is defined as 'a process through which parties who see different aspects of a problem can constructively explore their differences and search for solutions that go beyond their own limited vision of what is possible' (Gray, 1989, p. 5). Although many theories have been advanced on finding effective ways to engage stakeholders in tourism activities (Nunkoo, Smith, & Ramkissoon, 2013), there is little clarity on how best to achieve effective collaboration. The presence of multiple stakeholders with diverse perspectives makes the achievement of effective collaboration a challenge. It is, however, acknowledged that the unique contribution of each stakeholder can impact positively on accessible tourism development (Michopoulou & Buhalis, 2011).

Stakeholder collaboration is often a complex initiative (Jamal & Getz, 1995; O'Neill & Knight, 2000). In accessible tourism development, this complexity is magnified by the contentious and contextual nature of issues that must be addressed. The process can, therefore, be assisted by the careful identification and acknowledgement of key stakeholder groups (Clarkson, 1995). Studies have identified, analysed and evaluated stakeholder groups and their participation in tourism development (e.g. Butler, 1999; Byrd, 2007) and concluded that community residents, business owners and government officials form the key stakeholder groups involved in tourism development. Similarly, Michopoulou and Buhalis (2011) carried out an analysis of principal stakeholder groups in accessible tourism, and identified eight categories, highlighting the most prominent to be people with disabilities, disability organisations, H&T service providers and government agencies, a view similarly adopted by this study.

Bringing diverse stakeholders with disparate perspectives, interests and capabilities requires strong and reflective leadership (Waligo et al., 2013). Without leadership to drive collaboration, initiatives fall short of implementation due to a lack of concerted efforts from stakeholders (Michopoulou & Buhalis, 2011). Access and inclusion go beyond a single stakeholder group and become a community issue (Michopoulou et al., 2015; O'Neill & Knight, 2000; Shaw et al., 2005). Consequently, collaborative approaches to the sustainable development of accessible tourism would require a labyrinth of coordinated networks of stakeholder groups that have a holistic approach to participation. By becoming involved in the decision-making process, stakeholders become more aware of pertinent issues and gain a sense of responsibility, which enable them to build a greater degree of shared ownership (Cárdenas et al., 2015). It is essential, therefore, to identify a facilitator with clear roles and responsibilities who can direct the collaboration process and manage raised expectations beyond what can be realistically delivered (Bryd, 2007; Gray, 1989). In relation to disability and accessibility issues, this leadership role has predominantly been assumed by government agencies. Given the significant regulatory powers a government holds, the leadership role adopted by local government groups is critical to the collaborative process.

Effective collaboration requires insight into the perspectives and experiences that have shaped stakeholders' views regarding involvement in tourism-related activities. Collaboration can access localised knowledge and help ensure that decisions made are well informed and appropriate (Michopoulou & Buhalis, 2011), which has the advantage of building on the store of knowledge, insights and capabilities of stakeholders. Since people with disabilities are the stakeholder groups that have the greatest knowledge of disability and are most impacted by accessible tourism, it is imperative that their voices are heard. They need to be provided with a convivial platform to share their lived experiences and invited to discuss the issues that impact their quality of life as it pertains to utilising H&T services. In general, people with disabilities are underrepresented in community involvement (National People with Disabilities and Carer Council, 2009). This lack of participation as stakeholders may be attributed to the multiple barriers to meaningful participation they face in the community previously discussed. Hart and Sharma (2004) argue that the stakeholder groups considered powerless and isolated can provide valuable knowhow that can lead to innovative ways of solving problems. To enhance collaboration, other stakeholder groups within the network have to therefore find strategic and practical ways to work with people with disabilities to achieve common goals. This implies that the stakeholders considered powerful must be willing to share decision-making responsibilities with the 'silent voices' within their communities (Ryan, 2002, p. 23). Such a shift in behaviour would not only require a clear understanding of disability as socially imposed (Oliver

& Barnes, 2012; Shelton & Tucker, 2005), but also a shared understanding from all stakeholders as to how collaboration can work when dealing with marginalised groups that are perceived as 'invisible' (National People with Disabilities and Carer Council, 2009) or 'unimportant' (Hart & Sharma, 2004). Such pertinent social issues can be highly emotive, which may negatively impact on effective communication between stakeholders, and creative strategies for clearer communication may therefore be required.

Effective collaborative efforts require clarity about activities that should be undertaken and the depth of involvement considered appropriate (Cohen & Uphoff, 1980). Given that stakeholders possess diverse capabilities, assessing their level of involvement can be challenging. Arnstein's (1969) 'ladder of citizen participation' offers a three-category typology, which can be applied when articulating present and potential levels of stakeholder collaboration. The three groups depicting the levels of participation are: *Non-participation* – where the focus is on educating the citizen, with little attempt at engaging them in decision-making; *Degree of tokenism* – where the focus is on provision of information and soliciting for opinions and feedback, indicating the first step towards participation; and *Degree of citizen power* – where stakeholders can voice their ideas and thoughts, engage with and influence the decision-making process, indicating the highest level of participation. In tourism studies, Butler (1999) advanced five levels of participation, namely, imposition, petition, advice, representation and equality. These perspectives imply that the extent of participation falls on a continuum and is dynamically influenced by the environment in which individual stakeholders situate. To achieve a level of collaboration that engenders ownership, stakeholders should not be passive recipients of initial project information, but active participants in the decision-making process to a genuine level that elicits authentic feelings of involvement.

To summarise, literature concurs that a wide range of stakeholders need to be included in the development of accessible tourism, despite the complexities inherent in the process. In particular, the inclusion of people with disabilities is critical. To be effective, such an approach requires strategically coordinated planning and implementation (Buhalis & Darcy, 2011; Gillovic & McIntosh, 2015). If people with disabilities are centrally involved, stakeholder collaboration by those with vested interests may offer a way of overcoming previous challenges and achieving the desired objectives in access and inclusion.

Methods

The data we refer to in this paper is from an exploratory study on accessible tourism conducted in Margaret River, a town situated in the south-west of Western Australia. Margaret River is a tourist town three-hours' drive south of Perth and is home to, amongst other attractions, world-renowned vineyards, surfing locations, world's tallest trees and limestone caves. The diversity of tourist attractions in Margaret River, and its popularity as a tourist destination made it an ideal choice as a study site.

This study employed inductive qualitative approaches to investigate stakeholder collaboration, utilising in-depth interviews as a means of data collection. The inductive approach is appropriate for investigating phenomenon in naturally occurring situations (Miles, Huberman, & Saldana, 2014), provides opportunity to identify conceptual themes within participants' narratives and allows participants to share their experiences, thereby providing potential for new lines of inquiry to emerge (Denzin, 1973).

Participants

To recruit participants, a three-stage sampling technique was employed.

First, four key stakeholder groups were identified, namely, people with disabilities, organisations of people with disabilities, H&T service providers and government agencies. These groups have been highlighted in literature as key stakeholders in the development of accessible tourism (Michopoulou & Buhalis, 2011; O'Neill & Knight, 2000). Key stakeholders have the highest potential to provide deep and rich data (Miles et al., 2014), as they are most impacted by the implementation of the tourism initiatives. The researchers' justification for stakeholder identification is outlined in the following:

People with disabilities: These are people with visible or non-visible impairments (Thomas, 2007), who regularly, or occasionally, use H&T services. We also include in this category those who have never used such services – but would do so, if the H&T industry is able to better accommodate their particular access needs. Because of their lived experience of using H&T services (or being unable to do so because of access problems), people with disabilities have experiential knowledge that is invaluable to the H&T industry. This knowledge of where they have experienced difficulties in accessing H&T services or have been unable to do so for disability access reasons will be of particular value. In these situations, people with disabilities often have a strength of feeling or passion about disability access, which is not shared by the H&T industry – it is this passion that the industry needs to harness if access issues are to gain greater importance in the industry.

Organisations of people with disabilities: Organisations of people with disabilities represent the perspectives of people with disabilities and challenge negative, deficit-based knowledge about disability (Beresford, 2016). The primary allegiance of these organisations is to people with disabilities. This stakeholder group would bring advocacy to the collaborative table. By ensuring that they are as independent as possible and avoiding ties to government and businesses, these organisations are able to maintain their advocacy role.

H&T service providers: The H&T service providers, comprising of multiple interdependent operators (e.g. hotels, tourism attraction sites, restaurants, transport agencies, tourist bureaus and destination management organisations), are responsible for service and, therefore, contribute significantly to people with disabilities' H&T experience. H&T service providers bring this service expertise to stakeholder collaboration.

Government agencies: The government, through regulation and legislation, is typically responsible for managing the built environment – physical and adapted infrastructure – that is crucial to sustainable accessible tourism; and for keeping the public informed. Governments have the power, and the legislative knowledge to share with stakeholders, and can use their powerbase to be an effective bridge connecting stakeholders and in facilitating the collaborative effort.

Second, purposive sampling was applied to recruit participants who could provide insight into the study. Interviewees needed to be assessed by the researchers as belonging to one of the four stakeholder groups identified. Emphasis was placed on the heterogeneity of the sample, rather than equal representation of each stakeholder group. It was

Table 1. Participants' profile.

Code	Gender	Age	Stakeholder group
P#1GA	Female	30–40	Government agency
P#2PwD/DPO	Male	40–50	Person with disability
			Organisations of people with disabilities
P#3GA	Male	35–45	Government agency
P#4PwD/DPO	Female	50–60	Person with disability
			Organisations of people with disabilities
P#5DPO/H&T	Female	40–50	Organisations of people with disabilities
			H&T service provider
P#6PwD/GA	Female	40–50	Person with disability
			Government agency
P#7H&T/GA	Female	30–40	H&T service provider
			Government agency
P#8H&T/GA	Male	30–40	H&T service provider
			Government agency
P#9H&T/GA	Female	20–30	H&T service provider
			Government agency
P#10H&T/GA	Male	40–50	H&T service provider
			Government agency
P#11H&T/GA	Male	45–55	H&T service provider
			Government agency
P#12H&T/GA	Male	40–50	H&T service provider
			Government agency
P#13H&T	Male	30–40	H&T service provider
P#14DPO	Male	55–65	Organisations of people with disabilities
P#16PwD	Female	60–70	Person with disability
P#17DPO	Female	40–50	Organisations of people with disabilities
P#18H&T/GA	Female	30–40	H&T service provider
			Government agency
P#19H&T	Male	45–55	H&T service provider

important for the study to uncover not only the perceptions of people with disabilities about the subject under study, but explore the world views of other stakeholders about the issue. Some interviewees were identified as belonging to more than one stakeholder group. This diversity and overlap in stakeholder groups were appreciated as contributing enriched perspectives to the study.

Third, snowballing was used to recruit more interviewees based on recommendation from the initially recruited interviewees. This recruitment approach was suitable because it made it easier to access specifically people with disabilities and their advocates who were willing and able to participate in such demanding in-depth interviews. Following this sampling technique, a total of 19 participants, 10 females and 9 males, with ages ranging from 20 to 70 years, were recruited. One candidate later withdrew from the study leaving 18 participants. Table 1 outlines the demographics of the 18 interviewees.

Data collection

The interviews, which were audio-recorded, involved open-ended and non-leading questions that allowed participants to raise issues they felt were relevant to the discussion. The interviewer began by asking what the respondent felt were the important issues for disability and tourism in the region, directing conversation towards stakeholder involvement later in the interview. Key themes of interest were awareness about disability issues in H&T, community engagement and stakeholder involvement. Interviews, which lasted 1–1.5 hours, were conducted in locations convenient to the participants (i.e. at the participant's office, a public cafe or at the participant's home). Participants were encouraged to talk freely and deeply about their perceptions, feelings and attitudes towards accessible tourism based on their own experiences and acquired knowledge. The interviewer made supplementary notes during and after the interviews, which contributed to the triangulation of the data (Denzin, 1973). All interviews were digitally recorded and transcribed by a third party. The systematic sorting and analysis of data were carried out simultaneously with data collection (Miles et al., 2014).

Data analysis

A thematic approach to data analysis was applied (Corbin & Strauss, 2008; Saldaña, 2015).

In accordance with investigator triangulation process (Denzin, 1973), each co-researcher performed a separate analysis on the data and then systematically compared and contrasted their evaluation in team meetings. This was done over several intervals as the study progressed. Data analysis comprised of three phases. Phase 1 involved initial coding, which was carried out after the researchers were fully familiarised with the content through repeated review of the transcribed interview data. During this phase, sets of codes assessed as associated were assigned subcategory labels. Phase 2 involved focused coding and advanced the theoretical direction of the analysis. This involved a search for patterns within the data and allocation of categories to sets of subcategories.

Table 2 provides an example of how themes were developed during the two phases. In this example, during phase 1, a quote or sentence was coded *Barrier to inclusion* to indicate the obstacles faced by people with disabilities in participation when an interviewee highlighted a reason for non-participation in community affairs. Another piece of data was coded *People with disability as problem* in the same context. These two codes (including others deemed similar) resulted in a subcategory named *Challenges to participation*. In phase 2, several subcategories were grouped to create a yet more focused category. For example, a shared theme that included 'Challenges to participation' and other connected subcategories (e.g. *Building trust* and *Challenges to integration*) was identified and labelled as '*Promote integration and reciprocity*' because this set of subcategories depicted that there was a need for stakeholders to improve integration. A total of 12 *categories* of shared themes linked to different aspects deemed as describing shared experiences from the data-set were created.

Phase 3 involved theoretical coding, a process that comprised the analysis of shared themes and the consequent development of theory. Holding the core theme of stakeholder collaboration for the development of accessible tourism in mind, the researchers revisited the data (including reading notes made during the interviews and consulting post-interview reflective summaries) and searched for relationships between these shared themes so as to illuminate the shared aspects of the participants' lived experiences. Related categories were grouped together and given conceptual labels depicting tactical phases that denoted shared experiences across participant accounts (e.g. *Collaboration and Integration*). Consequently, four such phases were assigned (see Table 3).

Coding was continued until it was assessed that, for the purposes of the study, the appropriate degree of saturation had been attained (Corbin & Strauss, 2008). Saturation was gauged in three ways. First, at data collection, when the interviewer assessed that they had a full understanding of each participant's perspective (Legard, Keegan, & Ward, 2003); second, at data analysis, when coding was exhausted by each of the researchers,

Table 2. Example of coding.

Sample comments	Phase 1 initial coding		Phase 2 focused coding	Phase 3
	Code 1	Subcategories	Categories	Main themes/phases
'The untapped area is those disabilities that aren't as visible as physical and how you get communities to be welcoming of those sorts of people where it's not as overt'	Barriers to inclusion	Challenges to participation	Promote integration and reciprocity	Collaboration and integration
'I mean there are so many things that can be done, and really at not that much more of a cost, and that's something that really bugs me is, as soon as you put disability on anything, people put dollar signs on it, and that's really frustrating'	People with disability as problem			
'Some providers, businesses just see it as another hurdle that they have to jump through or another hoop they have to jump through – another cost – they don't see the benefit'	Trust issues	Building trust		
'I try to take a positive approach with them – an education type awareness type approach'	Sharing knowledge			
'Some [H&T providers] are more receptive than others and others just aren't interested'	No involvement	Challenges to integration		
'So I don't know if the industry has a platform or if they're doing a good enough job to communicate that'	Lack of communication			
			Build relationships Foster ownership	

Table 3. Theoretical coding.

Twelve categories	Four main themes forming the phases of the framework
Leadership	Control and coordination
Contributing to resources	
Creating a conducive environment	
Building awareness	Communication
Ensuring quality of information sources	
Eliminating misunderstandings	
Reducing complexity of information	Clarity of roles
Assisting in delivering common interpretation	
Encouraging action towards common goals	
Building relationships	Collaboration and integration
Promoting integration and reciprocity	
Fostering ownership and level of involvement	

and collectively as a group of researchers, and no new codes were emerging (Urquhart, 2012); and third, when it was assessed that no new themes were emerging from the data (Birks & Mills, 2015).

Limitations of the study

Although the findings have been developed from real-life accounts of lived experiences, our sample may be considered conservative in size, and findings cannot therefore be generalised. In addition, the participants were limited to four primary stakeholder groups. Notwithstanding the justification presented for our choices, the inclusion of secondary stakeholder groups may have presented perspectives that could have added further insight to our findings. It is also recognised that the study is exploratory, based in a country-specific location. Benchmarking across other locations may not be feasible and may require additional research in this area. Despite these limitations, our findings offer a sound contribution towards better understanding stakeholder collaboration at both practical and theoretical levels.

The inclusive tourism stakeholder collaboration framework

Based on findings from our exploratory empirical study and related literature, the inclusive tourism stakeholder collaboration framework is presented as an innovative strategy to increase stakeholder participation in accessible tourism development and to stimulate system changes that encourage the central involvement of people with disabilities. The framework comprises four interrelated and overlapping phases, and operationalises theory by building tactical strategic intent that encourages stakeholder interactions and recognises the specific objectives of each main theme. These phases are: *coordination and control*; *communication*; *clarity of roles and responsibilities*; and *collaboration and integration* (Figure 1).

Theoretically, the framework is designed to transform the stakeholder concept into practice by formulating the main emergent themes to achieve effective stakeholder collaboration. The stakeholder concept advocates legitimising primary stakeholders, working to build relationships and efficiently managing the transactions between stakeholders in order to operationalise effective stakeholder management (Freeman, 1984). Using the findings from the study, therefore, our framework applies these overarching concepts and translates them into tactical approaches that can be applied in practice.

In practice, the framework is an organic, circulatory and developmental mechanism that generates the pertinent issues impeding stakeholder collaboration and recognises that collaboration is a dynamic and emergent process (Gray, 1989) and is continuous and ongoing (Simmons, 1994). The inclusive tourism stakeholder collaboration framework becomes a live emergent process, providing a means to inform concrete ideas from stakeholder deliberations and translate them into actionable plans informed by practice in tandem with stakeholder collaborative processes. As depicted in Figure 1, the feedforward and feedback processes are assisted by the back and forth double arrows connecting the phases, whilst the dotted rectangle around the access and inclusion label, which illustrates amorphous passage of knowledge, allows for open access to ownership, advocacy and reciprocity. The framework works to systematically guide stakeholder deliberation processes that impact on the conceptualisation, implementation and operationalisation of the pertinent issues that drive accessible tourism development.

Findings and discussions

Findings of the present study demonstrate minimal collaboration between stakeholders, as there is little evidence of joint decision-making. These findings align with reports indicating that people with disabilities wish to be involved, but are often excluded from

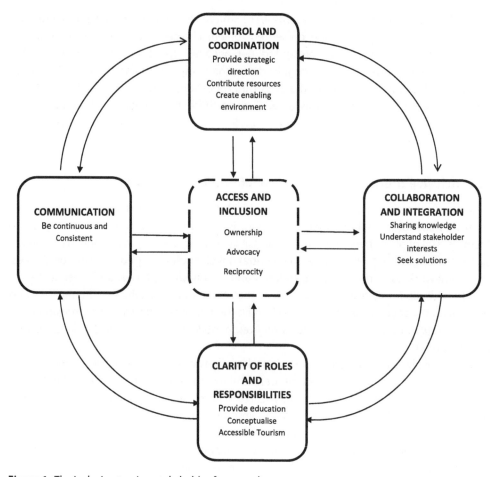

Figure 1. The inclusive tourism stakeholder framework.

participating in policy development (National People with Disabilities and Carer Council, 2009). The following section presents the practical and theoretical aspects of the framework. Each phase is highlighted and draws together the findings that have emerged from this study, supported by substantive literature as appropriate.

Coordination and control

The coordination and control phase is the first component we discuss within this circulatory framework and concerns the management and leadership of the collaborative initiative. Our research revealed a void in the area of leadership and coordination, and there appeared to be a lack of confidence about whether effective stakeholder collaboration could be achieved. One participant from a government agency remarked:

> I think probably the government probably has a role to play [in leadership], but in talking to other stakeholders, especially in my local communities, it's been whether or not we have the capacity to ... talk to people within the community. (P#3GA)

Evidence suggested that other stakeholders held parallel views about whether collaborative initiatives would be successful, from recognising that 'in terms of a coordinated approach I don't think there is one' (P#4PwD/DPO) to admitting that collaboration is 'not working the way that it should... So if that's the case then something is not right there' (P#7H&T/GA). These sentiments were surprising, given the hype surrounding government efforts to promote accessible tourism through legislation. It was apparent that much more needs to be done in terms of leadership to ensure effective collaboration. An effective stakeholder collaboration approach requires a facilitator as well as access to adequate resources (Byrd, 2007; Gray, 1989). Government, through its agencies, and given its role of managing the enactment of disability legislation, has a critical role to play here and is the most logical choice for a leadership role (Darcy, 2011; Gillovic & McIntosh, 2015; Shaw et al., 2005). The assumption, however, should not be that the government will necessarily fulfil this leadership role. Governments often view collaboration as risky and worry about the loss of control on decision-making (Jamal & Getz, 1995). Governments have also been found to harbour misconceptions and stereotypes that influence their attitudes and behaviours (National People with Disabilities and Carer Council, 2009), leaving participants wondering about people with 'those disabilities that aren't as visible as physical and how you get communities to be welcoming of those sorts of people' (P#2PwD). Holding such negative perspectives has consequences in policy creation and dissemination and can result in the ratification of policies and initiatives that act as barriers rather than offering solutions. Our research suggests that the responsibility of leadership or power should not lie solely with the government, but should be shared by members from other stakeholder groups, such as people with disabilities, or advocacy group members. This aligns with Gillovic and McIntosh's (2015) finding that a 'meeting-in-the-middle' approach to stakeholder participation would work best for accessible tourism development. Facilitation of such efforts could be made by placing members of stakeholder groups, other than the government, in leadership roles and ensuring that opportunities for leadership training are provided. Such endeavours would contribute to the creation of an enabling environment, which in turn could encourage collaboration and maintain momentum. Genuine involvement of stakeholders in collaborative efforts can help alleviate perceived power imbalances and move stakeholder networks towards more trusting relationships. The coordination and control phase is therefore critical to effective collaboration. It provides leadership, contributes to resources necessary for projects and creates an enabling environment for involvement. Its focus is to provide direction, seek buy-in and engender ownership. In practice, this phase is instrumental for getting people together, monitoring involvement, motivating stakeholders and addressing any issues that arise.

Communication

Communication is the second phase of the framework. This is an essential phase because access to information is vital for effective operationalisation of stakeholder collaboration. Given that accessible tourism continues to experience slow progress, it was not surprising to uncover from the study that communication was problematic. Across the board, concerns were raised about the lack of access to relevant information:

> People haven't realised the value of that information... finding the information is difficult. (P#5DPO/H&T)

> We aren't getting the information ...We don't know who else to call other than Access WA if we have a question. (P#8H&T/GA)
>
> I think we would be more inclined to get involved ...if we were clear on things. (P#2PwD/DPO)

Literature confirms that the lack of accessing relevant information is a major barrier to participation and social inclusion. Eichhorn et al. (2008) established that high fragmentation and lack of geographical reach of information were critical barriers that required deeper understanding of people with disabilities' differential needs. Similarly, Darcy (2010) found that information formats often did not consider the dimensions of disability and the level of support needs required to access information. This situation is disturbing, since the ability to access quality information facilitates more accurate decision-making about participation. It is important that information is consistent, continuous and in preferred formats that address the heterogeneous nature of disabilities, with clear intent to communicate a useful message articulately, and with best intentions. Participants reported that if accessed at all, information was often contradictory, irregular and complex. One local government participant stated:

> I just think that legislations have changed so much and so quickly and the communication back to the service providers hasn't happened or isn't continuous; it's a little bit hit and miss. ... (P#1GA)

As this is a long-standing and challenging issue, creative strategies must be initiated to resolve the quality of and access to information. One suggestion presented by several stakeholders to reduce misinterpretation and to improve accessibility was a central repository. Participants had visions of 'a database with current and up to date information' (P#7H&T/GA), emphasising the benefits of having 'one central resource that we can direct everyone to ...' (P #3GA) and 'one output source [that] everyone can link into' (P #14DPO). Whilst a central repository could improve information accessibility and help reduce misunderstandings, there are inherent financial and technological challenges. For example, all stakeholders, and in particular people with disabilities, would need accessible information technologies, such as computers or smartphones, which may need to be adapted to their particular needs. This could be challenging specifically for people with disabilities, given that they tend to have lower socio-economic status within communities (Schur, Kruse, & Blanck, 2013). This finding, however, underscored the lack of access to information as an impediment to effective stakeholder collaboration. Strategies that move information accessibility towards full inclusion need multifaceted and sophisticated approaches (Darcy, 2011; Eichhorn et al., 2008). In particular, the ability of people with disabilities to access relevant information about events, initiatives and deliberations is fundamental to their involvement. Therefore, a major purpose of the communication phase is to enhance the quality of information sources, eliminate misunderstandings and build awareness of relevant issues. In practice, this phase is tasked with ensuring that communication to all stakeholders is continuous and consistent and that the strategies employed undertake differential needs assessments and consider preferred formats, as appropriate.

Clarity of roles and responsibilities

Clarity of roles and responsibilities is the third phase of the framework. This phase offers support to the coordination and control phase by ensuring that the contribution of each stakeholder group to the collaboration process is transparently and collaboratively clarified and understood. Establishing the value of a stakeholder's contribution is a significant part of legitimising stakeholders within the collaborative process. Given the critical leadership role that the government can play in facilitating effective collaboration (Darcy, 2011; Gillovic & McIntosh, 2015), it was encouraging to reveal that the government, at least in theory if not in practice, appeared in general to be aware of their leadership role. One participant stated:

> Well I think local government certainly have a role to play, because most local government authorities would prescribe to that community...wanting to have all members of the community involved, because it creates a diverse and richer environment for everybody. (P#3GA)

However, a relational issue emerged between other stakeholder groups, indicating a need for role clarity and relationship building. People with disabilities and their advocates held the opinion that government and H&T providers were 'probably not aware of their obligations in some cases' (P#2PwD/DPO) and 'just aren't interested' (P#17DPO) in collaboration. On the other hand, H&T providers felt that 'Disability agencies need to be more involved' (P#10H&T/GA). This underscored the challenges that often face collaboration activities in practice. It was also apparent that a lack of comprehension about accessibility issues in H&T was contributing to misinterpretations of roles and responsibilities. For example, a person with disabilities from a government agency remarked:

> ... the new standards... they're really hard to navigate and to go through ... unless you actually know how to link them all up and do it – and it's very easy to miss things, and it's very easy not to get it right. (P#6DP/GA)

An H&T service provider commented:

> I'm sure there's a knowledge gap you know even for us in terms of understanding disabled tourists and the industry as well. (P#12H&T/GA)

It was clear that education and training would be critical. Although underrated in tourism development, education is a fundamental element to effective participation (Cárdenas et al., 2015). This is because active collaboration can only be achieved if stakeholders have the requisite knowledge (Simmons, 1994). It follows that awareness and understanding of critical issues that impact the implementation and operationalisation of accessible tourism must be encouraged. Consequently, in order to promote a common understanding of the term 'accessible tourism', a common conceptualisation of the concept is important (Darcy et al., 2010; Gillovic & McIntosh, 2015). Such an understanding allows multiple stakeholders to collectively address concerns and determine mutually agreed upon objectives that can benefit all stakeholders. Thus, this phase of the framework works to reduce the complexity of information, assist in achieving common interpretation and encourage action towards mutual objectives. In practice, the capacity of stakeholders to participate can be reviewed at this point, and education and training strategies utilised as appropriate. The framework can, therefore, be useful in facilitating role clarity between stakeholders so that each stakeholder can contribute strategically towards a common goal.

Collaboration and integration

This is the fourth phase presented in the framework. Collaborative efforts must begin to build a knowledge base that gels key stakeholders' divergent views and informs policy formulation. Stakeholders are, therefore, provided opportunities to exchange lived experiences on issues pertaining to accessible tourism. Opportunities to share knowledge become the platform from which the capacity for knowledge is created and strengthened. Yet, it was apparent that there was little cooperation happening between stakeholders to make knowledge-sharing better. A government employee remarked:

> ... It's a grim answer I guess but more engagement is definitely something that we could do more of, do differently. And I think that goes for all parties in government and in industry you know more and more engagement, more talking about the issue. (P#12H&T/GA)

This finding emphasised the current deficiencies in integration strategies. There are definite advantages however, when localised knowledge permeates decision-making processes and informs policy formulation. The decisions made about the development of accessible tourism should, therefore, include shared knowledge and experiences of all stakeholders (Cárdenas et al., 2015; Simmons, 1994). Moreover, and as advanced by Daruwalla and Darcy's (2005) study, understanding critical stakeholder issues can only be effectively done through the process of engagement and knowledge-sharing. To demonstrate the impact of non-collaboration, people with disabilities shared stories that confirmed the misconceptions surrounding accessibility. Their accounts demonstrated vast discrepancies between what they and the service providers considered to be an accessible environment. One respondent with disabilities explained:

> And they don't know ...and it's not until you know the right questions to ask and you start digging deeper that you actually realise, well no it's not [accessible]. And I've actually had people argue with me and say, well it is. And I'm like, well no it's not. So, you know, just because something has a bar in it, or there's no step into it doesn't mean that it's accessible. (P#6DP/GA)

The stories shared demonstrated the apparent gaps in policy formulation that inform the implementation of accessible tourism, suggesting a focus on explicit rather than tacit knowledge evaluation as a means to building knowledge capacities. Accessible tourism knowledge that is transferred into policy could benefit from more infusion of tacit knowledge from stakeholders. Further, harnessing tacit knowledge about the development of accessible tourism from people with the lived experience of disability and access issues would be a positive move towards inclusive tourism. The study revealed a sense of urgency from people with disabilities about acting to expedite the process to inclusion. They voiced considerable frustration and disappointment about the slow pace of change. One participant declared:

> People living with disabilities in Margaret River they need to sort of get together and gradually go and visit every hotel – [to confirm] yes they've got disabled access... no yes no yes. So that they meet some guidelines. (P#16PwD)

Despite this call to activism, there was an awareness that collaborative efforts and interaction would not be easy and would present challenges that would need to be overcome.

Participants seemed to recognise that the road to building relationships and creating an environment of trust through collaborative exchanges would be challenging and emotive. One participant remarked:

> ... people are going to get really pissed because they're being held, you know, or told they're not accessible, but then you know what, that's your choice, isn't' it, then you can actually then do something, at least then you know you're not accessible... (P #6PwD/GA)

In recognition of these challenges, the collaboration and integration phase could help promote integration and reciprocity, build relationships and foster ownership of the collaboration process. To progress accessible tourism, ownership and accountability during stakeholder deliberations are imperative (Gillovic & McIntosh, 2015). Appropriate engagement strategies that suit stakeholder needs and capabilities, and encourage open communication in an empathetic and respectful way, with the objective of building mutuality between stakeholders, need to be employed. In practice, this is the opportunity for knowledge-sharing, a time to identify and understand stakeholder interests and seek practical solutions. Practical initiatives could be using advocates or champions to hold workshops and events to facilitate collaboration, where stories can be shared, objectives set and achievements celebrated.

Conclusions

Stakeholder collaboration has the potential to improve the implementation and operationalisation of accessible tourism. However, the ways in which stakeholders collaborate (or not) in accessible tourism development have thus far remained underexamined. This study has started to address this gap in knowledge, by exploring how accessible tourism stakeholders collaborate in an area of Western Australia and opening up discussion of this important issue. The paper makes two key contributions. The paper contributes to the sparsely researched area of stakeholder collaboration in the development of accessible tourism. A framework that can be strategically applied in the implementation of collaborative approaches to the development of accessible tourism is also proposed. The findings suggest that when there are multiple and diverse stakeholders at play, an organic, circulatory and developmental approach to stakeholder collaboration should be adopted to innovatively move towards inclusive tourism. The development of accessible tourism requires more than passive participation. It requires strategic direction that will encourage active collaboration between stakeholder networks with an agenda to extend the accessible tourism concept to a more inclusive approach.

The framework offered in this paper has the potential to guide and direct stakeholders, with clear directions provided on how to approach the process and begin to work together. It also begins to clarify the lens through which the experiences of people with disabilities should be viewed – a lens focused clearly on the barriers to inclusion in mainstream tourism, rather than on perceived individual deficits. The framework advances practical strategies and recommendations, first and foremost being the central involvement of people with disabilities in the development of accessible tourism. The full involvement of people with disabilities in stakeholder deliberations will need resources in the form of time, effort and investment and involves a whole-of-life approach that includes social, political and economic initiatives. People with disabilities are less likely to engage in stakeholder collaboration efforts to solve community issues (Schur et al., 2013). This is also a group that will most likely have lower level resources to participate (such as income levels or education), greater isolation and lower likelihood of perceiving their contribution to such initiatives as valuable. Second, initiatives to encourage ownership and advocacy will be critical to the successful implementation of the framework. For example, champions from different stakeholder groups taking responsibility for different assignments, such as running workshops and delivering talks, could encourage integration. Third, stakeholders would need to make efforts to collaborate across stakeholder groups – for example, people with disabilities being invited as guest speakers during H&T operations training sessions to share their experiences.

The applicability of the framework is far-reaching. Social model understandings of disability and the central involvement of people with disabilities in stakeholder collaboration have universal application when we consider disability and accessible tourism as social constructs. Concerns for access and inclusion are significant globally. As many communities worldwide continue to contemplate access and inclusion, the role and voice of people with disabilities can offer valuable insights that could usefully be taken into account in policy formulation and development of accessible tourism. The proposed framework does not rely on country-specific legislation or characteristics. Thus, it can be applied for stakeholder collaboration at any destination worldwide, albeit with context-specific adjustments. Therefore, future research can test the relevant application of this framework in other regional or urban environments in other continents of the world. Gathering insights from stakeholders of other communities would also allow for international comparisons concerning stakeholder collaboration. Additional research that illustrates understandings of stakeholder collaborations where people with disabilities are holistically included would be particularly valuable, and applying the stakeholder theory to such research could contribute to further development of the theory by highlighting its applicability in accessible tourism development. Finally, the outcomes of this study contribute to the important agenda of advancing accessible tourism beyond access issues and towards inclusive tourism – an ideal that promotes full inclusion and participation in stakeholder collaborations, as well as equal access for all.

Disclosure statement

No potential conflict of interest was reported by the authors.

ORCID

Julie Nyanjom http://orcid.org/0000-0002-5878-4130

References

Arnstein, S. R. (1969). A ladder of citizen participation. *Journal of the American Institute of Planners, 35*(4), 216–224.
Beresford, P. (2016). *All our welfare: Towards participatory social policy*. Bristol: Policy Press.
Birks, M., & Mills, J. (2015). *Grounded theory: A practical guide*. London: Sage.
Boxall, K., Nyanjom, J., & Slaven, J. (2018). Disability, hospitality and the new sharing economy. *International Journal of Contemporary Hospitality Management, 30*(1), 539–556.
Buhalis, D., & Darcy, S. (Eds.). (2011). *Accessible tourism: Concepts and issues*. Bristol: Channel View Publications.
Butler, R. W. (1999). Sustainable tourism: A state-of-the-art review. *Tourism Geographies, 1*(1), 7–25.
Byrd, E. T. (2007). Stakeholders in sustainable tourism development and their roles: Applying stakeholder theory to sustainable tourism development. *Tourism Review, 62*(2), 6–13.
Chenoweth, L. (2000). Closing the doors: Insights and reflections on deinstitutionalisation. *Law in Context, 17*(2), 77.
Clarkson, M. E. (1995). A stakeholder framework for analyzing and evaluating corporate social performance. *Academy of Management Review, 20*(1), 92–117.
Cohen, J. M., & Uphoff, N. T. (1980). Participation's place in rural development: Seeking clarity through specificity. *World Development, 8*(3), 213–235.
Corbin, J., & Strauss, A. (2008). *Basics of qualitative research: Techniques and procedures for developing grounded theory* (3rd ed.). Thousand Oaks, CA: Sage.
Cárdenas, D. A., Byrd, E. T., & Duffy, L. N. (2015). An exploratory study of community awareness of impacts and agreement to sustainable tourism development principles. *Tourism and Hospitality Research, 15*(4), 254–266.
Darcy, S. (2010). Inherent complexity: Disability, accessible tourism and accommodation information preferences. *Tourism Management, 31*(6), 816–826.
Darcy, S. (2011). Developing sustainable approaches to accessible accommodation information provision: A foundation for strategic knowledge management. *Tourism Recreation Research, 36*(2), 141–157.
Darcy, S., & Dickson, T. J. (2009). A whole-of-life approach to tourism: The case for accessible tourism experiences. *Journal of Hospitality and Tourism Management, 16*(1), 32–44.
Darcy, S., & Pegg, S. (2011). Towards strategic intent: Perceptions of disability service provision amongst hotel accommodation managers. *International Journal of Hospitality Management, 30*(2), 468–476.
Darcy, S., Cameron, B., & Pegg, S. (2010). Accessible tourism and sustainability: A discussion and case study. *Journal of Sustainable Tourism, 18*(4), 515–537.
Daruwalla, P., & Darcy, S. (2005). Personal and societal attitudes to disability. *Annals of Tourism Research, 32*(3), 549–570.
Denzin, N. K. (1973). *The research act: A theoretical introduction to sociological methods*. New York, NY: Routledge.
Eichhorn, V., Miller, G., Michopoulou, E., & Buhalis, D. (2008). Enabling access to tourism through information schemes? *Annals of Tourism Research, 35*(1), 189–210.
Freeman, R. E. (1984). *Strategic management: A stakeholder approach*. Boston, MA: Pitman.
Gillovic, B., & McIntosh, A. (2015). Stakeholder perspectives of the future of accessible tourism in New Zealand. *Journal of Tourism Futures, 1*(3), 221–237.
Grady, J., & Ohlin, J. B. (2009). Equal access to hospitality services for guests with mobility impairments under the Americans with Disabilities Act: Implications for the hospitality industry. *International Journal of Hospitality Management, 28*(1), 161–169.
Gray, B. (1989). *Collaborating: Finding common ground for multiparty problems*. San Francisco, CA: Jossey-Bass.
Hart, S. L., & Sharma, S. (2004). Engaging fringe stakeholders for competitive imagination. *The Academy of Management Executive, 18*(1), 7–18.

Higgins-Desbiolles, F. (2006). More than an 'industry': The forgotten power of tourism as a social force. *Tourism Management, 27*, 1192–1208.

Jamal, T. B., & Getz, D. (1995). Collaboration theory and community tourism planning. *Annals of Tourism Research, 22*(1), 186–204.

Legard, R., Keegan, J., & Ward, K. (2003). In-depth interviews. In J. Ritchie & J. Lewis (Eds.), *Qualitative research practice: A guide for social science students and researchers* (pp. 138–169). London: Sage.

Michopoulou, E., & Buhalis, D. (2011). Stakeholder analysis of accessible tourism. In D. Buhalis & S. Darcy (Eds.), *Accessible tourism: Concepts and issues* (pp. 260–273). Bristol: Channel View Publications.

Michopoulou, E., Darcy, S., Ambrose, I., & Buhalis, D. (2015). Accessible tourism futures: The world we dream to live in and the opportunities we hope to have. *Journal of Tourism Futures, 1*(3), 179–188.

Miles, M. B., Huberman, A. M., & Saldana, J. (2014). *Qualitative data analysis: A methods sourcebook* (3rd ed.). Thousand Oaks, CA: Sage.

National People with Disabilities and Carer Council. (2009). *Shut out: The experience of people with disabilities and their families in Australia* (National Disability Strategy Consultation Report No.). Retrieved from Australian Government Department of Social Services website: https://www.dss.gov.au/sites/default/files/documents/05_2012/nds_report.pdf

Nunkoo, R., Smith, S. L., & Ramkissoon, H. (2013). Residents' attitudes to tourism: A longitudinal study of 140 articles from 1984 to 2010. *Journal of Sustainable Tourism, 21*(1), 5–25.

O'Neill, M., & Knight, J. (2000). Disability tourism dollars in Western Australia hotels. *Hospitality Review, 18*(2), 72–88.

Oliver, M., & Barnes, C. (2012). *The new politics of disablement*. Basingstoke: Palgrave Macmillan.

Patterson, I., Darcy, S., & Mönninghoff, M. (2012). Attitudes and experiences of tourism operators in Northern Australia towards people with disabilities. *World Leisure Journal, 54*(3), 215–229.

Poria, Y., Reichel, A., & Brandt, Y. (2011). Dimensions of hotel experience of people with disabilities: An exploratory study. *International Journal of Contemporary Hospitality Management, 23*(5), 571–591.

Rosen, A. (2006). The Australian experience of deinstitutionalization: Interaction of Australian culture with the development and reform of its mental health services. *Acta Psychiatrica Scandinavica, 113*(s429), 81–89.

Ryan, C. (2002). Equity, management, power sharing and sustainability—Issues of the 'new tourism'. *Tourism Management, 23*(1), 17–26.

Saldaña, J. (2015). *The coding manual for qualitative researchers*. Thousand Oaks, CA: Sage.

Scheyvens, R., & Biddulph, R. (2017). Inclusive tourism development. *Tourism Geographies*, 1–21, 10.1080/14616688.2017.1381985.

Schur, L., Kruse, D., & Blanck, P. (2013). *People with disabilities: Sidelined or mainstreamed?* New York, NY: Cambridge University Press. Retrieved from ProQuest Ebook Central, https://ebookcentral.proquest.com/lib/ECU/detail.action?docID=1357327.

Shaw, G., & Coles, T. (2004). Disability, holiday making and the tourism industry in the UK: A preliminary survey. *Tourism Management, 25*(3), 397–403.

Shaw, G., Veitch, C., & Coles, T. (2005). Access, disability, and tourism: Changing responses in the United Kingdom. *Tourism Review International, 8*(3), 167–176.

Shelton, E. J., & Tucker, H. (2005). Tourism and disability: Issues beyond access. *Tourism Review International, 8*, 211–219

Simmons, D. G. (1994). Community participation in tourism planning. *Tourism Management, 15*(2), 98–108.

Stumbo, N., & Pegg, S. (2005). Travelers and tourists with disabilities: A matter of priorities and loyalties. *Tourism Review International, 8*(3), 195–209.

Thomas, C. (2007). *Sociologies of disability and illness: Contested ideas in disability studies and medical sociology*. Basingstoke: Palgrave Macmillan.

Union of the Physically Impaired Against Segregation. (1976). *Fundamental principles of disability*, London union of the physically impaired against segregation/the disability alliance. Retrieved from http://disability-studies.leeds.ac.uk/files/library/UPIAS-fundamental-principles.pdf

Urquhart, C. (2012). *Grounded theory for qualitative research: A practical guide*. Thousand Oaks, CA: Sage.

Vernon, J., Essex, S., Pinder, D., & Curry, K. (2005). Collaborative policymaking: Local sustainable projects. *Annals of Tourism Research, 32*(2), 325–345.

Waligo, V. M., Clarke, J., & Hawkins, R. (2013). Implementing sustainable tourism: A multi-stakeholder involvement management framework. *Tourism Management, 36*, 342–353.

Yau, M., McKercher, B., & Packer, T. (2004). Traveling with a disability: More than an access issue. *Annals of Tourism Research, 31*(4), 946–960.

Index

Note: **Bold** page numbers refer to tables, *italic* page numbers refer to figures.

ABOUTAsia school programme 59
ABOUTAsia tours: enterprise, story of 59–60; future plans and challenges 60; social impacts 60
accessibility features 98
Accessibility of Monitoring and Control Regulations 104
accessibility provision 103
accessible tourism **13**, 13–14, 95, 99, 104; definition of 113; fundamental goal of 113–114; stakeholder collaboration in 116–118; stakeholder theory 116; understanding disabilities 114–115
activity stage 96, **97**, 98
adequate information systems 97
Aguiar, L. M. 74
Alegre, I. 53
'all-inclusives' tourism 8
Alter, K. 53
animal rights 40
Anna Cederberg Gerdrup 17
anti-foreigner political parties in Europe 19–20
Apollo 4, 30, 32–33; communication management department 33; CSR and sustainability management 33–34; ECPAT–code 34–35; outbound tour operator market 33; social components of **34**; SOS children's villages 35; statement of commitment on human rights 36–37; suppliers' code of conduct 36; travelife sustainability system 35–36
Apollo Nordic group 40
Arnstein, S. R. 118
Artisans Angkor: enterprise, story of 56; future plans and challenges 56; social impacts 56
Asociacion Espa nola de Gobernantas de Hotel y Otras Entidades (ASEGO) 79
Australia indigenous festivals 19
Australian ICOMOS Burra Charter 99
'avoiding reputational damage' 9

Backlund, Sandra 4
Bakker, M. 9
balancing interests 44–45
Barnes, C. 114
barrier to inclusion 121
Berbegal-Mirabent, J. 53
Biddulph, R. 3–5, 62, 73
Boxall, Kathy 4
Britton, S. 74
buffering/decoupling 42
Buhalis, D. 112, 117
business-centric approaches 10
business-to-business sustainability certification programme 35
Butler, G. 19, 118

Cape Town Declaration 15
Centre for Tourism in Gothenburg 2
Chancellor, H. C. 95
Chantiers-Ecoles de Formation Professionnelle (CEFP) 56
citizen power degree 118
class and gender sensitive approach 87
climate change 34
Cochrane, J. 53
codes of conduct 33
coding, example of 121, **122**
coercive isomorphism 38, 40
Cole, S. 95
collaboration and integration 127–129
collaborative platforms 43–44
collective interests, defence of 84–85
Commercial Sexual Exploitation of Children 34
communication 125–126
community based tourism 12, **13**, 15
community involvement 117
complex institutional environments 44–45
compromise and sense-making 43–44
coordination and control 124–125

corporate social responsibility (CSR) 3–4, 18, 30–30; Apollo, social components of **34**; and collaboration partners 32; inclusive tourism issues 4; and sustainability work 42–43; travelife certification system 40
Costoulas, Fotios 33
'critical case' approach 32
Crompton, J. L. 95
Cukier, J. 11
cultural desecration 2
cultural heritage sites 99
customer service 82

Dara, H. 57, 58
Darcy, S. 95, 97, 112, 126, 128
Daruwella, P. 128
data analysis 121–122
data collection 120–121
'decent work' concept 4, 73, 74
decision-making process 16, 64–65, 73, 116, 118
decision-making stage 96, **97**, 98
Delmas, M. A. 38
de-professionalisation 82–83
despite barriers 95
disability legislation 114
Dodge, M. 17
domestic tourism 17
Dubai 36, 37

economic benefits of tourism 19
economic development 9, 72
economic empowerment 23
economic geography of tourism 74
economic inequality 2
ECPAT–code 34–35
Eichhorn, V. 126
elements of inclusive tourism: decision-making 64–65; production of tourism 62–63; supporting self-representation 63–64; tourism map 65–66
emergency help program in Syria 35
Emmott, R. 53
employee wellbeing 4, 33
employment, insecurity 81–82
employment opportunities 9, 20, 73
Employment Ordinance for the Hospitality Industry 78
empowerment 19
environmental barriers 2, 95
ethical production and consumption 10
ethnic groups 19
European Industry Association Tour Operator Initiative 35
European social movements 53
European Union 35
European Union project 56
Evcil, A. N. 5, 100

exacerbating disability 115
exclusive tourism 2

Fair Trade in Tourism (FTT) 16
'feminisation' 75
filtering institutional pressures 41
financial crisis 72
Freeman, R. E. 116
French development assistance project 56

geography of tourism 73–74
German REWE-travel group 32
Gillovic, B. 125
government agencies 119
Grameen Credit Agricole Microfinance Foundation 57
group CSR strategy 34

Hall, Michael 4
Ha Long Bay, Vietnam 9
Hampton, M. 9
'handicapitalism' 103
Hanekom, Derek 19
Harvey, David 73
Haven, training restaurant: enterprise, story of 60–61; future plans and challenges 62; social impacts 61–62
health problems accentuation 83–84
Herod, Andrew 73
Higgins-Desbiolles, F. 19
historic place visiting **101**
hospitality agreement 80
Hospitality and Tourism (H&T) industry 112, 113, 119
hotel maid employment 36; collective interests, defence of 84–85; de-professionalisation 82–83; employment, insecurity 81–82; health problems accentuation 83–84; housekeepers 72; labour conditions 76; outsourcing processes 76; professional category loss 80; representation, capacity of 84–85; salary reduction 80; segmentation, hotel staff 83; Spanish hotel industry 78–79; timetables, insecurity 81–82; women housekeeping employees 75; workers' health 75; work overload 80–81; work schedule, insecurity 81–82
housekeepers 72
H&T service providers 119
2009 Human Development Report 10
human geography 74
human resource management 74
human rights 33, 34

ICOMOS (International Council of Monuments and Sites) 99
illegal labour 36

INDEX

immigrant workers 83
impairment (functional limitation) 115
inclusive business (IB) models 9
inclusive growth agenda 9
inclusive tourism: balancing interests 44–45; buffering/decoupling 42; coercive isomorphism 40; collaborative platforms 43–44; complex institutional environments 44–45; compromise and sense-making 43–44; concept of 2–3, 8–11; CSR and sustainability work 42–43; definition of 2, 8, 10–12; elements of 11, *12*; filtering institutional pressures 41; mimetic isomorphism 39–40; normative isomorphism 40–41; organizational responses 41; participation of 16–21; tourism and development 12–15; types of *29*; UNDP definition 10
inclusive tourism stakeholder framework **124**; clarity of roles and responsibilities 126–127; collaboration and integration 127–129; communication 125–126; coordination and control 124–125
information communication technology (ICT) 97
institutional isomorphic pressures concepts 38
institutional theory 37–39
intellectual disabilities 114–115
interactive barriers 95
International Centre for Responsible Tourism 15
International Labour Organisation (ILO) 4, 36, 73
International Social Tourism Organisation's (ISTO) Montreal Declaration 73
International Union of Architecture (UIA) 104
intrinsic barriers 95
investigator triangulation process 121
Ioannides, D. 74

Jeyacheya, J. 9

Khmer cultural heritage 56
Kitchin, R. 17
Kuoni group 4, 32, 34–37
Kuoni's Group CSR Strategy 33, 34
Kuoni Suppliers Code of Conduct 37

labour flexibility 75, 84
Labour Force Survey (LFS) 72
labour management 72
labour market reform 72, 78
labour policies 72
labour rights 4, 36
'ladder of citizen participation' 118
language of inclusive tourism 19
Law on Labour Relations 78
Lawson, V. 10
leisure: definition of 94; ravel motivations 95; and tourism activities 94; and tourism industries 96–99

Long, P. H. 9
lower wages 75

MacCannell, D. 63
McClain, L. 100
Mace, Ron 100
McGuire, F. 95
McIntosh, A. 125
'maintaining competitive position' 9
Maori people of New Zealand 20
marginalized people: mutual understanding 19–20; self-representation 20; self-representation of 73; as tourism consumers 16–17; in tourism decision-making 18–19; tourism map 17–18; as tourism producers 16; transforming power relations 20–21
Marques, J. C. 11
mass tourism 14, 15, 30
mass unemployment in Spain 75
Mayfield, S. 97
Mdee, A. 53
'meeting-in-the-middle' approach 125
mental illness 114–115
Messerli, H. R. 9
Michopoulou, E. 117
migrant workers 36, 37
mimetic isomorphism 39–40
Mowforth, M. 21
Moyo, A. M. 100
Munt, I. 21
Munyonga, E. 100
'must see places' 99

natural environment 33
negative social impacts 2
neoliberal capitalism 74
neoliberalism 21, 72
nineteenth-century cooperative movements 53
non-collaboration impact 128
non-governmental organizations (NGOs) 33, 100
non-participation 118
normative isomorphism 38, 40–41
Nyanjom, Julie 4

objectification process 20
Ochheuteal Beach in Cambodia 11
Oliver, M. 38, 41, 114
organisations of people with disabilities 119
organizational responses 41
outbound tour operators 29, 30, 33
outsourcing processes 76; collective interests, defence of 84–85; de-professionalisation 82–83; employment, insecurity 81–82; health problems accentuation 83–84; labour conditions 76; professional category loss 80; representation, capacity of 84–85;

salary reduction 80; segmentation, hotel staff 83; Spanish hotel industry 78–79; timetables, insecurity 81–82; work overload 80–81; work schedule, insecurity 81–82
ownership opportunities 16
Öztürk, Y. 104

Pappalepore, I. 19
participants methods: government agencies 119; H&T service providers 119; organisations of people with disabilities 119; people with disabilities 119; snowballing 120
participation lack 117, 118
Patterson, T. S. 96
peace through tourism 12, **13**, 14–15
Pearce, P. L. 18
people with disabilities (PWD) 94–95, 112, 119; accessible tourism 95, 99; despite barriers 95; environmental barriers 95; interactive barriers 95; intrinsic barriers 95; leisure and tourism industries 96–99; non-governmental organizations 100; as problem 121; social model of 115
Performing Arts School 57
Phare circus 56, 64, 65
phare performing social enterprise (PPSE): enterprise, story of 56–57; future plans and challenges 58; social impacts 57
Phare Ponleu Selpak Association (PPSA) 56–57
Phnom-Penh-based group Social Enterprise Cambodia 54
physical accessibility **101**
Physically Impaired Against Segregation 115
Pingeot, L. 18
political empowerment 72
'positive visibility' 19
Post-2015 agenda 18
poverty-alleviation/sustainability agenda 21
poverty reduction 9
poverty tourism 63, 72
practitioner-academic movement 14
Private-Community Partnerships in Uganda 21
production of tourism 62–63
professional category loss 80
profit maximization 18
pro-poor tourism (PPT) 9, 12, **13**, 14
'public space,' definition of 104
public transportation 98
push-and-pull model 95

'rational myths' 40
Ray, N. M. 98
refugee crisis 19–20
refugees, social inclusion of 23
remapping tourism process 17
representation, capacity of 84–85
responsible tourism **13**, 14, 15, 31

risk management 31
Rodriguez, P. R. 94
Rogerson, C. M. 19
Run project 20
'rural experiences' 65
Ryder, M. E. 98

Saarinen, J. 8
salary reduction 80
Scandinavia 32
Scheyvens, R. 3, 4, 62, 73
Schultz, K. 63
segmentation, hotel staff 83
self-representation 20
Sen, L. 97
'sense-making' 43
sexual exploitation of children 34
Shi, L. 95
Siem Reap's tourism sector 3, 52, **55**, 56–62
Slaven, Janine 4
Small, J. 97
Smith, A. 19
Smith, R. 95
social dialogue 73
social enterprise: ABOUTAsia tours 59–60; Artisans Angkor 56; elements of inclusive tourism 62–66; as emerging sector 52–54; Haven, training restaurant 60–62; phare performing social enterprise 56–58; Siem Reap's tourism sector **55**, 56–62; Soria Moria hotel 58–59
'social innovation' 53
social integration 18
social programme 56
social protection 73
social responsibility agenda 43
social sustainability 94
social tourism 12, **13**, 14
socio-economic goals 21
Solidarity Tourism Company 21
Somavía, Juan 73
Soria Moria hotel: enterprise, history of 58; future plans and challenges 59; social impacts 58–59
SOS children's villages 35
space tourism 2
Spain *see* hotel maid employment
Spanish Association of Head Housekeepers in Hotels and Other Organisations 79
Spanish hotel industry 78–79
Spanish job market 83
Spanish People's Party 78
staff management 79
stakeholder collaboration 112; accessible tourism development 117; citizen power degree 118; data analysis 121–122; data collection 120–121; definition of 116;

identification and legitimisation of 116; inclusive tourism 123; participation lack 117; relationship-building processes 116; stakeholder groups 117; stakeholder theory 116; theoretical coding 121–122; tokenism degree 118
stakeholder management 33
stakeholder theory 116
statement of commitment on human rights 36–37
Statute of Workers' Rights 78
Sultanahmet Square 94, 100, **101–103**
suppliers' codes of conduct 36, 42
supporting self-representation 63–64
sustainability 30–32; mapping and priority setting of 33; supply chain management 33, 34
sustainable development goals (SDGs) 8, 10, 18
sustainable products 33, 34
'symbolic compliance' 4
Syrian conflict 19–20

territorial dimension 17
thematic approach 121
theoretical coding 121, **122**
timetables, insecurity 81–82
Timothy, D. 18
Todd, C. 100
Toffel, W. M. 38
tokenism degree 118
tourism businesses 34
tourism consumers 16–17
tourism corporations 31
tourism decision-making 18–19
tourism employment 75
tourism-led inclusive growth 9
tourism map 65–66
tourism market 3, 9, 16, 63
tourism production 16
Tourism Workers Union 21
tour operator sector 30–32
tour package legislation 31–32
trade union organisations workers 79
'traditional hospitality' 63

transformational tourism 3
transforming power relations 20–21
travelife certification system 37
travelife sustainability system 35–37
Travelife system 33
travel market 29
Tren Ecuador 16, 22
Turkey 36
Turkish Disability Act 104

UN Convention on the Rights of PWD 97
UNDP 8, 10
unemployment 72, 80
Union of the Physically Impaired Against Segregation (UPIAS) 115
United Kingdom 17
Universal Declaration of Human Rights (Article 24, 1948) 94, 99
universal design principles 100
urban transformation 72
Useh, U. 100
US entrepreneur-driven model 53
Utting, P. 11

Var, T. 104, 105
'village tours' 65
Visual and Applied Arts School 57
volunteer tourism packages 53
von der Weppen, J. 53

Wallimann, Paul 59
whole-of-life approach 114
women housekeeping employees 75
worker–owner model 58, 65
workers' rights 73
work overload 80–81
work schedule, insecurity 81–82
Wu, M. Y. 18

Yaylı, A. 104
Yesiltas, M. 104

Zampoukos, K. 74
Zapata Campos, Maria Jose 4